THEY BATTLED IN EUROPE AND IN THE PACIFIC. ON LAND, ON SEA, IN THE AIR, THESE FIGHTING MEN WON THE MEDAL OF HONOR WITH THEIR BLOOD AND THEIR BRAVERY IN ACTS OF UNFORGETTABLE COURAGE, INCLUDING:

STAFF SERGEANT PAUL L. BOLDEN, who voluntarily attacked a Nazi strongpoint when his company was pinned down by heavy fire. Singlehandedly, he rushed the building, killed twenty SS troopers with machine-gun fire, was hit in the shoulder, chest, and stomach, then went back inside and wiped out fifteen remaining enemy soldiers.

PRIVATE 1st CLASS DESMOND T. DOSS, a company aide man who repeatedly risked death to rescue the wounded on Okinawa. Seriously wounded himself, he crawled off the litter, ordering rescuers to first save another man. Then, again struck by enemy fire, he bound his shattered arm to his rifle stock, and crawled 300 yards to safety.

LIEUTENANT WILLIAM R. LAWLEY, Air Corps pilot whose bomber was hit by enemy fire over Europe. With eight crew members wounded, seriously wounded himself and his plane on fire, he refused to bail out and leave the injured men. Still evading attacking enemy planes, he brought his crippled aircraft back to England and successfully crash-landed her.

Only three of the outstanding tales of gallantry in . . .
WORLD WAR II
THE NAMES, THE DEEDS
Volume I, A–L

THE CONGRESSIONAL MEDAL OF HONOR—THE NAMES, THE DEEDS on which this volume is based, has been highly acclaimed:

"A remarkable new book . . . an extraordinary job . . . a volume people will buy and read and thumb. . . . If you ever wonder about American heroism, this is a book to answer questions. It is more; it is a book to brighten in memory, to inspire, even to awe. It is the story of the brave."

—James Brady, *New York Post*

"This is an outstanding reference book, detailed, authentic, informative."

—*Infantry*

"If you have any interest in knowing what sort of person it took to gain the attention of Congress and be awarded this supreme recognition, then this book is certainly for you. . . . Simply put, this book contains everything you could possibly want to know about the Medal, its history, recipients, breakdowns of each branch of the service, alphabetical listings of recipients according to conflicts, and on and on. It is without a doubt the most up-to-date listing available."

—*Battle Cry*

"A valuable directory of our greatest heroes."

—*Aerospace Historian*

THE CONGRESSIONAL MEDAL OF HONOR LIBRARY

VIETNAM—The Names, The Deeds
WORLD WAR II—The Names, The Deeds, Volume I, A–L
WORLD WAR II—The Names, The Deeds, Volume II, M–Z

"The President may award, and present in the name of Congress, a medal of honor of appropriate design, with ribbons and appurtenances, to a person who, while a member of the [armed forces], distinguished himself conspicuously by gallantry and intrepidity at the risk of his life above and beyond the call of duty—

"(1) while engaged in an action against an enemy of the United States;

"(2) while engaged in military operations involving conflict with an opposing foreign force; or

"(3) while serving with friendly foreign forces engaged in an armed conflict against an opposing armed force in which the United States is not a belligerent party."

QUANTITY SALES

Most Dell Books are available at special quantity discounts when purchased in bulk by corporations, organizations, and special-interest groups. Custom imprinting or excerpting can also be done to fit special needs. For details write: Dell Publishing Co., Inc., 1 Dag Hammarskjold Plaza, New York, NY 10017, Attn.: Special Sales Dept., or phone: (212) 605-3319.

INDIVIDUAL SALES

Are there any Dell Books you want but cannot find in your local stores? If so, you can order them directly from us. You can get any Dell book in print. Simply include the book's title, author, and ISBN number, if you have it, along with a check or money order (no cash can be accepted) for the full retail price plus 75¢ per copy to cover shipping and handling. Mail to: Dell Readers Service, Dept. FM, P.O. Box 1000, Pine Brook, NJ 07058.

The Congressional Medal of Honor Library

❂

WORLD WAR II
The Names, The Deeds
Volume I, A-L

A DELL BOOK

Published by
Dell Publishing Co., Inc.
1 Dag Hammarskjold Plaza
New York, New York 10017

This work was extracted from *The Congressional Medal of Honor.*

Dell ® TM 681510, Dell Publishing Co., Inc.

ISBN: 0-440-11454-3

Reprinted by arrangement with Sharp and Dunnigan Publications

Printed in the United States of America

October 1986

10 9 8 7 6 5 4 3 2 1

WFH

Dedication

This book is dedicated to those whose deeds are recorded by name herein; to those whose deeds of valor were recognized by one of the honors listed; and to those whose deeds have neither record nor recognition, but who met the call of duty when duty itself was above and beyond.

Order of Precedence of Military Decorations

The following is the order of precedence for military decorations of the United States, based on degrees of valor and meritorious achievement, and the date each medal was established:

U.S. ARMY AND U.S. AIR FORCE

1. Medal of Honor (1862)
2. Distinguished Service Cross (1918); Air Force Cross (1960)
3. Defense Distinguished Service Medal (1970)
4. Distinguished Service Medal (1918)
5. Silver Star (1918)
6. Defense Superior Service Medal (1976)
7. Legion of Merit (1942)
8. Distinguished Flying Cross (1926)
9. Soldier's Medal (1926); Airman's Medal (1960)
10. Bronze Star Medal (1942)
11. Defense Meritorious Service Medal (1977)
12. Meritorious Service Medal (1969)
13. Air Medal (1942)
14. Joint Service Commendation Medal (1967)
15. Army Commendation Medal (formerly Commendation Ribbon)(1945); Air Force Commendation Medal (formerly Commendation Ribbon)
16. Army Achievement Medal (1981)/Air Force Achievement Medal (1981)
17. Purple Heart (1782)

U.S. NAVY AND U.S. MARINE CORPS

1. Medal of Honor (1862)
2. Navy Cross (1919)
3. Defense Distinguished Service Medal (1970)
4. Distinguished Service Medal (1918)
5. Silver Star (1918)
6. Defense Superior Service Medal (1976)

7. Legion of Merit (1942)
8. Distinguished Flying Cross (1956)
9. Navy and Marine Corps Medal (1956)
10. Bronze Star Medal (1942)
11. Meritorious Service Medal (1969)
12. Air Medal (1942)
13. Joint Service Commendation Medal (1963)
14. Navy Commendation Medal (formerly Navy Commendation Ribbon)(1944)
15. Navy Achievement Medal (1967)
16. Purple Heart (1782)

Preface

It is said that an American fights for three things:
His brothers in arms, who share his darkest hours,
His home,
and his country, regardless of the politics of the moment. He
always fights as a free man,
and he will lay his life on the line.

Acknowledgements

The publishers would like to thank the members of the Senate Committee on Veterans' Affairs, 96th Congress, for having the foresight and imagination to have commissioned, *MEDAL OF HONOR RECIPIENTS 1863-1978 "In the name of the Congress of the United States."*

And so it follows, our deep appreciation to those who carried out that directive, Specifically: "Sister Maria Veronica, IHM, Medal of Honor archivist, Freedoms Foundation at Valley Forge, Pennsylvania; the members of the Medal of Honor Roundtable and, in particular, Gerald F. White, national director, and Rudolph J. Frederick, editor-in-chief, both of the Medal of Honor History Roundtable; and GySgt. James McGinn and GySgt. David Kennedy, both of the ODASD(A)OSD(C), White House Correspondents."

The publishers would also like to express our gratitude to Edward A. Michalski, A.V. Division DDI, OASD(PA), Department of Defense and the Medals and Decorations sections of the United States Army and the United States Marine Corps.

Our thanks also to Congressional staff member Stephen Hardesty (former S/Sgt. USMC) and S/Sgt. Stuart Kelly USMC, for their effort on final update.

98th CONGRESS
2d Session

H.R. 5515

IN THE SENATE OF THE UNITED STATES

May 9 (legislative day, April 30), 1984
Received

May 10 (legislative day, April 30), 1984
Ordered held at the desk

AN ACT

To authorize the President to award the Medal of Honor to the unknown American who lost his life while serving in the Armed Forces of the United States in Southeast Asia during the Vietnam era and who has been selected to be buried in the Memorial Amphitheater at Arlington National Cemetery.

Be it enacted by the Senate and House of Representatives of the United States of America in Congress assembled, That the President may award, and present in the name of Congress, the Medal of Honor to the unknown American who lost his life while serving in Southeast Asia during the Vietnam era as a member of the Armed Forces of the United States and who has been selected to lie buried in the Memorial Amphitheater of the National Cemetery at Arlington, Virginia, as authorized by section 9 of the National Cemeteries Act of 1973 (Public Law 93-43).

May 3, 1984
Passed House by voice vote

May 16, 1984
Passed Senate without amendment by voice vote

May 25, 1984
Signed by the President. Became Public Law 98-301.

May 28, 1984
Memorial Day Services, Arlington National Cemetery,
Arlington, Virginia

"An American hero has returned home . . . Today, we simply say with pride, thank you dear son. May God cradle you in his arms.

"We present to you the Congressional Medal of Honor, for services above and beyond the call of duty – in action with the enemy during the Vietnam Era." — Ronald Reagan, President of the United States.

HISTORICAL BACKGROUND

THE MEDAL OF HONOR

The Medal of Honor is the highest military award for bravery that can be given to any individual in the United States of America. Conceived in the early 1860's and first presented in 1863, the medal has a colorful and inspiring history which has culminated in the standards applied today for awarding this respected honor.

In their provisions for judging whether a man is entitled to the Medal of Honor, each of the armed services has set up regulations which permit no margin of doubt or error. The deed of the person must be proved by incontestable evidence of at least two eyewitnesses; it must be so outstanding that it clearly distinguishes his gallantry beyond the call of duty from lesser forms of bravery; it must involve the risk of his life; and it must be the type of deed which, if he had not done it, would not subject him to any justified criticism.

A recommendation for the Army or Air Force Medal must be made within 2 years from the date of the deed upon which it depends. Award of the medal must be made within 3 years after the date of the deed. The recommendation for a Navy Medal of Honor must be made within 3 years and awarded within 5 years.

Apart from the great honor which it conveys, there are certain small privileges which accompany the Medal of Honor. Its recipients can, under certain conditions, obtain free air transportation on military aircraft within the continental United States on a "space available" basis. A veteran who has been awarded the medal for combat in any war is eligible for a special pension of $200 per month, starting from the date he applies for the pension.

The Medal of Honor is presented to its recipients by a high official "in the name of the Congress of the United States." For this reason it is sometimes called the Congressional Medal of Honor.

As a general rule, the Medal of Honor may be awarded for a deed of personal bravery or self-sacrifice above and beyond the call of duty only while the person is a member of the Armed Forces of the United States in action against an enemy of the United States, or while engaged in military operations involving conflict with an opposing foreign force, or while serving with friendly foreign forces engaged in armed conflict against an opposing armed force in which the United States is not a belligerent party. However, until passage of Public Law 88–77, the Navy could and did award Medals of Honor for bravery in the line of the naval profession. Such awards recognized bravery in saving life, and deeds of valor performed in submarine rescues, boiler explosions, turret fires, and other types of disaster unique to the naval profession.

Congress has often voted special medals for important victories and other contributions to the Nation, the first having been awarded to General Washington for his success at Boston in 1776. These are truly Congressional medals to honor individuals and events. By Congressional action, and signed by the President, the Medal of Honor was awarded to the following Unknown Soldiers: Britain and France, on March 4, 1921; United States—World War I, on August 24, 1921; Italy, on October 12, 1921; Belgium, on December 1, 1922; and Rumania, on June 6, 1923. On two occasions the Army Medal of Honor has been awarded by separate acts of Congress—the first being the act of December 1927 honoring Captain Charles A. Lindbergh; the second being the act of 21 March 1935 honoring Major General Adolphus W. Greely. In each case, the medal presented was the Army Medal of Honor in use at the time, not a special medal struck for the purpose expressed in each act of Congress. In addition, five members of the Navy—Machinist Floyd Bennett, Commander Richard E. Byrd, Jr., Boatswain's Mate George R. Cholister, Ensign

Henry C. Drexler, and Lieutenant Richmond P. Hobson, each received the Navy Medal of Honor by acts of Congress. By Congressional approval the Medal of Honor was also awarded to the American Unknown Soldier of World War II, on March 9, 1948; and to the American Unknown Soldier of the Korean conflict on August 31, 1957. On May 28, 1984 the medal was awarded to the Unknown American of the Vietnam era.

"IN THE NAME OF THE CONGRESS OF THE UNITED STATES"

The Medal of Honor was not the idea of any one American. Like most of the ideas which have flowered into institutions and practices in our Nation, it was the result of group thought and action and evolved in response to a need of the times.

In the winter of 1861–62, following the beginning of hostilities in the Civil War, there was much thought in Washington concerning the necessity for recognizing the deeds of the American soldiers, sailors, and marines who were distinguishing themselves in the fighting.

The American Nation, which had given little thought to its Armed Forces during times of peace, now found them to be the focal point of attention. The serviceman, unpublicized and isolated during the preceding years, many of which were spent guarding the national frontiers against Indian raids and the coastline against smugglers, now became a great looming figure in the fight to preserve the Union. Overnight, he ceased to be a man plying some remote and mysterious trade out on the plains of Kansas or North Dakota, or on some ship at sea. He was the boy next door, or indeed the son of the household, sent out to fight for a cause that, in a very real sense, lay close to home.

His contribution was not just in fighting, but in fighting gallantly, sometimes displaying a sheer heroism which, when looked upon by the Nation in whose name it was called forth, quite naturally caused that Nation to seek some means of rewarding him.

But the thought did not stop there. For the first time since the Revolution, Americans realized not only what important citizens its soldiers, sailors, and marines were, but how important they had always been. They realized that the far-off lonely trooper, walking his post on the frontier, or the equally lonely sailor or marine standing watch from the bridge of his ship at sea along the coast, during the years of "peace," had been doing the same essential work as that of the soldier, sailor, or marine of the Civil War—protecting the Nation. And they realized that in doing this work they had very often displayed a little-known and unrecognized heroism which, by its nature, rendered them capable of being killed in action in their posts of duty, just as they could have been during the winter of 1861–62.

In looking back for a precedent for honoring our servicemen, Americans could note the "Certificate of Merit," which had been authorized for soldiers in 1847. Originally this award did not provide a medal, but rather a certificate signed by the President. Later, in 1905, a medal and ribbon bar for wear on the uniform were authorized. Congress also passed a provision that holders of the certificate who were still in the service should have extra pay of $2 per month. But money alone could not honor the serviceman for his deed.

There also had been a method of honoring officers by means of the "brevet" system of promotions, whereby an officer mentioned for gallantry in dispatches could be granted a "brevet rank" higher than that of his actual rank, and be entitled to wear the insignia which went with the brevet. But this system had fallen victim to a series of political abuses, and by 1861 much of its honor had grown meaningless.

The best precedent for honoring servicemen—and the only precedent in our Nation's history which had involved the award of decorations—went back to 1782. On August 7 of that year, in Newburg, N.Y., George Washington had created the Purple Heart as a decoration for "singular meritorious action." Three men had received the award in 1783. The records show no others.

The philosophy behind the Purple Heart had been that since his honor is something which no true soldier, sailor or marine likes to talk about, those who sought to honor him should give him a token of that honor which he could wear without words.

A similar philosophy and purpose characterized the American

people and the Congress of the United States in 1861. Senator James W. Grimes, of Iowa, took the lead as chairman of the Senate Naval Committee. He introduced a bill to create a Navy medal. It was passed by both Houses of Congress and approved by President Abraham Lincoln on December 21, 1861. It established a Medal of Honor for enlisted men of the Navy and Marine Corps—the first decoration formally authorized by the American Government to be worn as a badge of honor.

Action on the Army medal was started 2 months later, when, on February 17, 1862, Senator Henry Wilson, of Massachusetts, introduced a Senate resolution providing for presentation of "medals of honor" to enlisted men of the Army and Voluntary Forces who "shall most distinguish themselves by their gallantry in action, and other soldierlike qualities."

President Lincoln's approval made the resolution law on July 12, 1862. It was amended by an act approved on March 3, 1863, which extended its provision to include officers as well as enlisted men, and made the provisions retroactive to the beginning of the Civil War.

This legislation was to stand as the basis upon which the Army Medal of Honor could be awarded until July 9, 1918, when it was superseded by a completely revised statute.

As soon as the Navy Medal of Honor had been authorized, Secretary of the Navy Gideon Welles wrote to James Pollock, Director of the U.S. Mint at Philadelphia, asking for his assistance in obtaining a design for the medal. Pollock had submitted five designs to the Navy by the time the Army bill had been introduced in the Senate. When he heard that a similar medal was being considered for the Army, Pollock wrote to Secretary of War Edwin M. Stanton, enclosing one of the designs prepared for the Navy, and pointing out that it would be appropriate for use by the Army as well. Two more designs were submitted to the Navy on May 6, 1862, and on May 9, the Navy approved one of them.

In bas-relief, on the star, the Union held a shield in her right hand against an attacker, who crouched to the left, holding forked-tongued serpents which struck at the shield. In the left hand of the Union was held the fasces, the ancient Roman symbol of unified authority, an ax bound in staves of wood—still a common symbol on many of our 10-cent pieces. The 34 stars which encircle these figures represent the number of States at the time the medal was designed. The reverse of the medal bore a blank for the name of the awardee and the date and place of his deed.

On November 17, 1862, the War Department contracted with the firm of William Wilson & Son, Philadelphia, where the Navy medals were being made, for 2,000 of the same type of medals for the Army. The only difference between the Army medal and that of the Navy was that the Army medal, instead of being attached to its ribbon by an anchor, was attached by means of the American Eagle symbol, standing on crossed cannon and cannon balls.

And now the Navy and the Army had a Medal of Honor. Heroic deeds would entitle their authors to the decoration. On March 25, 1863, the first Army medals were awarded "in the name of the Congress of the United States." A few days later, on April 3, 1863, the first Navy medals were awarded sailors and marines.

PROTECTING THE MEDAL

There were some sincere men who believed that the idea of a Medal of Honor would not prove popular with Americans. By the end of the Civil War, and in succeeding years, this view was definitely proved to be incorrect. If anything, the medal was too popular, and the glory which it conferred upon its recipients had the effect of inspiring the human emotion of envy in many breasts. A flood of imitations sprang up following the Civil War, and had the effect of causing Congress, eventually, to take steps to protect the dignity of the original medal.

The abuses and confusion as to who earned and who did not earn the Medal of Honor were stated as early as 1869, when M. H. Beaumont, publisher of a magazine named The Soldier's Friend, wrote from New York to the War Department, indicating that he had been repeatedly requested to publish the names of all Medal of Honor recipients.

"There are some who are using medals for the purpose of soliciting charity," he wrote, "who obtained them surreptitiously."

Adjutant General Townsend agreed that the publication of a list would be a good idea. He pointed out that some of the awardees had never applied for their medals, and that publication might help lead to their delivery. A list was sent to Beaumont on September 29, 1869, and published in The Soldier's Friend shortly afterward.

The number of abuses rose—with increased applications by ex-soldiers, who, following the Civil War, began to present claims for the Medal of Honor without any sound documentation, and after passage of an inordinate amount of time from the dates upon which they alleged to have been earned. These events led to the creation of boards of review, not only of individual acts, but of the whole policy involved in the award to the Medal of Honor.

Public interest in the history of the medal was quickened. Four editions of a book edited by Brig. Gen. Theophilus F. Rodenbaugh, himself a medal recipient, were published in rapid succession. These were entitled "Uncle Sam's Medal of Honor Men" (1886), "The Bravest Five Hundred of '61" (1891), "Fighting for Honor" (1893), and "Sabre and Bayonet" (1897).

President Harry S. Truman, in 1946, ordered the Navy and the Army to publish information on the Medal of Honor recipients in their respective services. In July 1948, the United States Army published the information in a book entitled "The Medal of Honor of the United States Army." In 1949, the Navy published a book entitled "Medal of Honor, the Navy." In compiling this report, the committee is indebted to both of these publications and has used a great deal of material from each.

Interest in perpetuating the ideals of the medal was mounting on the part of medal recipients themselves. On April 23, 1890, the Medal of Honor Legion was organized at Washington as a local society. It was made a national organization during the grand encampment of the Grand Army of the Republic in Boston, on August 14, 1890, and was incorporated by Act of Congress on August 4, 1955. Today it is known as the Legion of Valor of the United States of America. The objectives of the Legion of Valor are—

To promote true fellowship among our members;

To advance the best interests of members of the Armed Forces of the United States and to enhance their prestige and understanding by example and personal activity;

To extend all possible relief to needy members, their widows, and children; and

To stimulate patriotism in the minds of our youth and to engender a national pride and interest in the Armed Forces of the United States.

The Congressional Medal of Honor Society of the United States, was chartered by the 85th Congress under a legislative act signed into law by President Eisenhower on August 14, 1958. The purposes of the society are—

"To form a bond of friendship and comradeship among all holders of the Medal of Honor.

"To protect, uphold, and preserve the dignity and honor of the medal at all times and on all occasions.

"To protect the name of the medal, and individual holders of the medal from exploitation.

"To provide appropriate aid to all persons to whom the medal has been awarded, their widows or their children.

"To serve our country in peace as we did in war.

"To inspire and stimulate our youth to become worthy citizens of our country.

"To foster and perpetuate Americanism.

"The Society will *not* participate in local or national politics, nor will the Society lend its support for the purpose of obtaining special legislative considerations."

On June 26, 1897, the Secretary of War, R. A. Alger, announced that paragraph 177 of the Army regulations was revised, at the direction of President William McKinley, and that new regulations would henceforth define the award of the Medal of Honor.

The resulting regulations gave the War Department an authoritative and comprehensive system for dealing with award of the medal. Later, an act of Congress, approved on April 24, 1904, made it mandatory that all claims for the medal should be accompanied by official documents describing the deed involved.

At about the same time, the design of the Army Medal of Honor was changed. Initially, the Army and Navy Medal of Honor were the same design, except that the Navy medal was attached to its ribbon by an anchor while the Army medal was attached to its ribbon by means of the American Eagle, standing on crossed cannon and cannon balls.

Late in 1903, Brig. Gen. Horace Porter had several designs prepared by Messrs. Arthur, Bertrand & Berenger, of Paris, and sent them to the Adjutant General, recommending that one of them should be approved by the Medal of Honor Legion, which, at that time, was headed by Maj. Gen. Daniel E. Sickles. Following approval of this organization, the Secretary of War approved the new design and a rosette, fixing his signature to the plan on January 28, 1904.

Just 2 weeks earlier, Representative Cordell Hull, of Tennessee, had introduced the act of 1904, providing for the changes in issuance of the medal. It was approved on April 23, 1904, and it authorized "three thousand medals of honor prepared * * * upon a new design."

It remained only to protect the new design from abuse. Early in 1904, a patent was applied for, and on November 22, 1904, Gen. G. L. Gillespie was awarded Patent Serial No. 197,369, covering the new Medal of Honor, specified as U.S. Patent Office Design No. 37,236. The final step for protection of the new design was taken on December 19, 1904, when General Gillespie transferred the Medal of Honor patent "to W. H. Taft and his successor or successors as Secretary of War of the United States of America."

The medal as officially described is made of silver, heavily electroplated in gold. The chief feature of the old medal, the five-pointed star, has been retained, and in its center appears the head of the heroic Minerva, the highest symbol of wisdom and righteous war. Surrounding this central feature in circular form are the words "United States of America" representing nationality. An open laurel wreath, enameled in green, encircles the star, and the oak leaves at the bases of the prongs of the star are likewise enameled in green to give them prominence.

The medal is suspended by a blue silk ribbon, spangled with 13 white stars representing the original States, and this ribbon is attached to an eagle supported upon a horizontal bar. Upon the bar, which is attached to two points of the star, appears the word "Valor," indicative of the distinguished service represented by the medal.

The reverse of the medal is plain so that the name of the recipient may be engraved thereon. On the reverse of the bar are stamped the words "The Congress To."

The patent which had been taken out for protection of the design of the medal expired on November 21, 1918. When this situation was referred to the Judge Advocate General of the Army for an opinion, he stated that this method of protecting the design should be replaced by legislative action forbidding imitations on the part of Congress. A bill for this purpose was recommended by the War Department, passed Congress, and was approved by the President on February 24, 1923. Imitation of the design of the medal was now forbidden by law.

THE "PYRAMID OF HONOR"

The Medal of Honor, which had begun as an idea in the minds of a few people back in 1861, had become a reality occupying the attention and energies of many Americans by 1904. Not all of the extraordinary examples of courage or of service were of the type which would deserve the Medal of Honor. At the same time, all of them deserved recognition, and each degree of valor or service could be looked upon as a step in the direction of that extraordinary service of heroism above and beyond the call of duty which is rewarded, once it has been proved, by the award of the Medal of Honor.

The problem of recognition of these lesser deeds was solved by the creation of a system of decorations arranged in an ascending order, with the lowest awards being the most widely distributed —and the Medal of Honor as the final, supreme award, its distribution limited strictly to the handful of those meeting the most severe tests of heroism. Thus, between the medals most widely distributed—and the Medal of Honor, held by only a few, there came all the other awards of Americans in uniform—arranged as a "pyramid of honor," with the Medal of Honor being the highest point, at the very top.

The legislation of 1904 gave the medal the maximum protection it had yet achieved. Now thought began to turn to the matter of presentation of the medal as a means through which it could be further dignified.

There had been a few scattered instances in which the medal was presented by the President or other high official. The six survivors of the Mitchell Raid through Georgia were awarded the first Army Medals of Honor on March 25, 1863, by Secretary of War Stanton. After presentation of the medals in his office, Secretary Stanton then took the six to the White House for a visit with President Lincoln. A few days later, on April 3, 1863, the first Navy Medals of Honor were awarded to a number of sailors taking part in the attacks on Forts Jackson, Fisher, and St. Philip, on April 24, 1862.

When Ulysses S. Grant became President, he presented the medal in the White House on two separate occasions. While in some cases soldiers and sailors of the Civil War had been given their medals at military formations and mentioned in the orders of the day, there is only one occasion recorded in which this custom was continued after the Civil War.

In some cases, the medals had been sent to awardees by registered mail. And, unfortunately, in some cases these medals had been returned to the War and Navy Departments because the recipients who had earned them had been discharged and their whereabouts were unknown.

On December 9, 1904, Maj. William E. Birkhimer, who had been a brigadier general of volunteers during the Spanish-American War and who was himself a medal recipient, suggested to the Military Secretary in Washington that "every possible attention should be paid to formality and solemnity of circumstance" whenever the medal was given to its recipients. His suggestion was passed up through channels to the Chief of Staff, and after extensive exchanges of correspondence, President Theodore Roosevelt, on September 20, 1905, signed an Executive order directing that ceremonies of award "will always be made with formal and impressive ceremonial," and that the recipient "will, when practicable, be ordered to Washington, D.C., and the presentation will be made by the President, as Commander in Chief, or by such representative as the President may designate." If it should be impracticable for the awardee to come to Washington, the order provided, the Chief of Staff would prescribe the time and place of the ceremony in each case.

The first White House presentation of the medal under the terms of this order was made by President Roosevelt on January 10, 1906.

On April 27, 1916, Congress approved an act which provided for the creation of a "Medal of Honor Roll," upon which honorably discharged medal recipients who earned the medal in combat and who had attained the age of 65 years were to be recorded, with each enrolled person to receive a special pension of $10 per month for life. The primary purpose of this act was to give medal recipients the same special recognition shown to holders of similar British and French decorations for valor. Limiting the award to the nominal sum of $10 monthly emphasized that it was not given as a pension, but to provide a small amount for personal comforts in the advanced years of life, at a time when needs are generally not very acute, especially in cases in which the veteran is in receipt of pension benefits. The amount was not made larger both because it was contrary to the policy of Congress to recognize distinguished service by pensions, and because to combine an award for conspicuous gallantry with a pension would diminish the honor attached to the award of the medal.

The passage of this act marked the successful culmination of a 26-year effort by the Medal of Honor Legion—the organization of medal recipients which was formed back in 1890—to obtain, in the words of one of its first documents, "such legislation from Congress as will tend to give the Medal of Honor the same position among the military orders of the world which similar medals occupy." Bills aimed at this type of legislation had been introduced into Congress recurrently following the organization of the Medal of Honor Legion—none of them meeting with success.

The successful bill was introduced by Representative Isaac R. Sherwood, of New York, who was a Civil War veteran, breveted brigadier general by Lincoln. He had fought in 43 battles, being under fire 123 days, and had been complimented in special orders for gallantry in action six times. He had led a full-dress congressional discussion of the Medal of Honor question on the floor of the House on July 6, 1914.

The Medal of Honor Roll, established by an Act of Congress, 27 April 1916, provided that upon attaining age 65 each recipient of the Medal of Honor who was honorably discharged from the service by muster-out, resignation, or otherwise, would have his name entered on the Roll and be eligible for a special pension of $10 per month for life. The Act was amended 14 August 1961 to increase the amount of pension to $100 per month, decrease the age to 50 and remove the requirement of separation from the service. It was further amended 13 October 1964 to decrease the age to 40, and on 31 October 1965 to delete the age of the awardee as a requirement and, most recently, on 18 October 1978, to raise the amount of the special pension to $200 per month. In addition the act provided for enrollment "upon written application being made to the Secretary of the proper department"—War or Navy—"and subject to the conditions and requirements hereinafter contained," of "the name of each surviving person who has served in the military or naval service of the United States in any war, who has attained or shall attain the age of 65 years * * *." It then laid down the condition that the applicant's Medal of Honor should have been earned by action involving actual conflict with an enemy, distinguished by conspicuous gallantry or intrepidity, at the risk of life, above and beyond the call of duty.

The act specified that the Secretary of War or of the Navy would be responsible to decide whether each applicant would be entitled to the benefits of the act.

If the official award as originally made appeared to the War Department to conform to the criteria established by the statute, this automatically entitled the applicant to the pension without further investigation. If, on the other hand, a doubt arose as to whether or not the applicant was entitled to entry on the roll, then, to quote the act further, "all official correspondence, orders, reports, recommendations, requests, and other evidence now on file in any public office or department shall be considered."

What was to be done if, after the consideration of these documents, the War Department felt that the applicant was ineligible was defined on June 3, 1916, in section 122 of the Army reorganization bill. This act provided for appointment by the Secretary of War of a board of five retired general officers for the purpose of "investigating and reporting upon past awards or issue of the so-called congressional medal of honor by or through the War Department; this with a view to ascertain what medals of honor, if any, have been awarded or issued for any cause other than distinguished conduct * * * involving actual conflict with an enemy * * *."

"And in any case," this act continued, "in which said board shall find and report that said medal was issued for any cause other than that hereinbefore specified, the name of the recipient of the medal so issued shall be stricken permanently from the official Medal of Honor list. It shall be a misdemeanor for him to wear or publicly display such medal, and, if he shall still be in the Army, he shall be required to return said medal to the War Department for cancellation."

By October 16, 1916, the Board created by this act had met, gathered all Medal of Honor records, prepared statistics, classified cases and organized evidence which might be needed in its deliberations. Between October 16, 1916, and January 17, 1917, all of the 2,625 Medals of Honor which had been awarded up to that time were considered by the Board, and on February 15, 1917, 910 names were stricken from the list.

Of these 910 names, 864 were involved in one group—a case in which the medal had been given to members of a single regiment. The regiment's (27th Maine Volunteer Infantry) enlistment was to have expired in June of 1863. As an inducement to keep the regiment on active duty during a critical period, President Lincoln authorized Medals of Honor for any of its members who volunteered for another tour of duty. The 309 men who volunteered for extended duty, in the face of more action and possible death, certainly were demonstrating "soldierlike" qualities, and as such were entitled to the Medal under one proviso of the

World War II—The Names, The Deeds • 15

original law. But their act in no way measured up to the 1916 standards. A clerical error compounded the abuse. Not only did the 309 volunteers receive the medal, but the balance of the regiment, which had gone home in spite of the President's offer, was awarded it also. In this group case as well as in the remaining 46 scattered cases, the Board felt that the medal had not been properly awarded for distinguished services, by the definition of the act of June 3, 1916. Among the 46 others who lost their medal was William F. Cody, better known as Buffalo Bill.

In its final report, the Board indicated that in the large majority of cases "the medals have been awarded for distinguished conduct in action, measuring that term by the highest standard, and there can be no question as to the propriety of the award."

In some cases, the Board reported, the rewards the men received were "greater than would now be given for the same acts," but in the absence of evidence to the contrary, "and because there has been no high judicial interpretation of the Medal of Honor laws" the Board found that there were "but few instances where the medal has not been awarded for distinguished services."

The 910 cases which did not pass the Board's investigation were turned over to the War Department, and against each of the names involved was stamped the inscription, "Stricken from the list February 15, 1917, Adverse Action Medal of Honor Board—A. G. 2411162."

There have been no instances of cancellation of Medal of Honor awards within the naval service.

This Board had few legal definitions to guide it in its work. It had to work with a quantity of regulations and precedents in making its decisions, and this mass of information was uncoordinated and even, in some cases, conflicting. For example, the act of April 27, 1916, provided for a "Medal of Honor Roll" for those who met the definition of valor above and beyond the call of duty; whereas the original act creating the Medal on July 12, 1862, specified only gallantry in action and "other soldierlike qualities" as the basis for award.

In 1918, Congress decided to clear away any inconsistencies of the legislation which had grown around the Army medal and make a set of perfectly clear rules for its award. Only July 9, 1918, an act was approved which stated as follows:

"* * * the provisions of existing law relating to the award of Medals of Honor * * * are amended so that the President is authorized to present, in the name of the Congress, a Medal of Honor only to each person who, while an officer or enlisted man of the Army, shall hereafter, in action involving actual conflict with an enemy, distinguish himself conspicuously by gallantry and intrepidity at risk of his life above and beyond the call of duty."

At one stroke, by use of the word "hereafter," this legislation wiped out of existence the War Department's problem of acting on numerous ancient and complicated claims for medals originating as far back as the Civil War. At the same time, it clearly defined the type of deed which could earn a medal.

But these were not the only provisions of this 1918 act. It directed that enlisted men who were medal recipients should receive $2 per month extra in their military pay. This matter of an extra $2 per month was intertwined with the Certificate of Merit. The 1918 legislation abolished the Certificate of Merit and replaced it by a new medal—the Distinguished Service Medal—still retaining the extra pay feature.

The Distinguished Service Cross was brought into existence to more fully single out and honor combat gallantry. The committee on Military Affairs, which had prepared the bill, stated that, "It is believed that if a secondary medal * * * had been authorized in the past, the award of the * * * Medal of Honor would have been much more jealously guarded than it was for many years. And it is certain that the establishment of such a secondary medal now will go far toward removing the temptation to laxity with regard to future awards of the greater medal."

However, it would have been illogical to have a "secondary" medal which carried the old Certificate of Merit provision of $2 extra pay per month, while the "greater medal"—the Medal of Honor—had no such provision attached to it. Therefore, the extra pay feature was added to the award of the Medal of Honor.

But possibly the most important and far-reaching effect of this 1918 legislation was the fact that for the first time in American history it was established by law that there were degrees of service to the country, each worthy of recognition, but only *one* of which could be accorded supreme recognition. In addition to the Distinguished Service Cross, the 1918 act also created the Army Distinguished Service Medal and the Army Silver Star Citation, each of them lower in precedence. The Silver Star became a formal decoration, with its own distinctive ribbon, in 1932.

This legislation also made it clear that recommendations for such Army awards had to be made within 2 years after the act involved, and laid down the time limit of 3 years as that in which the medals involved could be issued, following the date of the act meriting their award. It provided that not more than one medal should be issued to any one person, but that for each succeeding act justifying the award a suitable bar or other device could be awarded by the President. The President was authorized to delegate award of all four medals with which this 1918 act was concerned—the Medal of Honor, Distinguished Service Cross, Distinguished Service Medal, and Silver Star—to commanding generals of armies or higher units in the field.

The act of July 9, 1918, was the genesis of what has been called the "Pyramid of Honor," a hierarchy of military decorations awarded for combat valor and meritorious service at the top of which is placed the Medal of Honor. The Medal of Honor is restricted to the few who qualify by the most rigid definition of courage and valor in combat. Next in order of precedence is the Distinguished Service Cross, with less rigid restrictions, allowing more to qualify for this award for combat valor. Beneath the Distinguished Service Cross is the Distinguished Service Medal, which can be awarded for exceptionally meritorious service. The complete hierarchy consists at present of 12 awards for valor and/or service, ranging from the Medal of Honor at the top to the Purple Heart at the base of the "Pyramid of Honor."

A second Medal of Honor, commonly referred to as the (new) Medal of Honor, was approved by act of Congress of February 4, 1919, for award to any person in the naval service of the United States who while in action involving "actual conflict" with the enemy distinguished himself conspicuously by gallantry and intrepidity at the risk of his life above and beyond the call of duty and without detriment to the mission. The old Medal of Honor was retained for noncombat service.

The new Navy Medal of Honor was designed by Tiffany & Company of New York—hence the reference to it as the "Tiffany Cross"—and is a gold cross pattee, 35 millimeters across, on a wreath of oak and laurel leaves. The center of the cross bears the eagle design from the United States seal within an octagon bearing the inscription, "United States Navy, 1917–1918." A plain anchor appears on each arm of the cross. Except for the embossed words, "Awarded to," the reverse is plain. The medal is suspended from a ribbon consisting of a triple chevron of 13 white stars on a light blue field, the star at the point of the chevron being uppermost. At the crest of the ribbon is a bar which bears the single word "Valour." It is worn at the neck as a pendant, suspended from the band by means of its ribbon. The ribbon bar worn in lieu of either the original Medal of Honor or the second Medal of Honor is light blue and is embroidered with 5 white stars.

The act of Congress, approved February 4, 1919, which established the new Navy Medal of Honor, also provided for the adoption of a Navy Distinguished Service Medal, a Navy Cross and a gold star to be awarded in lieu of a second or additional award of any Navy decoration.

The new Navy Medal of Honor was made obsolete by an act of Congress approved August 7, 1942. This act restored the dual status of the old Navy Medal of Honor, thereby authorizing its award for combat or noncombat service above and beyond the call of duty. It also reversed the relative position of the Distinguished Service Medal and Navy Cross and established the Silver Star, the Legion of Merit, and the Navy and Marine Corps Medal as Navy decorations. In addition, it also abolished duplication of awards.

In order to insure fairness to all, Gen. John J. Pershing issued instructions to various commanding officers of the American Expeditionary Forces to submit recommendations for award of the Medal of Honor, Distinguished Service Cross, and Distinguished Service Medal. Recommendations were to come from regimental commanders, or, in the cases of men not in regiments, from the commanders corresponding as nearly as possible to the grade of regimental commander. General Pershing also appointed a board of officers at his headquarters to consider recommendations for the decorations. The recommendations so screened were then passed on to the Commander in Chief.

From these procedures there evolved the methods of examining possible awards which were used throughout World War II. Among the major requirements established at Headquarters, AEF, was one which specified that each recommendation for a Medal of Honor must cite a specific action on a particular day or in a particular engagement, giving the place and details of the action and the numbers of troops involved. It was also specified that each recommendation must be accompanied by sworn statements of two or more persons who were eyewitnesses of the action for which the medal was recommended.

Five days after the Armistice, General Pershing not only directed that a careful review be made of each case which had been submitted for award of the Distinguished Service Cross, but he also sent to headquarters of each division an officer thoroughly familiar with the forms necessary to substantiate awards of the Medal of Honor. He ordered that these officers were to be given every possible assistance in obtaining necessary evidence for Medal of Honor award in these cases, so that the Distinguished Service Cross would not be given when a case merited the Medal of Honor.

Up to November 23, 1918, 24 Medal of Honor recommendations had been received in the Personnel Bureau, AEF, and 4 approved, as mentioned above. As of that date, the Personnel Bureau became the Personnel Division of The Adjutant General's Office, U.S. Army, and Lt. Col. J. A. Ulio continued as chief of the Decorations Section within this new Division.

Medal of Honor recommendations and those pertaining to other decorations were handled at General Pershing's headquarters at Chaumont, France, between November 1918 and July 1919. They were submitted to the War Department, and during this period 78 Medal of Honor awards were made.

General Pershing personally reviewed each recommendation and the supporting documents.

Until June 30, 1921, the Badge and Medal Section in The Adjutant General's Office functioned within very limited areas of administration. On that date, the Secretary of War directed The Adjutant General to take over all operating functions connected with the award of Army medals and decorations.

The last Medal of Honor which could be awarded under the legislations of 1918—which specified that the award could be made not more than 3 years from the date of the act which won it —was presented to the American Unknown Soldier on Armistice Day of 1921. The bill which allowed it to be awarded to an unidentified soldier was signed by the President on August 24, 1921.

The medal was pinned on the flag draping the coffin of the Unknown Soldier at Arlington National Cemetery by President Warren G. Harding, at services in the amphitheater of the cemetery. At the same time, the President pinned to the flag high awards of Great Britain, France, Belgium, Italy, Rumania, Czechoslovakia, and Poland. All of these nations had authorized award of their highest decorations to the American Unknown Soldier, and the ceremony was attended by dignitaries of each of these countries.

During the post-World War I period special congressional action and Executive orders allowed the award of the Medal of Honor to Unknown Soldiers of nations which had been our allies in the conflict. On March 4, 1921, an act was approved awarding the medal to the Unknown British and French Soldiers, and on October 12, 1921, a similar act awarded it to the Italian Unknown Soldier.

Authorization to award the medal to the Belgian Unknown Soldier was given by Executive order of the President on December 1, 1922, and a similar authorization was given in the case of the Unknown Rumanian Soldier on June 6, 1923.

The Medal of Honor was also awarded to the Unknown American of World War II by act of Congress approved March 9, 1948, and to the Unknown American of the Korean conflict by act of Congress approved August 31, 1957, and of the Vietnam era on May 28, 1984.

In the winter of 1919–20, there was some discussion of changing the design of the Army medal once again, in order to beautify it, but the prevailing opinion was in favor of leaving it unchanged, and the design remained the same as it is today.

During the period of 1927–30, the Army War College, which has the mission of training selected officers for duty with the General Staff of the War Department and for high command, made studies of the principles and technical aspects of administration of Medal of Honor awards. Ten student officers had been assigned to make a study of the system of rewards in the Army as early as 1924. Three years later, in 1927, using the earlier study as a guide and source of material, a study of greater scope was finished at the War College.

A third study of the subject was made later.

When the time limitation on awards of the medal—contained in the 1918 legislation—expired for the second time, on April 7, 1923, many applications for War Department decorations which already had been filed with the Department during the first 4 postwar years still remained pending in the archives of The Adjutant General and the General Staff. On May 26, 1928, an extension was made part of an act of Congress in order to allow clearing up of these cases. It provided for consideration of recommendations pending at that date in the War and Navy Departments and the Marine Corps, with awards to be made in such cases as could be shown worthy.

On October 14, 1927, The Permanent Board of Awards was established by the Secretary of the Navy Curtis D. Wilbur to consider recommendations for awards of naval decorations to members of the military forces and to those attached to or serving with the Navy in any capacity. The Board was composed of two rear admirals of the line of the Navy and a brigadier general of the Marine Corps, with a lieutenant commander of the line of the Navy who served as recorder. The ranks and the number of members composing the Board have varied through the years, depending on conditions of world affairs, and the name of the Board was changed to Navy Department Board of Decorations and Medals.

During World War II and the Korean conflict, the Secretary of the Navy delegated authority to certain designated commands in the theaters of operations to award decorations without reference to the Secretary of the Navy (Navy Department Board of Decorations and Medals). Such authority excluded the Medal of Honor, the Distinguished Service Medal, all awards to flag officers, the Navy and Marine Corps Medal, and unit awards.

All of these procedures and policies, based upon congressional legislation, may seem dry and uninteresting. Legal terminology does not make for glamour. Records of proceedings of a board of review do not lend themselves to heroics. And the precise wording of regulations and bulletins, spelling out the law with care and repetition hardly constitutes the material of an adventure story. But it is precisely *because* of these legalistic safeguards that the Medal of Honor is a symbol of such glorious tradition today. The hours which were spent—thousands of them—from 1861 to the present day in the work of legislation, definition, administration, review of applications and recommendations, were unglamorous hours which painfully built the firm base for the pinnacle which bears the Medal of Honor. As a result of this painstaking work, the Nation was prepared, when World War II struck, to administer a swift and accurate reward for many provable cases of valor in action. Since World War II, through both the Korean conflict and the Vietnam era, these procedures have stood intact to continue to provide the Nation with an efficient manner of rewarding such conspicuous valor.

The Air Force Medal of Honor was established by Congress on July 6, 1960. Designed by the Institute of Heraldry, U.S. Army, the medal is a gold finished five pointed bronze star (one point down) 2″ in diameter. Its points are tipped with trefoils and joined by a green enamel laurel wreath edged in gold. In the center of the star is a likeness of the head of the Statue of Liberty surrounded by an amulet of 34 stars (the number of states in 1862). The star is suspended from a gold design of thunderbolts taken from the Air Force coat of arms. This in turn is attached to a horizontal bar bearing the word "Valor". The bar is suspended from a light blue silk-moiré neck ribbon behind an octagonal shaped pad of the ribbon bearing 13 white stars.

WORLD WAR II

ADAMS, LUCIAN

Rank and organization: Staff Sergeant, U.S. Army, 30th Infantry, 3d Infantry Division. *Place and date:* Near St. Die, France, 28 October 1944. *Entered service at:* Port Arthur, Tex. *Birth:* Port Arthur, Tex. *G.O. No.:* 20, 29 March 1945. *Citation:* For conspicuous gallantry and intrepidity at risk of life above and beyond the call of duty on 28 October 1944, near St. Die, France. When his company was stopped in its effort to drive through the Mortagne Forest to reopen the supply line to the isolated third battalion, S/Sgt. Adams braved the concentrated fire of machineguns in a lone assault on a force of German troops. Although his company had progressed less than 10 yards and had lost 3 killed and 6 wounded, S/Sgt. Adams charged forward dodging from tree to tree firing a borrowed BAR from the hip. Despite intense machinegun fire which the enemy directed at him and rifle grenades which struck the trees over his head showering him with broken twigs and branches, S/Sgt. Adams made his way to within 10 yards of the closest machinegun and killed the gunner with a handgrenade. An enemy soldier threw handgrenades at him from a position only 10 yards distant; however, S/Sgt. Adams dispatched him with a single burst of BAR fire. Charging into the vortex of the enemy fire, he killed another machinegunner at 15 yards range with a handgrenade and forced the surrender of 2 supporting infantrymen. Although the remainder of the German group concentrated the full force of its automatic weapons fire in a desperate effort to knock him out, he proceeded through the woods to find and exterminate 5 more of the enemy. Finally, when the third German machinegun opened up on him at a range of 20 yards, S/Sgt. Adams killed the gunner with BAR fire. In the course of the action, he personally killed 9 Germans, eliminated 3 enemy machineguns, vanquished a specialized force which was armed with automatic weapons and grenade launchers, cleared the woods of hostile elements, and reopened the severed supply lines to the assault companies of his battalion.

*AGERHOLM, HAROLD CHRIST

Rank and organization: Private First Class, U.S. Marine Corps Reserve. *Born:* 29 January 1925, Racine, Wis. *Accredited to:* Wisconsin. *Citation:* For conspicuous gallantry and intrepidity at the risk of his life above and beyond the call of duty while serving with the 4th Battalion, 10th Marines, 2d Marine Division, in action against enemy Japanese forces on Saipan, Marianas Islands, 7 July 1944. When the enemy launched a fierce, determined counterattack against our positions and overran a neighboring artillery battalion, Pfc. Agerholm immediately volunteered to assist in the efforts to check the hostile attack and evacuate our wounded. Locating and appropriating an abandoned ambulance jeep, he repeatedly made extremely perilous trips under heavy rifle and mortar fire and single-handedly loaded and evacuated approximately 45 casualties, working tirelessly and with utter disregard for his own safety during a gruelling period of more than 3 hours. Despite intense, persistent enemy fire, he ran out to aid 2 men whom he believed to be wounded marines but was himself mortally wounded by a Japanese sniper while carrying out his hazardous mission. Pfc. Agerholm's brilliant initiative, great personal valor and self-sacrificing efforts in the face of almost certain death reflect the highest credit upon himself and the U.S. Naval Service. He gallantly gave his life for his country.

ANDERSON, BEAUFORT T.

Rank and organization: Technical Sergeant, U.S. Army, 381st Infantry, 96th Infantry Division. *Place and date:* Okinawa, 13 April 1945. *Entered service at:* Soldiers Grove, Wis. *Birth:* Eagle, Wis. *G.O. No.:* 63, 27 June 1946. *Citation:* He displayed conspicuous gallantry and intrepidity above and beyond the call of duty. When a powerfully conducted predawn Japanese counterattack struck his unit's flank, he ordered his men to take cover in an old tomb, and then, armed only with a carbine, faced the onslaught alone. After emptying 1 magazine at pointblank range into the screaming attackers, he seized an enemy mortar dud and threw it back among the charging Japs, killing several as it burst. Securing a box of mortar shells, he extracted the safety pins, banged the bases upon a rock to arm them and proceeded alternately to hurl shells and fire his piece among the fanatical foe, finally forcing them to withdraw. Despite the protests of his comrades, and bleeding profusely from a severe shrapnel wound, he made his way to his company commander to report the action. T/Sgt. Anderson's intrepid conduct in the face of overwhelming odds accounted for 25 enemy killed and several machineguns and knee mortars destroyed, thus singlehandedly removing a serious threat to the company's flank.

*ANDERSON, RICHARD BEATTY

Rank and organization: Private First Class, U.S. Marine Corps. *Born:* 26 June 1921, Tacoma, Wash. *Accredited to:* Washington. *Citation:* For conspicuous gallantry and intrepidity at the risk of his life above and beyond the call of duty while serving with the 4th Marine Division during action against enemy Japanese forces on Roi Island, Kwajalein Atoll, Marshall Islands, 1 February 1944. Entering a shell crater occupied by 3 other marines, Pfc. Anderson was preparing to throw a grenade at an enemy position when it slipped from his hands and rolled toward the men at the bottom of the hole. With insufficient time to retrieve the armed weapon and throw it, Pfc. Anderson fearlessly chose to sacrifice himself and save his companions by hurling his body upon the grenade and taking the full impact of the explosion. His personal valor and exceptional spirit of loyalty in the face of almost certain death were in keeping with the highest traditions of the U.S. Naval Service. He gallantly gave his life for his country.

*ANTOLAK, SYLVESTER

Rank and organization: Sergeant, U.S. Army, Company B, 15th Infantry, 3d Infantry Division. *Place and date:* Near Cisterna di Littoria, Italy, 24 May 1944. *Entered service at:* St. Clairsville, Ohio. *Birth:* St. Clairsville, Ohio. *G.O. No.:* 89, 19 October 1945. *Citation:* Near Cisterna di Littoria, Italy, he charged 200 yards over flat, coverless terrain to destroy an enemy machinegun nest during the second day of the offensive which broke through the German cordon of steel around the Anzio beachhead. Fully 30 yards in advance of his squad, he ran into withering enemy machinegun, machine-pistol and rifle fire. Three times he was struck by bullets and knocked to the ground, but each time he struggled to his feet to continue his relentless advance. With one shoulder deeply gashed and his right arm shattered, he continued to rush directly into the enemy fire concentration with his submachinegun wedged under his uninjured arm until within 15 yards of the enemy strongpoint, where he opened fire at deadly close range, killing 2 Germans and forcing the remaining 10 to surrender. He reorganized his men and, refusing to seek medical attention so badly needed, chose to lead the way toward another strongpoint 100 yards distant. Utterly disregarding the hail of bullets concentrated upon him, he had stormed ahead nearly three-fourths of the space between strongpoints when he was instantly killed by hostile enemy fire. Inspired by his example, his squad went on to overwhelm the enemy troops. By his supreme sacrifice, superb fighting courage, and heroic devotion to the attack, Sgt. Antolak was directly responsible for eliminating 20 Germans, capturing an enemy machinegun, and clearing the path for his company to advance.

ANTRIM, RICHARD NOTT

Rank and organization: Commander, U.S. Navy. *Place and date:* Makassar, Celebes, Netherlands East Indies, April 1942. *Entered service at:* Indiana. *Born:* 17 December 1907, Peru, Ind. *Citation:* For conspicuous gallantry and intrepidity at the risk of his life above and beyond the call of duty while interned as a prisoner of war of the enemy Japanese in the city of Makassar, Celebes, Netherlands East Indies, in April 1942. Acting instantly on behalf of a naval officer who was subjected to a vicious clubbing by a frenzied Japanese guard venting his insane wrath upon the helpless prisoner, Comdr. (then Lt.) Antrim boldly intervened, attempting to quiet the guard and finally persuading him to discuss the charges against the officer. With the entire Japanese force assembled and making extraordinary preparations for the threatened beating, and with the tension heightened by 2,700 Allied prisoners rapidly closing in, Comdr. Antrim courageously appealed to the fanatic enemy, risking his own life in a desperate effort to mitigate the punishment. When the other had been beaten unconscious by 15 blows of a hawser and was repeatedly kicked by 3 soldiers to a point beyond which he could not survice, Comdr. Antrim gallantly stepped forward and indicated to the perplexed guards that he would take the remainder of the punishment, throwing the Japanese completely off balance in their amazement and eliciting a roar of acclaim from the suddenly inspired Allied prisoners. By his fearless leadership and valiant concern for the welfare of another, he not only saved the life of a fellow officer and stunned the Japanese into sparing his own life but also brought about a new respect for American officers and men and a great improvement in camp living conditions. His heroic conduct throughout reflects the highest credit upon Comdr. Antrim and the U.S. Naval Service.

ATKINS, THOMAS E.

Rank and organization: Private First Class, U.S. Army, Company A, 127th Infantry, 32d Infantry Division. *Place and date:* Villa Verde Trail, Luzon, Philippine Islands, 10 March 1945. *Entered service at:* Campobello, S.C. *Birth:* Campobello, S.C. *G.O. No.:* 95, 30 October 1945. *Citation:* He fought gallantly on the Villa Verde Trail, Luzon, Philippine Islands. With 2 companions he occupied a position on a ridge outside the perimeter defense established by the 1st Platoon on a high hill. At about 3 a.m., 2 companies of Japanese attacked with rifle and machinegun fire, grenades, TNT charges, and land mines, severely wounding Pfc. Atkins and killing his 2 companions. Despite the intense hostile fire and pain from his deep wound, he held his ground and returned heavy fire. After the attack was repulsed, he remained in his precarious position to repel any subsequent assaults instead of returning to the American lines for medical treatment. An enemy machinegun, set up within 20 yards of his foxhole, vainly attempted to drive him off or silence his gun. The Japanese repeatedly made fierce attacks, but for 4 hours Pfc. Atkins determinedly remained in his foxhole, bearing the brunt of each assault and maintaining steady and accurate fire until each charge was repulsed. At 7 a.m., 13 enemy dead lay in front of his position; he had fired 400 rounds, all he and his 2 dead companions possessed, and had used 3 rifles until each had jammed too badly for further operation. He withdrew during a lull to secure a rifle and more ammunition, and was persuaded to remain for medical treatment. While waiting, he saw a Japanese within the perimeter and, seizing a nearby rifle, killed him. A few minutes later, while lying on a litter, he discovered an enemy group moving up behind the platoon's lines. Despite his severe wound, he sat up, delivered heavy rifle fire against the group and forced them to withdraw. Pfc. Atkins' superb bravery and his fearless determination to hold his post against the main force of repeated enemy attacks, even though painfully wounded, were major factors in enabling his comrades to maintain their lines against a numerically superior enemy force.

*BAILEY, KENNETH D.

Rank and organization: Major, U.S. Marine Corps. *Born:* 21 October 1910, Pawnee, Okla. *Appointed from:* Illinois. *Other Navy awards:* Silver Star Medal. *Citation:* For extraordinary courage and heroic conduct above and beyond the call of duty as Commanding Officer of Company C, 1st Marine Raider Battalion, during the enemy Japanese attack on Henderson Field, Guadalcanal, Solomon Islands, on 12–13 September 1942. Completely reorganized following the severe engagement of the night before, Maj. Bailey's company, within an hour after taking its assigned position as reserve battalion between the main line and the coveted airport, was threatened on the right flank by the penetration of the enemy into a gap in the main line. In addition to repulsing this threat, while steadily improving his own desperately held position, he used every weapon at his command to cover the forced withdrawal of the main line before a hammering assault by superior enemy forces. After rendering invaluable service to the battalion commander in stemming the retreat, reorganizing the troops and extending the reverse position to the left, Maj. Bailey, despite a severe head wound, repeatedly led his troops in fierce hand-to-hand combat for a period of 10 hours. His great personal valor while exposed to constant and merciless enemy fire, and his indomitable fighting spirit inspired his troops to heights of heroic endeavor which enabled them to repulse the enemy and hold Henderson Field. He gallantly gave his life in the service of his country.

*BAKER, ADDISON E. (Air Mission)

Rank and organization: Lieutenant Colonel, U.S. Army Air Corps, 93d Heavy Bombardment Group. *Place and date:* Ploesti Raid, Rumania, 1 August 1943. *Entered service at:* Akron, Ohio. *Born:* 1 January 1907, Chicago, Ill. *G.O. No.:* 20, 11 March 1944. *Citation:* For conspicuous gallantry and intrepidity above and beyond the call of duty in action with the enemy on 1 August 1943. On this date he led his command, the 93d Heavy Bombardment Group, on a daring low-level attack against enemy oil refineries and installations at Ploesti, Rumania. Approaching the target, his aircraft was hit by a large caliber antiaircraft shell, seriously damaged and set on fire. Ignoring the fact he was flying over terrain suitable for safe landing, he refused to jeopardize the mission by breaking up the lead formation and continued unswervingly to lead his group to the target upon which he dropped his bombs with devastating effect. Only then did he leave formation, but his valiant attempts to gain sufficient altitude for the crew to escape by parachute were unavailing and his aircraft crashed in flames after his successful efforts to avoid other planes in formation. By extraordinary flying skill, gallant leadership and intrepidity, Lt. Col. Baker rendered outstanding, distinguished, and valorous service to our Nation.

*BAKER, THOMAS A.

Rank and organization: Sergeant, U.S. Army, Company A, 105th Infantry, 27th Infantry Division. *Place and date:* Saipan, Mariana Islands, 19 June to 7 July 1944. *Entered service at:* Troy, N.Y. *Birth:* Troy, N.Y. *G.O. No.:* 35, 9 May 1945. *Citation:* For conspicuous gallantry and intrepidity at the risk of his life above and beyond the call of duty at Saipan, Mariana Islands, 19 June to 7 July 1944. When his entire company was held up by fire from automatic weapons and small-arms fire from strongly fortified enemy positions that commanded the view of the company, Sgt. (then Pvt.) Baker voluntarily took a bazooka and dashed alone to within 100 yards of the enemy. Through heavy rifle and machine-gun fire that was directed at him by the enemy, he knocked out the strongpoint, enabling his company to assault the ridge. Some days later while his company advanced across the open field flanked with obstructions and places of concealment for the enemy, Sgt. Baker again voluntarily took up a position in the rear to protect the company against surprise attack and came upon 2 heavily fortified enemy pockets manned by 2 officers and 10 enlisted men which had been bypassed. Without regard for such superior numbers, he unhesitatingly attacked and killed all of them. Five hundred yards farther, he discovered 6 men of the enemy who had concealed themselves behind our lines and destroyed all of them. On 7 July 1944, the perimeter of which Sgt. Baker was a part was attacked from 3 sides by from 3,000 to 5,000 Japanese. During the early stages of this attack, Sgt. Baker was seriously wounded but he insisted on remaining in the line and fired at the enemy at ranges sometimes as close as 5 yards until his ammunition ran out. Without ammunition and with his own weapon battered to uselessness from hand-to-hand combat, he was carried about 50 yards to the rear by a comrade, who was then himself wounded. At this point Sgt. Baker refused to be moved any farther stating that he preferred to be left to die rather than risk the lives of any more of his friends. A short time later, at his request, he was placed in a sitting position against a small tree. Another comrade, withdrawing, offered assistance. Sgt. Baker refused, insisting that he be left alone and be given a soldier's pistol with its remaining 8 rounds of ammunition. When last seen alive, Sgt. Baker was propped against a tree, pistol in hand, calmly facing the foe. Later Sgt. Baker's body was found in the same position, gun empty, with 8 Japanese lying dead before him. His deeds were in keeping with the highest traditions of the U.S. Army.

BARFOOT, VAN T.

Rank and organization: Second Lieutenant, U.S. Army, 157th Infantry, 45th Infantry Division. *Place and date:* Near Carano, Italy, 23 May 1944. *Entered service at:* Carthage, Miss. *Birth:* Edinburg, Miss. *G.O. No.:* 79, 4 October 1944. *Citation:* For conspicuous gallantry and intrepidity at the risk of life above and beyond the call of duty on 23 May 1944, near Carano, Italy. With his platoon heavily engaged during an assault against forces well entrenched on commanding ground, 2d Lt. Barfoot (then Tech. Sgt.) moved off alone upon the enemy left flank. He crawled to the proximity of 1 machinegun nest and made a direct hit on it with a handgrenade, killing 2 and wounding 3 Germans. He continued along the German defense line to another machinegun emplacement, and with his tommygun killed 2 and captured 3 soldiers. Members of another enemy machinegun crew then abandoned their position and gave themselves up to Sgt. Barfoot.

Leaving the prisoners for his support squad to pick up, he proceeded to mop up positions in the immediate area, capturing more prisoners and bringing his total count to 17. Later that day, after he had reorganized his men and consolidated the newly captured ground, the enemy launched a fierce armored counterattack directly at his platoon positions. Securing a bazooka, Sgt. Barfoot took up an exposed position directly in front of 3 advancing Mark VI tanks. From a distance of 75 yards his first shot destroyed the track of the leading tank, effectively disabling it, while the other 2 changed direction toward the flank. As the crew of the disabled tank dismounted, Sgt. Barfoot killed 3 of them with his tommygun. He continued onward into enemy terrain and destroyed a recently abandoned German fieldpiece with a demolition charge placed in the breech. While returning to his platoon position, Sgt. Barfoot, though greatly fatigued by his herculean efforts, assisted 2 of his seriously wounded men 1,700 yards to a position of safety. Sgt. Barfoot's extraordinary heroism, demonstration of magnificent valor, and aggressive determination in the face of pointblank fire are a perpetual inspiration to his fellow soldiers.

BARRETT, CARLTON W.

Rank and organization: Private, U.S. Army, 18th Infantry, 1st Infantry Division. *Place and date:* Near St. Laurent-sur-Mer, France, 6 June 1944. *Entered service at:* Albany, N.Y. *Birth:* Fulton, N.Y. *G.O. No.:* 78, 2 October 1944. *Citation:* For gallantry and intrepidity at the risk of his life above and beyond the call of duty on 6 June 1944, in the vicinity of St. Laurent-sur-Mer, France. On the morning of D-day Pvt. Barrett, landing in the face of extremely heavy enemy fire, was forced to wade ashore through neck-deep water. Disregarding the personal danger, he returned to the surf again and again to assist his floundering comrades and save them from drowning. Refusing to remain pinned down by the intense barrage of small-arms and mortar fire poured at the landing points, Pvt. Barrett, working with fierce determination, saved many lives by carrying casualties to an evacuation boat lying offshore. In addition to his assigned mission as guide, he carried dispatches the length of the fire-swept beach; he assisted the wounded; he calmed the shocked; he arose as a leader in the stress of the occasion. His coolness and his dauntless daring courage while constantly risking his life during a period of many hours had an inestimable effect on his comrades and is in keeping with the highest traditions of the U.S. Army.

BASILONE, JOHN

Rank and organization: Sergeant, U.S. Marine Corps. *Born:* 4 November 1916, Buffalo, N.Y. *Accredited to:* New Jersey. *Other Navy award:* Navy Cross. *Citation:* For extraordinary heroism and conspicuous gallantry in action against enemy Japanese forces, above and beyond the call of duty, while serving with the 1st Battalion, 7th Marines, 1st Marine Division in the Lunga Area, Guadalcanal, Solomon Islands, on 24 and 25 October 1942. While the enemy was hammering at the Marines' defensive positions, Sgt. Basilone, in charge of 2 sections of heavy machineguns, fought valiantly to check the savage and determined assault. In a fierce frontal attack with the Japanese blasting his guns with grenades and mortar fire, one of Sgt. Basilone's sections, with its guncrews, was put out of action, leaving only 2 men able to carry on. Moving an extra gun into position, he placed it in action, then, under continual fire, repaired another and personally manned it, gallantly holding his line until replacements arrived. A little later, with ammunition critically low and the supply lines cut off, Sgt. Basilone, at great risk of his life and in the face of continued enemy attack, battled his way through hostile lines with urgently needed shells for his gunners, thereby contributing in large measure to the virtual annihilation of a Japanese regiment. His great personal valor and courageous initiative were in keeping with the highest traditions of the U.S. Naval Service.

*BAUER, HAROLD WILLIAM

Rank and organization: Lieutenant Colonel, U.S. Marine Corps. *Born:* 20 November 1908, Woodruff, Kans. *Appointed from:* Nebraska. *Citation:* For extraordinary heroism and conspicuous courage as Squadron Commander of Marine Fighting Squadron 212 in the South Pacific Area during the period 10 May to 14 November 1942. Volunteering to pilot a fighter plane in defense of our positions on Guadalcanal, Lt. Col. Bauer participated in 2 air battles against enemy bombers and fighters outnumbering our force more than 2 to 1, boldly engaged the enemy and destroyed 1 Japanese bomber in the engagement of 28 September and shot down 4 enemy fighter planes in flames on 3 October, leaving a fifth smoking badly. After successfully leading 26 planes on an over-water ferry flight of more than 600 miles on 16 October, Lt. Col. Bauer, while circling to land, sighted a squadron of enemy planes attacking the U.S.S. *McFarland*. Undaunted by the formidable opposition and with valor above and beyond the call of duty, he engaged the entire squadron and, although alone and his fuel supply nearly exhausted, fought his plane so brilliantly that 4 of the Japanese planes were destroyed before he was forced down by lack of fuel. His intrepid fighting spirit and distinctive ability as a leader and an airman, exemplified in his splendid record of combat achievement, were vital factors in the successful operations in the South Pacific Area.

*BAUSELL, LEWIS KENNETH

Rank and organization: Corporal, U.S. Marine Corps. *Born:* 17 April 1924, Pulaski, Va. *Accredited to:* District of Columbia. *Citation:* For conspicuous gallantry and intrepidity at the risk of his life above and beyond the call of duty while serving with the 1st Battalion, 5th Marines, 1st Marine Division, during action against enemy Japanese forces on Peleliu Island, Palau Group, 15 September 1944. Valiantly placing himself at the head of his squad, Cpl. Bausell led the charge forward against a hostile pillbox which was covering a vital sector of the beach and, as the first to reach the emplacement, immediately started firing his automatic into the aperture while the remainder of his men closed in on the enemy. Swift to act, as a Japanese grenade was hurled into their midst, Cpl. Bausell threw himself on the deadly weapon, taking the full blast of the explosion and sacrificing his own life to save his men. His unwavering loyalty and inspiring courage reflect the highest credit upon Cpl. Bausell and the U.S. Naval Service. He gallantly gave his life for his country.

*BEAUDOIN, RAYMOND O.

Rank and organization: First Lieutenant, U.S. Army, Company F, 119th Infantry, 30th Infantry Division. *Place and date:* Hamelin, Germany, 6 April 1945. *Entered service at:* Holyoke, Mass. *Birth:* Holyoke, Mass. *G.O. No.:* 9, 25 January 1946. *Citation:* He was leading the 2d Platoon of Company F over flat, open terrain to Hamelin, Germany, when the enemy went into action with machineguns and automatic weapons, laying down a devastating curtain of fire which pinned his unit to the ground. By rotating men in firing positions he made it possible for his entire platoon to dig in, defying all the while the murderous enemy fire to encourage his men and to distribute ammunition. He then dug in himself at the most advanced position, where he kept up a steady fire, killing 6 hostile soldiers, and directing his men in inflicting heavy casualties on the numerically superior opposing force. Despite these defensive measures, however, the position of the platoon became more precarious, for the enemy had brought up strong reinforcements and was preparing a counterattack. Three men, sent back at intervals to obtain ammunition and reinforcements, were killed by sniper fire. To relieve his command from the desperate situation, 1st Lt. Beaudoin decided to make a 1-man attack on the most damaging enemy sniper nest 90 yards to the right flank, and thereby divert attention from the runner who would attempt to pierce the enemy's barrier of bullets and secure help. Crawling over completely exposed ground, he relentlessly advanced, undeterred by 8 rounds of bazooka fire which threw mud and stones over him or by rifle fire which ripped his uniform. Ten yards from the enemy position he stood up and charged. At point-blank range he shot and killed 2 occupants of the nest; a third, who tried to bayonet him, he overpowered and killed with the butt of his carbine; and the fourth adversary was cut down by the platoon's rifle fire as he attempted to flee. He continued his attack by running toward a dugout, but there he was struck and killed by a burst from a machinegun. By his intrepidity, great fighting skill, and supreme devotion to his responsibility for the well-being of his platoon, 1st Lt. Beaudoin singlehandedly accomplished a mission that enabled a messenger to secure help which saved the stricken unit and made possible the decisive defeat of the German forces.

BELL, BERNARD P.

Rank and organization: Technical Sergeant, U.S. Army, Company I, 142d Infantry, 36th Infantry Division. *Place and date:* Mittelwihr, France, 18 December 1944. *Entered service at:* New York, N.Y. *Birth:* Grantsville, W. Va. *G.O. No.:* 73, 30 August 1945. *Citation:* For fighting gallantly at Mittelwihr, France. On the morning of 18 December 1944, he led a squad against a schoolhouse held by enemy troops. While his men covered him, he dashed toward the building, surprised 2 guards at the door and took them prisoner without firing a shot. He found that other Germans were in the cellar. These he threatened with handgrenades, forcing 26 in all to emerge and surrender. His squad then occupied the building and prepared to defend it against powerful enemy action. The next day, the enemy poured artillery and mortar barrages into the position, disrupting communications which T/Sgt. Bell repeatedly repaired under heavy small-arms fire as he crossed dangerous terrain to keep his company commander informed of the squad's situation. During the day, several prisoners were taken and other Germans killed when hostile forces were attracted to the schoolhouse by the sound of captured German weapons fired by the Americans. At dawn the next day the enemy prepared to assault the building. A German tank fired round after round into the structure, partially demolishing the upper stories. Despite this heavy fire, T/Sgt. Bell climbed to the second floor and directed artillery fire which forced the hostile tank to withdraw. He then adjusted mortar fire on large forces of enemy foot soldiers attempting to reach the American position and, when this force broke and attempted to retire, he directed deadly machinegun and rifle fire into their disorganized ranks. Calling for armored support to blast out the German troops hidden behind a wall, he unhesitatingly exposed himself to heavy small-arms fire to stand beside a friendly tank and tell its occupants where to rip holes in walls protecting approaches to the school building. He then trained machineguns on the gaps and mowed down all hostile troops attempting to cross the openings to get closer to the school building. By his intrepidity and bold, aggressive leadership, T/Sgt. Bell enabled his 8-man squad to drive back approximately 150 of the enemy, killing at least 87 and capturing 42. Personally, he killed more than 20 and captured 33 prisoners.

BENDER, STANLEY

Rank and organization: Staff Sergeant, U.S. Army, Company E, 7th Infantry, 3d Infantry Division. *Place and date:* Near La Lande, France, 17 August 1944. *Entered service at:* Chicago, Ill. *Born:* 31 October 1909, Carlisle, W. Va. *G.O. No.:* 7, 1 February 1945. *Citation:* For conspicuous gallantry and intrepidity at risk of life above and beyond the call of duty. On 17 August 1944, near La Lande, France, he climbed on top of a knocked-out tank, in the face of withering machinegun fire which had halted the advance of his company, in an effort to locate the source of this fire. Although bullets ricocheted off the turret at his feet, he nevertheless remained standing upright in full view of the enemy for over 2 minutes. Locating the enemy machineguns on a knoll 200 yards away, he ordered 2 squads to cover him and led his men down an irrigation ditch, running a gauntlet of intense machinegun fire, which completely blanketed 50 yards of his advance and wounded 4 of his men. While the Germans hurled handgrenades at the ditch, he stood his ground until his squad caught up with him, then advanced alone, in a wide flanking approach, to the rear of the knoll. He walked deliberately a distance of 40 yards, without cover, in full view of the Germans and under a hail of both enemy and friendly fire, to the first machinegun and knocked it out with a single short burst. Then he made his way through the strongpoint, despite bursting handgrenades, toward the second machinegun, 25 yards distant, whose 2-man crew swung the machinegun around and fired two bursts at him, but he walked calmly through the fire and, reaching the edge of the emplacement, dispatched the crew. Signaling his men to rush the rifle pits, he then walked 35 yards further to kill an enemy rifleman and returned to lead his squad in the destruction of the 8 remaining Germans in the strongpoint. His audacity so inspired the remainder of the assault company that the men charged out of their positions, shouting and yelling, to overpower the enemy roadblock and sweep into town, knocking out 2 antitank guns, killing 37 Germans and capturing 26 others. He had sparked and led the assault company in an attack which overwhelmed the enemy, destroying a roadblock, taking a town, seizing intact 3 bridges over the Maravenne River, and capturing commanding terrain which dominated the area.

*BENJAMIN, GEORGE, Jr.

Rank and organization: Private First Class, U.S. Army, Company A, 306th Infantry, 77th Infantry Division. *Place and date:* Leyte, Philippine Islands, 21 December 1944. *Entered service at:* Carney's Point, N.J. *Birth:* Philadelphia, Pa. *G.O. No.:* 49, 28 June 1945. *Citation:* He was a radio operator, advancing in the rear of his company as it engaged a well-defended Japanese strongpoint holding up the progress of the entire battalion. When a rifle platoon supporting a light tank hesitated in its advance, he voluntarily and with utter disregard for personal safety left his comparatively secure position and ran across bullet-whipped terrain to the tank, waving and shouting to the men of the platoon to follow. Carrying his bulky radio and armed only with a pistol, he fearlessly penetrated intense machinegun and rifle fire to the enemy position, where he killed 1 of the enemy in a foxhole and moved on to annihilate the crew of a light machinegun. Heedless of the terrific fire now concentrated on him, he continued to spearhead the assault, killing 2 more of the enemy and exhorting the other men to advance, until he fell mortally wounded. After being evacuated to an aid station, his first thought was still of the American advance. Overcoming great pain he called for the battalion operations officer to report the location of enemy weapons and valuable tactical information he had secured in his heroic charge. The unwavering courage, the unswerving devotion to the task at hand, the aggressive leadership of Pfc. Benjamin were a source of great and lasting inspiration to his comrades and were to a great extent responsible for the success of the battalion's mission.

BENNETT, EDWARD A.

Rank and organization: Corporal, U.S. Army, Company B, 358th Infantry, 90th Infantry Division. *Place and date:* Heckhuscheid, Germany, 1 February 1945. *Entered service at:* Middleport, Ohio. *Birth:* Middleport, Ohio. *G.O. No.:* 95, 30 October 1945. *Citation:* He was advancing with Company B across open ground to assault Heckhuscheid, Germany, just after dark when vicious enemy machinegun fire from a house on the outskirts of the town pinned down the group and caused several casualties. He began crawling to the edge of the field in an effort to flank the house, persisting in this maneuver even when the hostile machinegunners located him by the light of burning buildings and attempted to cut him down as he made for the protection of some trees. Reaching safety, he stealthily made his way by a circuitous route to the rear of the building occupied by the German gunners. With his trench knife he killed a sentry on guard there and then charged into the darkened house. In a furious hand-to-hand struggle he stormed about a single room which harbored 7 Germans. Three he killed with rifle fire, another he clubbed to death with the butt of his gun, and the 3 others he dispatched with his .45 caliber pistol. The fearless initiative, stalwart combat ability, and outstanding gallantry of Cpl. Bennett eliminated the enemy fire which was decimating his company's ranks and made it possible for the Americans to sweep all resistance from the town.

*BENNION, MERVYN SHARP

Rank and organization: Captain, U.S. Navy. *Born:* 5 May 1887, Vernon, Utah. *Appointed from:* Utah. *Citation:* For conspicuous devotion to duty, extraordinary courage, and complete disregard of his own life, above and beyond the call of duty, during the attack on the Fleet in Pearl Harbor, by Japanese forces on 7 December 1941. As Commanding Officer of the U.S.S. *West Virginia,* after being mortally wounded, Capt. Bennion evidenced apparent concern only in fighting and saving his ship, and strongly protested against being carried from the bridge.

*BERRY, CHARLES JOSEPH

Rank and organization: Corporal, U.S. Marine Corps. *Born:* 10 July 1923, Lorain, Ohio. *Accredited to:* Ohio. *Citation:* For conspicuous gallantry and intrepidity at the risk of his life above and beyond the call of duty as member of a machinegun crew, serving with the 1st Battalion, 26th Marines, 5th Marine Division, in action against enemy Japanese forces during the seizure of Iwo Jima in the Volcano Islands, on 3 March 1945. Stationed in the front lines, Cpl. Berry manned his weapon with alert readiness as he maintained a constant vigil with other members of his guncrew during the hazardous night hours. When infiltrating Japanese soldiers launched a surprise attack shortly after midnight in an attempt to overrun his position, he engaged in a pitched handgrenade duel, returning the dangerous weapons with prompt and deadly accuracy until an enemy grenade landed in the foxhole. Determined to save his comrades, he unhesitatingly chose to sacrifice himself and immediately dived on the deadly missile, absorbing the shattering violence of the exploding charge in his own body and protecting the others from serious injury. Stouthearted and indomitable, Cpl. Berry fearlessly yielded his own life that his fellow marines might carry on the relentless battle against a ruthless enemy and his superb valor and unfaltering devotion to duty in the face of certain death reflect the highest credit upon himself and upon the U.S. Naval Service. He gallantly gave his life for his country.

BERTOLDO, VITO R.

Rank and organization: Master Sergeant, U.S. Army, Company A, 242d Infantry, 42d Infantry Division. *Place and date:* Hatten, France, 9–10 January 1945. *Entered service at:* Decatur,

Ill. *Born:* 1 December 1916, Decatur, Ill. *G.O. No.:* 5, 10 January 1946. *Citation:* He fought with extreme gallantry while guarding 2 command posts against the assault of powerful infantry and armored forces which had overrun the battalion's main line of resistance. On the close approach of enemy soldiers, he left the protection of the building he defended and set up his gun in the street, there to remain for almost 12 hours driving back attacks while in full view of his adversaries and completely exposed to 88-mm., machinegun and small-arms fire. He moved back inside the command post, strapped his machinegun to a table and covered the main approach to the building by firing through a window, remaining steadfast even in the face of 88-mm. fire from tanks only 75 yards away. One shell blasted him across the room, but he returned to his weapon. When 2 enemy personnel carriers led by a tank moved toward his position, he calmly waited for the troops to dismount and then, with the tank firing directly at him, leaned out of the window and mowed down the entire group of more than 20 Germans. Some time later, removal of the command post to another building was ordered. M/Sgt. Bertoldo voluntarily remained behind, covering the withdrawal of his comrades and maintaining his stand all night. In the morning he carried his machinegun to an adjacent building used as the command post of another battalion and began a day-long defense of that position. He broke up a heavy attack, launched by a self-propelled 88-mm. gun covered by a tank and about 15 infantrymen. Soon afterward another 88-mm. weapon moved up to within a few feet of his position, and, placing the muzzle of its gun almost inside the building, fired into the room, knocking him down and seriously wounding others. An American bazooka team set the German weapon afire, and M/Sgt. Bertoldo went back to his machinegun dazed as he was and killed several of the hostile troops as they attempted to withdraw. It was decided to evacuate the command post under the cover of darkness, but before the plan could be put into operation the enemy began an intensive assault supported by fire from their tanks and heavy guns. Disregarding the devastating barrage, he remained at his post and hurled white phosphorous grenades into the advancing enemy troops until they broke and retreated. A tank less than 50 yards away fired at his stronghold, destroyed the machinegun and blew him across the room again but he once more returned to the bitter fight and, with a rifle, singlehandedly covered the withdrawal of his fellow soldiers when the post was finally abandoned. With inspiring bravery and intrepidity M/Sgt. Bertoldo withstood the attack of vastly superior forces for more than 48 hours without rest or relief, time after time escaping death only by the slightest margin while killing at least 40 hostile soldiers and wounding many more during his grim battle against the enemy hordes.

BEYER, ARTHUR O.

Rank and organization: Corporal, U.S. Army, Company C, 603d Tank Destroyer Battalion. *Place and date:* Near Arloncourt, Belgium, 15 January 1945. *Entered service at:* St. Ansgar, Iowa. *Born:* 20 May 1909, Rock Township, Mitchell County, Iowa. *G.O. No.:* 73, 30 August 1945. *Citation:* He displayed conspicuous gallantry in action. His platoon, in which he was a tank-destroyer gunner, was held up by antitank, machinegun, and rifle fire from enemy troops dug in along a ridge about 200 yards to the front. Noting a machinegun position in this defense line, he fired upon it with his 76-mm. gun killing 1 man and silencing the weapon. He dismounted from his vehicle and, under direct enemy observation, crossed open ground to capture the 2 remaining members of the crew. Another machinegun, about 250 yards to the left, continued to fire on him. Through withering fire, he advanced on the position. Throwing a grenade into the emplacement, he killed 1 crewmember and again captured the 2 survivors. He was subjected to concentrated small-arms fire but, with great bravery, he worked his way a quarter mile along the ridge, attacking hostile soldiers in their foxholes with his carbine and grenades. When he had completed his self-imposed mission against powerful German forces, he had destroyed 2 machinegun positions, killed 8 of the enemy and captured 18 prisoners, including 2 bazooka teams. Cpl. Beyer's intrepid action and unflinching determination to close with and destroy the enemy eliminated the German defense line and enabled his task force to gain its objective.

*BIANCHI, WILLIBALD C.

Rank and organization: First Lieutenant, U.S. Army, 45th Infantry, Philippine Scouts. *Place and date:* Near Bagac, Bataan Province, Philippine Islands, 3 February 1942. *Entered service at:* New Ulm, Minn. *Birth:* New Ulm, Minn. *G.O. No.:* 11, 5 March 1942. *Citation:* For conspicuous gallantry and intrepidity above and beyond the call of duty in action with the enemy on 3 February 1942, near Bagac, Province of Bataan, Philippine Islands. When the rifle platoon of another company was ordered to wipe out 2 strong enemy machinegun nests, 1st Lt. Bianchi voluntarily and of his own initiative, advanced with the platoon leading part of the men. When wounded early in the action by 2 bullets through the left hand, he did not stop for first aid but discarded his rifle and began firing a pistol. He located a machinegun nest and personally silenced it with grenades. When wounded the second time by 2 machinegun bullets through the chest muscles, 1st Lt. Bianchi climbed to the top of an American tank, manned its antiaircraft machinegun, and fired into strongly held enemy position until knocked completely off the tank by a third severe wound.

BIDDLE, MELVIN E.

Rank and organization: Private First Class, U.S. Army, Company B, 517th Parachute Infantry Regiment. *Place and date:* Near Soy, Belgium, 23–24 December 1944. *Entered service at:* Anderson, Ind. *Birth:* Daleville, Ind. *G.O. No.:* 95, 30 October 1945. *Citation:* He displayed conspicuous gallantry and intrepidity in action against the enemy near Soy, Belgium, on 23 and 24 December 1944. Serving as lead scout during an attack to relieve the enemy-encircled town of Hotton, he aggressively penetrated a densely wooded area, advanced 400 yards until he came within range of intense enemy rifle fire, and within 20 yards of enemy positions killed 3 snipers with unerring marksmanship. Courageously continuing his advance an additional 200 yards, he discovered a hostile machinegun position and dispatched its 2 occupants. He then located the approximate position of a well-concealed enemy machinegun nest, and crawling forward threw handgrenades which killed two Germans and fatally wounded a third. After signaling his company to advance, he entered a determined line of enemy defense, coolly and deliberately shifted his position, and shot 3 more enemy soldiers. Undaunted by enemy fire, he crawled within 20 yards of a machinegun nest, tossed his last handgrenade into the position, and after the explosion charged the emplacement firing his rifle. When night fell, he scouted enemy positions alone for several hours and returned with valuable information which enabled our attacking infantry and armor to knock out 2 enemy tanks. At daybreak he again led the advance and, when flanking elements were pinned down by enemy fire, without hesitation made his way toward a hostile machinegun position and from a distance of 50 yards killed the crew and 2 supporting riflemen. The remainder of the enemy, finding themselves without automatic weapon support, fled panic stricken. Pfc. Biddle's intrepid courage and superb daring during his 20-hour action enabled his battalion to break the enemy grasp on Hotton with a minimum of casualties.

*BIGELOW, ELMER CHARLES

Rank and organization: Watertender First Class, U.S. Naval Reserve. *Born:* 12 July 1920, Hebron, Ill. *Accredited to:* Illinois. *Citation:* For conspicuous gallantry and intrepidity at the risk of his life above and beyond the call of duty while serving on board the U.S.S. *Fletcher* during action against enemy Japanese forces off Corregidor Island in the Philippines, 14 February 1945. Standing topside when an enemy shell struck the *Fletcher,* Bigelow, acting instantly as the deadly projectile exploded into fragments which penetrated the No. 1 gun magazine and set fire to several powder cases, picked up a pair of fire extinguishers and rushed below in a resolute attempt to quell the raging flames. Refusing to waste the precious time required to don rescue-breathing apparatus, he plunged through the blinding smoke billowing out of the magazine hatch and dropped into the blazing compartment. Despite the acrid, burning powder smoke which seared his lungs with every agonizing breath, he worked rapidly and with instinctive sureness and succeeded in quickly extinguishing the fires and in cooling the cases and bulkheads, thereby preventing further damage to the stricken ship. Although he succumbed to his injuries on the following day, Bigelow, by his dauntless valor, unfaltering skill and prompt action in the critical emergency, had averted a magazine explosion which undoubtedly would have left his ship wallowing at the mercy of the furiously pounding Japanese guns on Corregidor, and his heroic spirit of self-sacrifice in the face of almost certain death enhanced and sustained the highest traditions of the U.S. Naval Service. He gallantly gave his life in the service of his country.

BJORKLUND, ARNOLD L.

Rank and organization: First Lieutenant, U.S. Army, 36th Infantry Division. *Place and date:* Near Altavilla, Italy, 13 September 1943. *Entered service at:* Seattle, Wash. *Birth:* Clinton, Wash. *G.O. No.:* 73, 6 September 1944. *Citation:* For conspicuous gallantry and intrepidity at the risk of life above and beyond the call of duty in action with the enemy near Altavilla, Italy, 13 September 1943. When his company attacked a German position on Hill 424, the first platoon, led by 1st Lt. Bjorklund, moved forward on the right flank to the slope of the hill where it was pinned down by a heavy concentration of machinegun and rifle fire. Ordering his men to give covering fire, with only 3 handgrenades, he crept and crawled forward to a German machinegun position located on a terrace along the forward slope. Approaching within a few yards of the position, and while continuously exposed to enemy fire, he hurled 1 grenade into the nest, destroyed the gun and killed 3 Germans. Discovering a second machinegun 20 yards to the right on a higher terrace, he moved under intense enemy fire to a point within a few yards and threw a second grenade into this position, destroying it and killing 2 more Germans. The first platoon was then able to advance 150 yards further up the slope to the crest of the hill, but was again stopped by the fire from a heavy enemy mortar on the reverse slope. 1st Lt. Bjorklund located the mortar and worked his way under little cover to within 10 yards of its position and threw his third grenade, destroying the mortar, killing 2 of the Germans, and forcing the remaining 3 to flee. His actions permitted the platoon to take its objective.

BLOCH, ORVILLE EMIL

Rank and organization: First Lieutenant, U.S. Army, Company E, 338th Infantry, 85th Infantry Division. *Place and date:* Near Firenzuola, Italy, 22 September 1944. *Entered service at:* Streeter, N. Dak. *Birth:* Big Falls, Wis. *G.O. No.:* 9, 10 February 1945. *Citation:* For conspicuous gallantry and intrepidity at risk of life above and beyond the call of duty. 1st Lt. Bloch undertook the task of wiping out 5 enemy machinegun nests that had held up the advance in that particular sector for 1 day. Gathering 3 volunteers from his platoon, the patrol snaked their way to a big rock, behind which a group of 3 buildings and 5 machinegun nests were located. Leaving the 3 men behind the rock, he attacked the first machinegun nest alone charging into furious automatic fire, kicking over the machinegun, and capturing the machinegun crew of 5. Pulling the pin from a grenade, he held it ready in his hand and dashed into the face of withering automatic fire toward this second enemy machinegun nest located at the corner of an adjacent building 15 yards distant. When within 20 feet of the machinegun he hurled the grenade, wounding the machinegunner, the other 2 members of the crew fleeing into a door of the house. Calling one of his volunteer group to accompany him, they advanced to the opposite end of the house, there contacting a machinegun crew of 5 running toward this house. 1st Lt. Bloch and his men opened fire on the enemy crew, forcing them to abandon this machinegun and ammunition and flee into the same house. Without a moment's hesitation, 1st Lt. Bloch, unassisted, rushed through the door into a hail of small-arms fire, firing his carbine from the hip, and captured the 7 occupants, wounding 3 of them. 1st Lt. Bloch with his men then proceeded to a third house where they discovered an abandoned enemy machinegun and detected another enemy machinegun nest at the next corner of the building. The crew of 6 spotted 1st Lt. Bloch the instant he saw them. Without a moment's hesitation he dashed toward them. The enemy fired pistols wildly in his direction and vanished through a door of the house, 1st Lt. Bloch following them through the door, firing his carbine from the hip, wounding 2 of the enemy and capturing 6. Altogether 1st Lt. Bloch had singlehandedly captured 19 prisoners, wounding 6 of them and eliminating a total of 5 enemy machinegun nests. His gallant and heroic actions saved his company many casualties and permitted them to continue the attack with new inspiration and vigor.

BOLDEN, PAUL L.

Rank and organization: Staff Sergeant, U.S. Army, Company I, 120th Infantry, 30th Infantry Division. *Place and date:* Petit-Coo, Belgium, 23 December 1944. *Entered service at:* Madison, Ala. *Birth:* Hobbes Island, Iowa. *G.O. No.:* 73, 30 August 1945. *Citation:* He voluntarily attacked a formidable enemy strongpoint in Petit-Coo, Belgium, on 23 December 1944, when his company was pinned down by extremely heavy automatic and small-arms fire coming from a house 200 yards to the front. Mortar and tank artillery shells pounded the unit, when S/Sgt. Bolden and a comrade, on their own initiative, moved forward into a hail of bullets to eliminate the ever-increasing fire from the German position. Crawling ahead to close with what they knew was a powerfully armed, vastly superior force, the pair reached the house and took up assault positions, S/Sgt. Bolden under a window, his comrade across the street where he could deliver covering fire. In rapid succession, S/Sgt. Bolden hurled a fragmentation grenade and a white phosphorous grenade into the building; and then, fully realizing that he faced tremendous odds, rushed to the door, threw it open and fired into 35 SS troopers who were trying to reorganize themselves after the havoc wrought by the grenades. Twenty Germans died under fire of his submachinegun before he was struck in the shoulder, chest, and stomach by part of a burst which killed his comrade across the street. He withdrew from the house, waiting for the surviving Germans to come out and surrender. When none appeared in the doorway, he summoned his ebbing strength, overcame the extreme pain he suffered and boldly walked back into the house, firing as he went. He had killed the remaining 15 enemy soldiers when his ammunition ran out. S/Sgt. Bolden's heroic advance against great odds, his fearless assault, and his magnificent display of courage in reentering the building where he had been severely wounded cleared the path for his company and insured the success of its mission.

BOLTON, CECIL H.

Rank and organization: First Lieutenant, U.S. Army, Company E, 413th Infantry, 104th Infantry Division. *Place and date:* Mark River, Holland, 2 November 1944. *Entered service at:* Huntsville, Ala. *Birth:* Crawfordsville, Fla. *G.O. No.:* 74, 1 September 1945. *Citation:* As leader of the weapons platoon of Company E, 413th Infantry, on the night of 2 November 1944, he fought gallantly in a pitched battle which followed the crossing of the Mark River in Holland. When 2 machineguns pinned down his company, he tried to eliminate, with mortar fire, their grazing fire which was inflicting serious casualties and preventing the company's advance from an area rocked by artillery shelling. In the moonlight it was impossible for him to locate accurately the enemy's camouflaged positions; but he continued to direct fire until wounded severely in the legs and rendered unconscious by a German shell. When he recovered consciousness he instructed his unit and then crawled to the forward rifle platoon positions. Taking a two-man bazooka team on his voluntary mission, he advanced chest deep in chilling water along a canal toward 1 enemy machinegun. While the bazooka team covered him, he approached alone to within 15 yards of the hostile emplacement in a house. He charged the remaining distance and killed the 2 gunners with handgrenades. Returning to his men he led them through intense fire over open ground to assault the second German machinegun. An enemy sniper who tried to block the way was dispatched, and the trio pressed on. When discovered by the machinegun crew and subjected to direct fire, 1st Lt. Bolton killed 1 of the 3 gunners with carbine fire, and his 2 comrades shot the others. Continuing to disregard his wounds, he led the bazooka team toward an 88-mm. artillery piece which was having telling effect on the American ranks, and approached once more through icy canal water until he could dimly make out the gun's silhouette. Under his fire direction, the two soldiers knocked out the enemy weapon with rockets. On the way back to his own lines he was again wounded. To prevent his men being longer subjected to deadly fire, he refused aid and ordered them back to safety, painfully crawling after them until he reached his lines, where he collapsed. 1st Lt. Bolton's heroic assaults in the face of vicious fire, his inspiring leadership, and continued aggressiveness even through suffering from serious wounds, contributed in large measure to overcoming strong enemy resistance and made it possible for his battalion to reach its objective.

BONG, RICHARD I. (Air Mission)

Rank and organization: Major, U.S. Army Air Corps. *Place and date:* Over Borneo and Leyte, 10 October to 15 November 1944. *Entered service at:* Poplar, Wis. *Birth:* Poplar, Wis. *G.O. No.:* 90, 8 December 1944. *Citation:* For conspicuous gallantry and intrepidity in action above and beyond the call of duty in the Southwest Pacific area from 10 October to 15 November 1944. Though assigned to duty as gunnery instructor and neither required nor expected to perform combat duty, Maj. Bong voluntarily and at his own urgent request engaged in repeated combat missions, including unusually hazardous sorties over Balikpapan, Borneo, and in the Leyte area of the Philippines. His aggressiveness and daring resulted in his shooting down 8 enemy airplanes during this period.

*BONNYMAN, ALEXANDER, Jr.

Rank and organization: First Lieutenant, U.S. Marine Corps Reserves. *Born:* 2 May 1910, Atlanta, Ga. *Accredited to:* New Mexico. *Citation:* For conspicuous gallantry and intrepidity at the risk of his life above and beyond the call of duty as Executive Officer of the 2d Battalion Shore Party, 8th Marines, 2d Marine

Division, during the assault against enemy Japanese-held Tarawa in the Gilbert Islands, 20–22 November 1943. Acting on his own initiative when assault troops were pinned down at the far end of Betio Pier by the overwhelming fire of Japanese shore batteries, 1st Lt. Bonnyman repeatedly defied the blasting fury of the enemy bombardment to organize and lead the besieged men over the long, open pier to the beach and then, voluntarily obtaining flame throwers and demolitions, organized his pioneer shore party into assault demolitionists and directed the blowing of several hostile installations before the close of D-day. Determined to effect an opening in the enemy's strongly organized defense line the following day, he voluntarily crawled approximately 40 yards forward of our lines and placed demolitions in the entrance of a large Japanese emplacement as the initial move in his planned attack against the heavily garrisoned, bombproof installation which was stubbornly resisting despite the destruction early in the action of a large number of Japanese who had been inflicting heavy casualties on our forces and holding up our advance. Withdrawing only to replenish his ammunition, he led his men in a renewed assault, fearlessly exposing himself to the merciless slash of hostile fire as he stormed the formidable bastion, directed the placement of demolition charges in both entrances and seized the top of the bombproof position, flushing more than 100 of the enemy who were instantly cut down, and effecting the annihilation of approximately 150 troops inside the emplacement. Assailed by additional Japanese after he had gained his objective, he made a heroic stand on the edge of the structure, defending his strategic position with indomitable determination in the face of the desperate charge and killing 3 of the enemy before he fell, mortally wounded. By his dauntless fighting spirit, unrelenting aggressiveness and forceful leadership throughout 3 days of unremitting, violent battle, 1st Lt. Bonnyman had inspired his men to heroic effort, enabling them to beat off the counterattack and break the back of hostile resistance in that sector for an immediate gain of 400 yards with no further casualties to our forces in this zone. He gallantly gave his life for his country.

*BOOKER, ROBERT D.

Rank and organization: Private, U.S. Army, 34th Infantry Division. *Place and date:* Near Fondouk, Tunisia, 9 April 1943. *Entered service at:* Callaway, Nebr. *Born:* 11 July 1920, Callaway, Nebr. *G.O. No.:* 34, 25 April 1944. *Citation:* For conspicuous gallantry and intrepidity at risk of life above and beyond the call of duty in action. On 9 April 1943 in the vicinity of Fondouk, Tunisia, Pvt. Booker, while engaged in action against the enemy, carried a light machinegun and a box of ammunition over 200 yards of open ground. He continued to advance despite the fact that 2 enemy machineguns and several mortars were using him as an individual target. Although enemy artillery also began to register on him, upon reaching his objective he immediately commenced firing. After being wounded he silenced 1 enemy machinegun and was beginning to fire at the other when he received a second mortal wound. With his last remaining strength he encouraged the members of his squad and directed their fire. Pvt. Booker acted without regard for his own safety. His initiative and courage against insurmountable odds are an example of the highest standard of self-sacrifice and fidelity to duty.

*BORDELON, WILLIAM JAMES

Rank and organization: Staff Sergeant, U.S. Marine Corps. *Born:* 25 December 1920, San Antonio, Tex. *Accredited to:* Texas. *Citation:* For valorous and gallant conduct above and beyond the call of duty as a member of an assault engineer platoon of the 1st Battalion, 18th Marines, tactically attached to the 2d Marine Division, in action against the Japanese-held atoll of Tarawa in the Gilbert Islands on 20 November 1943. Landing in the assault waves under withering enemy fire which killed all but 4 of the men in his tractor, S/Sgt. Bordelon hurriedly made demolition charges and personally put 2 pillboxes out of action. Hit by enemy machinegun fire just as a charge exploded in his hand while assaulting a third position, he courageously remained in action and, although out of demolition, provided himself with a rifle and furnished fire coverage for a group of men scaling the seawall.

Disregarding his own serious condition, he unhesitatingly went to the aid of one of his demolition men, wounded and calling for help in the water, rescuing this man and another who had been hit by enemy fire while attempting to make the rescue. Still refusing first aid for himself, he again made up demolition charges and singlehandedly assaulted a fourth Japanese machinegun position but was instantly killed when caught in a final burst of fire from the enemy. S/Sgt. Bordelon's great personal valor during a critical phase of securing the limited beachhead was a contributing factor in the ultimate occupation of the island, and his heroic determination throughout 3 days of violent battle reflects the highest credit upon the U.S. Naval Service. He gallantly gave his life for his country.

*BOYCE, GEORGE W. G., Jr.

Rank and organization: Second Lieutenant, U.S. Army, 112th Cavalry Regimental Combat Team. *Place and date:* Near Afua, New Guinea, 23 July 1944. *Entered service at:* Town of Cornwall, Orange County, N.Y. *Birth:* New York City, N.Y. *G.O. No.:* 25, 7 April 1945. *Citation:* For conspicuous gallantry and intrepidity at risk of his life above and beyond the call of duty near Afua, New Guinea, on 23 July 1944. 2d Lt. Boyce's troop, having been ordered to the relief of another unit surrounded by superior enemy forces, moved out, and upon gaining contact with the enemy, the two leading platoons deployed and built up a firing line. 2d Lt. Boyce was ordered to attack with his platoon and make the main effort on the right of the troop. He launched his attack but after a short advance encountered such intense rifle, machinegun, and mortar fire that the forward movement of his platoon was temporarily halted. A shallow depression offered a route of advance and he worked his squad up this avenue of approach in order to close with the enemy. He was promptly met by a volley of handgrenades, 1 falling between himself and the men immediately following. Realizing at once that the explosion would kill or wound several of his men, he promptly threw himself upon the grenade and smothered the blast with his own body. By thus deliberately sacrificing his life to save those of his men, this officer exemplified the highest traditions of the U.S. Armed Forces.

BOYINGTON, GREGORY

Rank and organization: Major, U.S. Marine Corps Reserve, Marine Squadron 214. *Place and date:* Central Solomons area, from 12 September 1943 to 3 January 1944. *Entered service at:* Washington. *Born:* 4 December 1912, Coeur D'Alene, Idaho. *Other Navy award:* Navy Cross. *Citation:* For extraordinary heroism and valiant devotion to duty as commanding officer of Marine Fighting Squadron 214 in action against enemy Japanese forces in the Central Solomons area from 12 September 1943 to 3 January 1944. Consistently outnumbered throughout successive hazardous flights over heavily defended hostile territory, Maj. Boyington struck at the enemy with daring and courageous persistence, leading his squadron into combat with devastating results to Japanese shipping, shore installations, and aerial forces. Resolute in his efforts to inflict crippling damage on the enemy, Maj. Boyington led a formation of 24 fighters over Kahili on 17 October and, persistently circling the airdrome where 60 hostile aircraft were grounded, boldly challenged the Japanese to send up planes. Under his brilliant command, our fighters shot down 20 enemy craft in the ensuing action without the loss of a single ship. A superb airman and determined fighter against overwhelming odds, Maj. Boyington personally destroyed 26 of the many Japanese planes shot down by his squadron and, by his forceful leadership, developed the combat readiness in his command which was a distinctive factor in the Allied aerial achievements in this vitally strategic area.

BRILES, HERSCHEL F.

Rank and organization: Staff Sergeant, U.S. Army, Co. C, 899th Tank Destroyer Battalion. *Place and date:* Near Scherpenseel, Germany, 20 November 1944. *Entered service at:* Fort Des Moines, Iowa. *Birth:* Colfax, Iowa. *G.O. No.:* 77, 10 September 1945. *Citation:* He was leading a platoon of destroyers across an exposed slope near Scherpenseel, Germany, on 20 November 1944, when they came under heavy enemy artillery fire. A direct hit was scored on 1 of the vehicles, killing 1 man, seriously wounding 2 others, and setting the destroyer afire. With a comrade, S/Sgt. Briles left the cover of his own armor and raced across ground raked by artillery and small-arms fire to the rescue of the men in the shattered destroyer. Without hesitation, he lowered himself into the burning turret, removed the wounded and then extinguished the fire. From a position he assumed the next morning, he observed hostile infantrymen advancing. With his machinegun, he poured such deadly fire into the enemy ranks that an entire pocket of 55 Germans surrendered, clearing the way for a junction between American units which had been held up for 2 days. Later that day, when another of his destroyers was hit by a concealed enemy tank, he again left protection to give assistance. With the help of another soldier, he evacuated two wounded under heavy fire and, returning to the burning vehicle, braved death from exploding ammunition to put out the flames. By his heroic initiative and complete disregard for personal safety, S/Sgt. Briles was largely responsible for causing heavy enemy casualties, forcing the surrender of 55 Germans, making possible the salvage of our vehicles, and saving the lives of wounded comrades.

BRITT, MAURICE L.

Rank and organization: Captain (then Lieutenant), U.S. Army, 3d Infantry Division. *Place and date:* North of Mignano, Italy, 10 November 1943. *Entered service at:* Lonoke, Ark. *Born:* 29 June 1919, Carlisle, Ark. *G.O. No.:* 23, 24 March 1944. *Citation:* For conspicuous gallantry and intrepidity at the risk of his life above and beyond the call of duty. Disdaining enemy handgrenades and close-range machine pistol, machinegun, and rifle, Lt. Britt inspired and led a handful of his men in repelling a bitter counterattack by approximately 100 Germans against his company positions north of Mignano, Italy, the morning of 10 November 1943. During the intense fire fight, Lt. Britt's canteen and field glasses were shattered; a bullet pierced his side; his chest, face, and hands were covered with grenade wounds. Despite his wounds, for which he refused to accept medical attention until ordered to do so by his battalion commander following the battle, he personally killed 5 and wounded an unknown number of Germans, wiped out one enemy machinegun crew, fired 5 clips of carbine and an undetermined amount of M1 rifle ammunition, and threw 32 fragmentation grenades. His bold, aggressive actions, utterly disregarding superior enemy numbers, resulted in capture of 4 Germans, 2 of them wounded, and enabled several captured Americans to escape. Lt. Britt's undaunted courage and prowess in arms were largely responsible for repulsing a German counterattack which, if successful, would have isolated his battalion and destroyed his company.

*BROSTROM, LEONARD C.

Rank and organization: Private First Class, U.S. Army, Company F, 17th Infantry, 7th Infantry Division. *Place and date:* Near Dagami, Leyte, Philippine Islands, 28 October 1944. *Entered service at:* Preston, Idaho. *Birth:* Preston, Idaho. *G.O. No.:* 104, 15 November 1945. *Citation:* He was a rifleman with an assault platoon which ran into powerful resistance near Dagami, Leyte, Philippine Islands, on 28 October 1944. From pillboxes, trenches, and spider holes, so well camouflaged that they could be detected at no more than 20 yards, the enemy poured machinegun and rifle fire, causing severe casualties in the platoon. Realizing that a key pillbox in the center of the strong point would have to be knocked out if the company were to advance, Pfc. Brostrom, without orders and completely ignoring his own safety, ran forward to attack the pillbox with grenades. He immediately became the prime target for all the riflemen in the area, as he rushed to the rear of the pillbox and tossed grenades through the entrance. Six enemy soldiers left a trench in a bayonet charge against the heroic American, but he killed 1 and drove the others off with rifle fire. As he threw more grenades from his completely exposed position he was wounded several times in the abdomen and knocked to the ground. Although suffering intense pain and rapidly weakening from loss of blood, he slowly rose to his feet and once more hurled his deadly missiles at the pillbox. As he collapsed, the enemy began fleeing from the fortification and were killed by riflemen of his platoon. Pfc. Brostrom died while being carried from the battlefield, but his intrepidity and unhesitating willingness to sacrifice himself in a 1-man attack against overwhelming odds enabled his company to reorganize against attack, and annihilate the entire enemy position.

BROWN, BOBBIE E.

Rank and organization: Captain, U.S. Army, Company C, 18th Infantry, 1st Infantry Division. *Place and date:* Crucifix Hill, Aachen, Germany, 8 October 1944. *Entered service at:* Atlanta, Ga. *Born:* 2 September 1903, Dublin, Ga. *G.O. No.:* 74, 1 September 1945. *Citation:* He commanded Company C, 18th Infantry Regiment, on 8 October 1944, when it, with the Ranger Platoon of the 1st Battalion, attacked Crucifix Hill, a key point in the enemy's defense of Aachen, Germany. As the leading rifle platoon assaulted the first of many pillboxes studding the rising ground, heavy fire from a flanking emplacement raked it. An intense artillery barrage fell on the American troops which had been pinned down in an exposed position. Seeing that the pillboxes must be neutralized to prevent the slaughter of his men, Capt. Brown obtained a pole charge and started forward alone toward the first pillbox, about 100 yards away. Hugging the ground while enemy bullets whipped around him, he crawled and then ran toward the aperture of the fortification, rammed his explosive inside and jumped back as the pillbox and its occupants were blown up. He rejoined the assault platoon, secured another pole charge, and led the way toward the next pillbox under continuous artillery mortar, automatic, and small-arms fire. He again ran forward and placed his charge in the enemy fortification, knocking it out. He then found that fire from a third pillbox was pinning down his company; so he returned to his men, secured another charge, and began to creep and crawl toward the hostile emplacement. With heroic bravery he disregarded opposing fire and worked ahead in the face of bullets streaming from the pillbox. Finally reaching his objective, he stood up and inserted his explosive, silencing the enemy. He was wounded by a mortar shell but refused medical attention and, despite heavy hostile fire, moved swiftly among his troops exhorting and instructing them in subduing powerful opposition. Later, realizing the need for information of enemy activity beyond the hill, Capt. Brown went out alone to reconnoiter. He observed possible routes of enemy approach and several times deliberately drew enemy fire to locate gun emplacements. Twice more, on this self-imposed mission, he was wounded; but he succeeded in securing information which led to the destruction of several enemy guns and enabled his company to throw back 2 powerful counterattacks with heavy losses. Only when Company C's position was completely secure did he permit treatment of his 3 wounds. By his indomitable courage, fearless leadership, and outstanding skill as a soldier, Capt. Brown contributed in great measure to the taking of Crucifix Hill, a vital link in the American line encircling Aachen.

BULKELEY, JOHN DUNCAN

Rank and organization: Lieutenant Commander, Commander of Motor Torpedo Boat Squadron 3, U.S. Navy. *Place and date:* Philippine waters, 7 December 1941 to 10 April 1942. *Entered service at:* Texas. *Born:* 19 August 1911, New York, N.Y. *Other awards:* Navy Cross, Distinguished Service Cross, Silver Star, Legion of Merit. *Citation:* For extraordinary heroism, distinguished service, and conspicuous gallantry above and beyond the call of duty as commander of Motor Torpedo Boat Squadron 3, in Philippine waters during the period 7 December 1941 to 10 April 1942. The remarkable achievement of Lt. Comdr. Bulkeley's command in damaging or destroying a notable number of Japanese enemy planes, surface combatant and merchant ships, and in dispersing landing parties and land-based enemy forces during the 4 months and 8 days of operation without benefit of repairs, overhaul, or maintenance facilities for his squadron, is believed to be without precedent in this type of warfare. His dynamic forcefulness and daring in offensive action, his brilliantly planned and skillfully executed attacks, supplemented by a unique resourcefulness and ingenuity, characterize him as an outstanding leader of men and a gallant and intrepid seaman. These qualities coupled with a complete disregard for his own personal safety reflect great credit upon him and the Naval Service.

BURKE, FRANK (also known as FRANCIS X. BURKE)

Rank and organization: First Lieutenant, U.S. Army, 15th Infantry, 3d Infantry Division. *Place and date:* Nuremberg, Germany, 17 April 1945. *Entered service at:* Jersey City, N.J. *Born:* 29 September 1918, New York, N.Y. *G.O. No.:* 4, 9 January 1946. *Citation:* He fought with extreme gallantry in the streets of wartorn Nuremberg, Germany, where the 1st Battalion, 15th Infantry, was engaged in rooting out fanatical defenders of the citadel of Nazism. As battalion transportation officer he had gone forward to select a motor-pool site, when, in a desire to perform more than his assigned duties and participate in the fight, he advanced beyond the lines of the forward riflemen. Detecting a group of about 10 Germans making preparations for a local counterattack, he rushed back to a nearby American company, secured a light machinegun with ammunition, and daringly opened fire on this superior force, which deployed and returned his fire with machine pistols, rifles, and rocket launchers. From another angle a German machinegun tried to blast him from his emplacement, but 1st Lt. Burke killed this guncrew and drove off the survivors of the unit he had originally attacked. Giving his next attention to enemy infantrymen in ruined buildings, he picked up a rifle dashed more than 100 yards through intense fire and engaged the Germans from behind an abandoned tank. A sniper nearly hit him from a cellar only 20 yards away, but he dispatched this adversary by running directly to the basement window, firing a full clip into it and then plunging through the darkened aperture to complete the job. He withdrew from the fight only long enough to replace his jammed rifle and secure grenades, then reengaged the Germans. Finding his shots ineffective, he pulled the pins from 2 grenades, and, holding 1 in each hand, rushed the enemy-held building, hurling his missiles just as the enemy threw a potato masher grenade at him. In the triple explosion the Germans were wiped out and 1st Lt. Burke was dazed; but he emerged from the shower of debris that engulfed him, recovered his rifle, and went on to kill 3 more Germans and meet the charge of a machine pistolman, whom he cut down with 3 calmly delivered shots. He then retired toward the American lines and there assisted a platoon in a raging, 30-minute fight against formidable armed hostile forces. This enemy group was repulsed, and the intrepid fighter moved to another friendly group which broke the power of a German unit armed with a 20-mm. gun in a fierce fire fight. In 4 hours of heroic action, 1st Lt. Burke singlehandedly killed 11 and wounded 3 enemy soldiers and took a leading role in engagements in which an additional 29 enemy were killed or wounded. His extraordinary bravery and superb fighting skill were an inspiration to his comrades, and his entirely voluntary mission into extremely dangerous territory hastened the fall of Nuremberg, in his battalion's sector.

*BURR, ELMER J.

Rank and organization: First Sergeant, U.S. Army, Company I, 127th Infantry, 32d Infantry Division. *Place and date:* Buna, New Guinea, 24 December 1942. *Entered service at:* Menasha, Wis. *Birth:* Neenah, Wis. *G.O. No.:* 66, 11 Oct. 1943. *Citation:* For conspicuous gallantry and intrepidity in action above and beyond the call of duty. During an attack near Buna, New Guinea, on 24 December 1942, 1st Sgt. Burr saw an enemy grenade strike near his company commander. Instantly and with heroic self-sacrifice he threw himself upon it, smothering the explosion with his body. 1st Sgt. Burr thus gave his life in saving that of his commander.

BURR, HERBERT H.

Rank and organization: Staff Sergeant, U.S. Army, Company C, 41st Tank Battalion, 11th Armored Division. *Place and date:* Near Dorrmoschel, Germany, 19 March 1945. *Entered service at:* Kansas City, Mo. *Birth:* St. Joseph, Mo. *G.O. No.:* 73, 30 August 1945. *Citation:* He displayed conspicuous gallantry during action when the tank in which he was bow gunner was hit by an enemy rocket, which severely wounded the platoon sergeant and forced the remainder of the crew to abandon the vehicle. Deafened, but otherwise unhurt, S/Sgt. Burr immediately climbed into the driver's seat and continued on the mission of entering the town to reconnoiter road conditions. As he rounded a turn he encountered an 88-mm. antitank gun at pointblank range. Realizing that he had no crew, no one to man the tank's guns, he heroically chose to disregard his personal safety in a direct charge on the German weapon. At considerable speed he headed straight for the loaded gun, which was fully manned by enemy troops who had only to pull the lanyard to send a shell into his vehicle. So unexpected and daring was his assault that he was able to drive his tank completely over the gun, demolishing it and causing its crew to flee in confusion. He then skillfully sideswiped a large truck, overturned it, and wheeling his lumbering vehicle, returned to his company. When medical personnel who had been summoned to treat the wounded sergeant could not locate him, the valiant soldier ran through a hail of sniper fire to direct them to his stricken comrade. The bold, fearless determination of S/Sgt. Burr, his skill and courageous devotion to duty, resulted in the completion of his mission in the face of seemingly impossible odds.

BURT, JAMES M.

Rank and organization: Captain, U.S. Army, Company B, 66th Armored Regiment, 2d Armored Division. *Place and date:* Near Wurselen, Germany, 13 October 1944. *Entered service at:* Lee, Mass. *Birth:* Hinsdale, Mass. *G.O. No.:* 95, 30 October 1945. *Citation:* Capt. James M. Burt was in command of Company B, 66th Armored Regiment on the western outskirts of Wurselen, Germany, on 13 October 1944, when his organization participated in a coordinated infantry-tank attack destined to isolate the large German garrison which was tenaciously defending the city of Aachen. In the first day's action, when infantrymen ran into murderous small-arms and mortar fire, Capt. Burt dismounted from his tank about 200 yards to the rear and moved forward on foot beyond the infantry positions, where, as the enemy concentrated a tremendous volume of fire upon him, he calmly motioned his tanks into good firing positions. As our attack gained momentum, he climbed aboard his tank and directed the action from the rear deck, exposed to hostile volleys which finally wounded him painfully in the face and neck. He maintained his dangerous post despite pointblank self-propelled gunfire until friendly artillery knocked out these enemy weapons, and then proceeded to the advanced infantry scouts' positions to deploy his tanks for the defense of the gains which had been made. The next day, when the enemy counterattacked, he left cover and went 75 yards through heavy fire to assist the infantry battalion commander who was seriously wounded. For the next 8 days, through rainy, miserable weather and under constant, heavy shelling, Capt. Burt held the combined forces together, dominating and controlling the critical situation through the sheer force of his heroic example. To direct artillery fire, on 15 October, he took his tank 300 yards into the enemy lines, where he dismounted and remained for 1 hour giving accurate data to friendly gunners. Twice more that day he went into enemy territory under deadly fire on reconnaissance. In succeeding days he never faltered in his determination to defeat the strong German forces opposing him. Twice the tank in which he was riding was knocked out by enemy action, and each time he climbed aboard another vehicle and continued the fight. He took great risks to rescue wounded comrades and inflicted prodigious destruction on enemy personnel and materiel even though suffering from the wounds he received in the battle's opening phase. Capt. Burt's intrepidity and disregard of personal safety were so complete that his own men and the infantry who attached themselves to him were inspired to overcome the wretched and extremely hazardous conditions which accompanied one of the most bitter local actions of the war. The victory achieved closed the Aachen gap.

BUSH, RICHARD EARL

Rank and organization: Corporal, U.S. Marine Corps Reserve, 1st Battalion, 4th Marines, 6th Marine Division. *Place and date:* Mount Yaetake on Okinawa, Ryukyu Islands, 16 April 1945.

Entered service at: Kentucky. *Born:* 23 December 1923, Glasgow, Ky. *Citation:* For conspicuous gallantry and intrepidity at the risk of his life above and beyond the call of duty as a squad leader serving with the 1st Battalion, 4th Marines, 6th Marine Division, in action against enemy Japanese forces, during the final assault against Mount Yaetake on Okinawa, Ryukyu Islands, 16 April 1945. Rallying his men forward with indomitable determination, Cpl. Bush boldly defied the slashing fury of concentrated Japanese artillery fire pouring down from the gun-studded mountain fortress to lead his squad up the face of the rocky precipice, sweep over the ridge, and drive the defending troops from their deeply entrenched position. With his unit, the first to break through to the inner defense of Mount Yaetake, he fought relentlessly in the forefront of the action until seriously wounded and evacuated with others under protecting rocks. Although prostrate under medical treatment when a Japanese handgrenade landed in the midst of the group, Cpl. Bush, alert and courageous in extremity as in battle, unhesitatingly pulled the deadly missile to himself and absorbed the shattering violence of the exploding charge in his body, thereby saving his fellow marines from severe injury or death despite the certain peril to his own life. By his valiant leadership and aggressive tactics in the face of savage opposition, Cpl. Bush contributed materially to the success of the sustained drive toward the conquest of this fiercely defended outpost of the Japanese Empire. His constant concern for the welfare of his men, his resolute spirit of self-sacrifice, and his unwavering devotion to duty throughout the bitter conflict enhance and sustain the highest traditions of the U.S. Naval Service.

BUSH, ROBERT EUGENE

Rank and organization: Hospital Apprentice First Class, U.S. Naval Reserve, serving as Medical Corpsman with a rifle company, 2d Battalion, 5th Marines, 1st Marine Division. *Place and date:* Okinawa Jima, Ryukyu Islands, 2 May 1945. *Entered service at:* Washington. *Born:* 4 October 1926, Tacoma, Wash. *Citation:* For conspicuous gallantry and intrepidity at the risk of his life above and beyond the call of duty while serving as Medical

Corpsman with a rifle company, in action against enemy Japanese forces on Okinawa Jima, Ryukyu Islands, 2 May 1945. Fearlessly braving the fury of artillery, mortar, and machinegun fire from strongly entrenched hostile positions, Bush constantly and unhesitatingly moved from 1 casualty to another to attend the wounded falling under the enemy's murderous barrages. As the attack passed over a ridge top, Bush was advancing to administer blood plasma to a marine officer lying wounded on the skyline when the Japanese launched a savage counterattack. In this perilously exposed position, he resolutely maintained the flow of life-giving plasma. With the bottle held high in 1 hand, Bush drew his pistol with the other and fired into the enemy's ranks until his ammunition was expended. Quickly seizing a discarded carbine, he trained his fire on the Japanese charging pointblank over the hill, accounting for 6 of the enemy despite his own serious wounds and the loss of 1 eye suffered during his desperate battle in defense of the helpless man. With the hostile force finally routed, he calmly disregarded his own critical condition to complete his mission, valiantly refusing medical treatment for himself until his officer patient had been evacuated, and collapsing only after attempting to walk to the battle aid station. His daring initiative, great personal valor, and heroic spirit of self-sacrifice in service of others reflect great credit upon Bush and enhance the finest traditions of the U.S. Naval Service.

*BUTTS, JOHN E.

Rank and organization: Second Lieutenant, U.S. Army, Co. E, 60th Infantry, 9th Infantry Division. *Place and date:* Normandy, France, 14, 16, and 23 June 1944. *Entered service at:* Buffalo, N.Y. *Birth:* Medina, N.Y. *G.O. No.:* 58, 19 July 1945. *Citation:* Heroically led his platoon against the enemy in Normandy, France, on 14, 16, and 23 June 1944. Although painfully wounded on the 14th near Orglandes and again on the 16th while spearheading an attack to establish a bridgehead across the Douve River, he refused medical aid and remained with his platoon. A week later, near Flottemanville Hague, he led an assault on a tactically important and stubbornly defended hill studded with tanks, antitank guns, pillboxes, and machinegun emplacements, and protected by concentrated artillery and mortar fire. As the attack was launched, 2d Lt. Butts, at the head of his platoon, was critically wounded by German machinegun fire. Although weakened by his injuries, he rallied his men and directed 1 squad to make a flanking movement while he alone made a frontal assault to draw the hostile fire upon himself. Once more he was struck, but by grim determination and sheer courage continued to crawl ahead. When within 10 yards of his objective, he was killed by direct fire. By his superb courage, unflinching valor and inspiring actions, 2d Lt. Butts enabled his platoon to take a formidable strong point and contributed greatly to the success of his battalion's mission.

*CADDY, WILLIAM ROBERT

Rank and organization: Private First Class, U.S. Marine Corps Reserve. *Born:* 8 August 1925, Quincy, Mass. *Accredited to:* Massachusetts. *Citation:* For conspicuous gallantry and intrepidity at the risk of his life above and beyond the call of duty while serving as a rifleman with Company I, 3d Battalion, 26th Marines, 5th Marine Division, in action against enemy Japanese forces during the seizure of Iwo Jima in the Volcano Islands, 3 March 1945. Consistently aggressive, Pfc. Caddy boldly defied shattering Japanese machinegun and small-arms fire to move forward with his platoon leader and another marine during the determined advance of his company through an isolated sector and, gaining the comparative safety of a shell hole, took temporary cover with his comrades. Immediately pinned down by deadly sniper fire from a well-concealed position, he made several unsuccessful attempts to again move forward and then, joined by his platoon leader, engaged the enemy in a fierce exchange of handgrenades until a Japanese grenade fell beyond reach in the shell hole. Fearlessly disregarding all personal danger, Pfc. Caddy instantly dived on the deadly missile, absorbing the exploding charge in his own body and protecting the others from serious injury. Stouthearted and indomitable, he unhesitatingly yielded his own life that his fellow marines might carry on the relentless battle against a fanatic enemy. His dauntless courage and valiant spirit of self-sacrifice in the face of certain death reflect the highest credit upon Pfc. Caddy and upon the U.S. Naval Service. He gallantly gave his life for his comrades.

*CALLAGHAN, DANIEL JUDSON

Rank and organization: Rear Admiral, U.S. Navy. *Born:* 26 July 1892, San Francisco, Calif. *Appointed from:* California. *Entered service at:* Oakland, Calif. *Other Navy award:* Distinguished Service Medal. *Citation:* For extraordinary heroism and conspicuous intrepidity above and beyond the call of duty during action against enemy Japanese forces off Savo Island on the night of 12–13 November 1942. Although out-balanced in strength and numbers by a desperate and determined enemy, Rear Adm. Callaghan, with ingenious tactical skill and superb coordination of the units under his command, led his forces into battle against tremendous odds, thereby contributing decisively to the rout of a powerful invasion fleet, and to the consequent frustration of a formidable Japanese offensive. While faithfully directing close-range operations in the face of furious bombardment by superior enemy fire power, he was killed on the bridge of his flagship. His courageous initiative, inspiring leadership, and judicious foresight in a crisis of grave responsibility were in keeping with the finest traditions of the U.S. Naval Service. He gallantly gave his life in the defense of his country.

CALUGAS, JOSE

Rank and organization: Sergeant, U.S. Army, Battery B, 88th Field Artillery, Philippine Scouts. *Place and date:* At Culis, Bataan Province, Philippine Islands, 16 January 1942. *Entered service at:* Fort Stotsenburg, Philippine Islands. *Born:* 29 December 1907, Barrio Tagsing, Leon, Iloilo, Philippine Islands. *G.O. No.:* 10, 24 February 1942. *Citation:* The action for which the award was made took place near Culis, Bataan Province, Philippine Islands, on 16 January 1942. A battery gun position was bombed and shelled by the enemy until 1 gun was put out of commission and all the cannoneers were killed or wounded. Sgt. Calugas, a mess sergeant of another battery, voluntarily and without orders ran 1,000 yards across the shell-swept area to the gun position. There he organized a volunteer squad which placed the gun back in commission and fired effectively against the enemy, although the position remained under constant and heavy Japanese artillery fire.

*CANNON, GEORGE HAM

Rank and organization: First Lieutenant, U.S. Marine Corps. *Born:* 5 November 1915, Webster Groves, Mo. *Entered service at:* Michigan. *Citation:* For distinguished conduct in the line of his profession, extraordinary courage and disregard of his own condition during the bombardment of Sand Island, Midway Islands, by Japanese forces on 7 December 1941. 1st Lt. Cannon, Battery Commander of Battery H, 6th Defense Battalion, Fleet Marine Force, U.S. Marine Corps, was at his command post when he was mortally wounded by enemy shellfire. He refused to be evacuated from his post until after his men who had been wounded by the same shell were evacuated, and directed the reorganization of his command post until forcibly removed. As a result of his utter disregard of his own condition he died from loss of blood.

*CAREY, ALVIN P.

Rank and organization: Staff Sergeant, U.S. Army, 38th Infantry, 2d Infantry Division. *Place and date:* Near Plougastel, Brittany, France, 23 August 1944. *Entered service at:* Laughlinstown, Pa. *Born:* 16 August 1916, Lycippus, Pa. *G.O. No.:* 37, 11 May 1945. *Citation:* For conspicuous gallantry and intrepidity at the risk of his life, above and beyond the call of duty, on 23 August 1944. S/Sgt. Carey, leader of a machinegun section, was advancing with his company in the attack on the strongly held enemy hill 154, near Plougastel, Brittany, France. The advance was held up when the attacking units were pinned down by intense enemy machinegun fire from a pillbox 200 yards up the hill. From his position covering the right flank, S/Sgt. Carey displaced his guns to an advanced position and then, upon his own initiative, armed himself with as many handgrenades as he could carry and without regard for his personal safety started alone up the hill toward the pillbox. Crawling forward under its withering fire, he proceeded 150 yards when he met a German rifleman whom he killed with his carbine. Continuing his steady forward movement until he reached grenade-throwing distance, he hurled his grenades at the pillbox opening in the face of intense enemy fire which wounded him mortally. Undaunted, he gathered his strength and continued his grenade attack until one entered and exploded within the pillbox, killing the occupants and putting their guns out of action. Inspired by S/Sgt. Carey's heroic act, the riflemen quickly occupied the position and overpowered the remaining enemy resistance in the vicinity.

*CAREY, CHARLES F., JR.

Rank and organization: Technical Sergeant, U.S. Army, 379th Infantry, 100th Infantry Division. *Place and date:* Rimling, France, 8–9 January 1945. *Entered service at:* Cheyenne, Wyo. *Birth:* Canadian, Okla. *G.O. No.:* 53, July 1945. *Citation:* He was in command of an antitank platoon when about 200 enemy infantrymen and 12 tanks attacked his battalion, overrunning part of its position. After losing his guns, T/Sgt. Carey, acting entirely on his own initiative, organized a patrol and rescued 2 of his squads from a threatened sector, evacuating those who had been wounded. He organized a second patrol and advanced against an enemy-held house from which vicious fire issued, preventing the free movement of our troops. Covered by fire from his patrol, he approached the house, killed 2 snipers with his rifle, and threw a grenade in the door. He entered alone and a few minutes later emerged with 16 prisoners. Acting on information he furnished, the American forces were able to capture an additional 41 Germans in adjacent houses. He assembled another patrol, and, under covering fire, moved to within a few yards of an enemy tank and damaged it with a rocket. As the crew attempted to leave their burning vehicle, he calmly shot them with his rifle, killing 3 and wounding a fourth. Early in the morning of 9 January, German infantry moved into the western part of the town and encircled a house in which T/Sgt. Carey had previously posted a squad. Four of the group escaped to the attic. By maneuvering an old staircase against the building, T/Sgt. Carey was able to rescue these men. Later that day, when attempting to reach an outpost, he was struck down by sniper fire. The fearless and aggressive leadership of T/Sgt. Carey, his courage in the face of heavy fire from superior enemy forces, provided an inspiring example for his comrades and materially helped his battalion to withstand the German onslaught.

CARR, CHRIS (name legally changed from CHRISTOS H. KARABERIS, under which name the medal was awarded)

Rank and organization: Sergeant, U.S. Army, Company L, 337th Infantry, 85th Infantry Division. *Place and date:* Near Guignola, Italy, 1–2 October 1944. *Entered service at:* Manchester, N.H. *Birth:* Manchester, N.H. *G.O. No.:* 97, 1 November 1945. *Citation:* Leading a squad of Company L, he gallantly cleared the way for his company's approach along a ridge toward its objective, the Casoni di Remagna. When his platoon was pinned down by heavy fire from enemy mortars, machineguns, machine pistols, and rifles, he climbed in advance of his squad on a maneuver around the left flank to locate and eliminate the enemy gun positions. Undeterred by deadly fire that ricocheted off the barren rocky hillside, he crept to the rear of the first machinegun and charged, firing his submachinegun. In this surprise attack he captured 8 prisoners and turned them over to his squad before striking out alone for a second machinegun. Discovered in his advance and subjected to direct fire from the hostile weapon, he leaped to his feet and ran forward, weaving and crouching, pouring automatic fire into the emplacement that killed 4 of its defenders and forced the surrender of a lone survivor. He again moved forward through heavy fire to attack a third machinegun. When close to the emplacement, he closed with a nerve-shattering shout and burst of fire. Paralyzed by his whirlwind attack, all 4 gunners immediately surrendered. Once more advancing aggressively in the face of a thoroughly alerted enemy, he approached a point of high ground occupied by 2 machineguns which were firing on his company on the slope below. Charging the first of these weapons, he killed 4 of the crew and captured 3 more. The 6 defenders of the adjacent position, cowed by the savagery of his assault, immediately gave up. By his 1-man attack, heroically and voluntarily undertaken in the face of tremendous risks, Sgt. Karaberis captured 5 enemy machinegun positions, killed 8 Germans, took 22 prisoners, cleared the ridge leading to his company's objective, and drove a deep wedge into the enemy line, making it possible for his battalion to occupy important, commanding ground.

*CARSWELL, HORACE S., Jr. (Air Mission)

Rank and organization: Major, 308th Bombardment Group, U.S. Army Air Corps. *Place and date:* Over South China Sea, 26 October 1944. *Entered service at:* San Angelo, Tex. *Birth:* Fort Worth, Tex. *G.O. No.:* 14, 4 February 1946. *Citation:* He piloted a B-24 bomber in a one-plane strike against a Japanese convoy in the South China Sea on the night of 26 October 1944. Taking the enemy force of 12 ships escorted by at least 2 destroyers by surprise, he made 1 bombing run at 600 feet, scoring a near miss on 1 warship and escaping without drawing fire. He circled, and fully realizing that the convoy was thoroughly alerted and would meet his next attack with a barrage of antiaircraft fire, began a second low-level run which culminated in 2 direct hits on a large tanker. A hail of steel from Japanese guns, riddled the bomber, knocking out 2 engines, damaging a third, crippling the hydraulic system, puncturing 1 gasoline tank, ripping uncounted holes in the aircraft, and wounding the copilot; but by magnificent display of flying skill, Maj. Carswell controlled the plane's plunge toward the sea and carefully forced it into a halting climb in the direction of the China shore. On reaching land, where it would have been possible to abandon the staggering bomber, one of the crew discovered that his parachute had been ripped by flak and rendered useless; the pilot, hoping to cross mountainous terrain and reach a base, continued onward until the third engine failed. He ordered the crew to bail out while he struggled to maintain altitude, and, refusing to save himself, chose to remain with his comrade and attempt a crash landing. He died when the airplane struck a mountainside and burned. With consummate gallantry and intrepidity, Maj. Carswell gave his life in a supreme effort to save all members of his crew. His sacrifice, far beyond that required of him, was in keeping with the traditional bravery of America's war heroes.

CASAMENTO, ANTHONY

Rank and organization: Corporal, Company D, First Battalion, Fifth Marines, First Marine Division. *Place and date:* Guadalcanal, Solomon Islands. *Entered service at:* Manhattan, New York. *Date and place of birth:* 16 November 1920, Manhattan, New York. *Citation:* For conspicuous gallantry and intrepidity at the risk of his life above and beyond the call of duty while serving with Company "D," First Battalion, Fifth Marines, First Marine Division on Guadalcanal, British Solomon Islands, in action against the enemy Japanese forces on 1 November 1942. Serving as a leader of a machine gun section, Corporal Casamento directed his unit to advance along a ridge near the Matanikau River where they engaged the enemy. He positioned his section to provide covering fire for two flanking units and to provide direct support for the main force of his company which was behind him. During the course of this engagement, all members of his section were either killed or severely wounded and he himself suffered multiple, grievous wounds. Nonetheless, Corporal Casamento continued to provide critical supporting fire for the attack and in defense of his position. Following the loss of all effective personnel, he set up, loaded, and manned his unit's machine gun, tenaciously holding the enemy forces at bay. Corporal Casamento single-handedly engaged and destroyed one machine gun emplacement to his front and took under fire the other emplacement on the flank. Despite the heat and ferocity of the engagement, he continued to man his weapon and repeatedly repulsed multiple assaults by the enemy forces, thereby protecting the flanks of the adjoining companies and holding his position until the arrival of his main attacking force. Corporal Casamento's courageous fighting spirit, heroic conduct, and unwavering dedication to duty reflected great credit upon himself and were in keeping with the highest traditions of the Marine Corps and the United States Naval Service.

*CASTLE, FREDERICK W. (Air Mission)

Rank and organization: Brigadier General, Assistant Commander, 4th Bomber Wing, U.S. Army Air Corps. *Place and date:* Germany, 24 December 1944. *Entered service at:* Mountain Lake, N.J. *Born:* 14 October 1908, Manila, P.I. *G.O. No.:* 22, 28 February 1947. *Citation:* He was air commander and leader of more than 2,000 heavy bombers in a strike against German airfields on 24 December 1944. En route to the target, the failure of 1 engine forced him to relinquish his place at the head of the formation. In order not to endanger friendly troops on the ground below, he refused to jettison his bombs to gain speed maneuverability. His lagging, unescorted aircraft became the target of numerous enemy fighters which ripped the left wing with cannon shells, set the oxygen system afire, and wounded 2 members of the crew. Repeated attacks started fires in 2 engines, leaving the Flying Fortress in imminent danger of exploding. Realizing the hopelessness of the situation, the bail-out order was given. Without regard for his personal safety he gallantly remained alone at the controls to afford all other crewmembers an opportunity to escape. Still another attack exploded gasoline tanks in the right wing, and the bomber plunged earthward, carrying Gen. Castle to his death. His intrepidity and willing sacrifice of his life to save members of the crew were in keeping with the highest traditions of the military service.

CHAMBERS, JUSTICE M.

Rank and organization: Colonel, U.S. Marine Corps Reserve, 3rd Assault Battalion Landing Team, 25th Marines, 4th Marine Division. *Place and date:* On Iwo Jima, Volcano Islands, from 19 to 22 February 1945. *Entered service at:* Washington, D.C. *Born:* 2 February 1908, Huntington, W. Va. *Citation:* For conspicuous gallantry and intrepidity at the risk of his life above and beyond the call of duty as commanding officer of the 3d Assault Battalion Landing Team, 25th Marines, 4th Marine Division, in action against enemy Japanese forces on Iwo Jima, Volcano Islands, from 19 to 22 February 1945. Under a furious barrage of enemy machinegun and small-arms fire from the commanding cliffs on the right, Col. Chambers (then Lt. Col.) landed immediately after the initial assault waves of his battalion on D-day to find the momentum of the assault threatened by heavy casualties from withering Japanese artillery, mortar rocket, machinegun, and rifle fire. Exposed to relentless hostile fire, he coolly reorganized his battle-weary men, inspiring them to heroic efforts by his own valor and leading them in an attack on the critical, impregnable high ground from which the enemy was pouring an increasing volume of fire directly onto troops ashore as well as amphibious craft in succeeding waves. Constantly in the frontlines encouraging his men to push forward against the enemy's savage resistance, Col. Chambers led the 8-hour battle to carry the flanking ridge top and reduce the enemy's fields of aimed fire, thus protecting the vital foothold gained. In constant defiance of hostile fire while reconnoitering the entire regimental combat team zone of action, he maintained contact with adjacent units and forwarded vital information to the regimental commander. His zealous fighting spirit undiminished despite terrific casualties and the loss of most of his key officers, he again reorganized his troops for renewed attack against the enemy's main line of resistance and was directing the fire of the rocket platoon when he fell, critically wounded. Evacuated under heavy Japanese fire, Col. Chambers, by forceful leadership, courage, and fortitude in the face of staggering odds, was directly instrumental in insuring the success of subsequent operations of the 5th Amphibious Corps on Iwo Jima, thereby sustaining and enhancing the finest traditions of the U.S. Naval Service.

*CHELI, RALPH (Air Mission)

Rank and organization: Major, U.S. Army Air Corps. *Place and date:* Near Wewak, New Guinea, 18 August 1943. *Entered service at:* Brooklyn, N.Y. *Birth:* San Francisco, Calif. *G.O. No.:* 72, 28 October 1943. *Citation:* For conspicuous gallantry and intrepidity above and beyond the call of duty in action with the enemy. While Maj. Cheli was leading his squadron in a dive to attack the heavily defended Dagua Airdrome, intercepting enemy aircraft centered their fire on his plane, causing it to burst into flames while still 2 miles from the objective. His speed would have enabled him to gain necessary altitude to parachute to safety, but this action would have resulted in his formation becoming disorganized and exposed to the enemy. Although a crash was inevitable, he courageously elected to continue leading the attack in his blazing plane. From a minimum altitude, the squadron made a devastating bombing and strafing attack on the target. The mission completed, Maj. Cheli instructed his wingman to lead the formation and crashed into the sea.

CHILDERS, ERNEST

Rank and organization: Second Lieutenant, U.S. Army, 45th Infantry Division. *Place and date:* At Oliveto, Italy, 22 September 1943. *Entered service at:* Tulsa, Okla. *Birth:* Broken Arrow, Okla. *G.O. No.:* 30, 8 April 1944. *Citation:* For conspicuous gallantry and intrepidity at risk of life above and beyond the call of duty in action on 22 September 1943, at Oliveto, Italy. Although 2d Lt. Childers previously had just suffered a fractured instep he, with 8 enlisted men, advanced up a hill toward enemy machinegun nests. The group advanced to a rock wall overlooking a cornfield and 2d Lt. Childers ordered a base of fire laid across the field so that he could advance. When he was fired upon by 2 enemy snipers from a nearby house he killed both of them. He moved behind the machinegun nests and killed all occupants of the nearer one. He continued toward the second one and threw rocks into it. When the 2 occupants of the nest raised up, he shot 1. The other was killed by 1 of the 8 enlisted men. 2d Lt. Childers continued his advance toward a house farther up the hill, and singlehanded, captured an enemy mortar observer. The exceptional leadership, initiative, calmness under fire, and conspicuous gallantry displayed by 2d Lt. Childers were an inspiration to his men.

CHOATE, CLYDE L.

Rank and organization: Staff Sergeant, U.S. Army, Company C, 601st Tank Destroyer Battalion. *Place and date:* Near Bruyeres, France, 25 October 1944. *Entered service at:* Anna, Ill. *Born:* 28 June 1920, West Frankfort, Ill. *G.O. No.:* 75, 5 September 1945. *Citation:* He commanded a tank destroyer near Bruyeres, France, on 25 October 1944. Our infantry occupied a position on a wooded hill when, at dusk, an enemy Mark IV tank and a company of infantry attacked, threatening to overrun the American position and capture a command post 400 yards to the rear. S/Sgt. Choate's tank destroyer, the only weapon available to oppose the German armor, was set afire by 2 hits. Ordering his men to abandon the destroyer, S/Sgt. Choate reached comparative safety. He returned to the burning destroyer to search for comrades possibly trapped in the vehicle risking instant death in an explosion which was imminent and braving enemy fire which ripped his jacket and tore the helmet from his head. Completing the search and seeing the tank and its supporting infantry overrunning our infantry in their shallow foxholes, he secured a bazooka and ran after the tank, dodging from tree to tree and passing through the enemy's loose skirmish line. He fired a rocket from a distance of 20 yards, immobilizing the tank but leaving it able to spray the area with cannon and machinegun fire. Running back to our infantry through vicious fire, he secured another rocket, and, advancing against a hail of machinegun and small-arms fire reached a position 10 yards from the tank. His second shot shattered the turret. With his pistol he killed 2 of the crew as they emerged from the tank; and then running to the crippled Mark IV while enemy infantry sniped at him, he dropped a grenade inside the tank and completed its destruction. With their armor gone, the enemy infantry became disorganized and was driven back. S/Sgt. Choate's great daring in assaulting an enemy tank singlehanded, his determination to follow the vehicle after it had passed his position, and his skill and crushing thoroughness in the attack prevented the enemy from capturing a battalion command post and turned a probable defeat into a tactical success.

*CHRISTENSEN, DALE ELDON

Rank and organization: Second Lieutenant, U.S. Army, Troop E, 112th Cavalry Regiment. *Place and date:* Driniumor River, New Guinea, 16–19 July 1944. *Entered service at:* Gray, Iowa. *Birth:* Cameron Township, Iowa. *G.O. No.:* 36, 10 May 1945. *Citation:* For conspicuous gallantry and intrepidity at the risk of his life above and beyond the call of duty along the Driniumor River, New Guinea, from 16–19 July 1944. 2d Lt. Christensen repeatedly distinguished himself by conspicuous gallantry above and beyond the call of duty in the continuous heavy fighting which occurred in this area from 16–19 July. On 16 July, his platoon engaged in a savage fire fight in which much damage was caused by 1 enemy machinegun effectively placed. 2d Lt. Christensen ordered his men to remain under cover, crept forward under fire, and at a range of 15 yards put the gun out of action with handgrenades. Again, on 19 July, while attacking an enemy position strong in mortars and machineguns, his platoon was pinned to the ground by intense fire. Ordering his men to remain under cover, he crept forward alone to locate definitely the enemy automatic weapons and the best direction from which to attack. Although his rifle was struck by enemy fire and knocked from his hands he continued his reconnaissance, located 5 enemy machineguns, destroyed 1 with handgrenades, and rejoined his platoon. He then led his men to the point selected for launching the attack and, calling encouragement, led the charge. This assault was successful and the enemy was driven from the positions with a loss of 4 mortars and 10 machineguns and leaving many dead on the field. On 4 August 1944, near Afua, Dutch New Guinea, 2d Lt. Christensen was killed in action about 2 yards from his objective while leading his platoon in an attack on an enemy machinegun position. 2d Lt. Christensen's leadership, intrepidity, and repeatedly demonstrated gallantry in action at the risk of his life, above and beyond the call of duty, exemplify the highest traditions of the U.S. Armed Forces.

*CHRISTIAN, HERBERT F.

Rank and organization: Private, U.S. Army, 15th Infantry, 3d Infantry Division. *Place and date:* Near Valmontone, Italy, 2–3 June 1944. *Entered service at:* Steubenville, Ohio. *Birth:* Byersville, Ohio. *G.O. No.:* 43, 30 May 1945. *Citation:* For conspicuous gallantry and intrepidity at risk of life above and beyond the call of duty. On 2–3 June 1944, at 1 a.m., Pvt. Christian elected to sacrifice his life in order that his comrades might extricate themselves from an ambush. Braving massed fire of about 60 riflemen, 3 machineguns, and 3 tanks from positions only 30 yards distant, he stood erect and signaled to the patrol to withdraw. The whole area was brightly illuminated by enemy flares. Although his right leg was severed above the knee by cannon fire, Pvt. Christian advanced on his left knee and the bloody stump of his right thigh, firing his submachinegun. Despite excruciating pain, Pvt. Christian continued on his self-assigned mission. He succeeded in distracting the enemy and enabled his 12 comrades to escape. He killed 3 enemy soldiers almost at once. Leaving a trail of blood behind him, he made his way forward 20 yards, halted at a point within 10 yards of the enemy, and despite intense fire killed a machine-pistol man. Reloading his weapon, he fired directly into the enemy position. The enemy appeared enraged at the success of his ruse, concentrated 20-mm. machinegun, machine-pistol and rifle fire on him, yet he refused to seek cover. Maintaining his erect position, Pvt. Christian fired his weapon to the very last. Just as he emptied his submachinegun, the enemy bullets found their mark and Pvt. Christian slumped forward dead. The courage and spirit of self-sacrifice displayed by this soldier were an inspiration to his comrades and are in keeping with the highest traditions of the armed forces.

*CICCHETTI, JOSEPH J.

Rank and organization: Private First Class, U.S. Army, Company A, 148th Infantry, 37th Infantry Division. *Place and date:* South Manila, Luzon, Philippine Islands, 9 February 1945. *Entered service at:* Waynesburg, Ohio. *Birth:* Waynesburg, Ohio. *G.O. No.:* 115, 8 December 1945. *Citation:* He was with troops assaulting the first important line of enemy defenses. The Japanese had converted the partially destroyed Manila Gas Works and adjacent buildings into a formidable system of mutually supporting strongpoints from which they were concentrating machinegun, mortar, and heavy artillery fire on the American forces. Casualties rapidly mounted, and the medical aid men, finding it increasingly difficult to evacuate the wounded, called for volunteer litter bearers. Pfc. Cicchetti immediately responded, organized a litter team and skillfully led it for more than 4 hours in rescuing 14 wounded men, constantly passing back and forth over a 400-yard route which was the impact area for a tremendous volume of the most intense enemy fire. On 1 return trip the path was blocked by machinegun fire, but Pfc. Cicchetti deliberately exposed himself to draw the automatic fire which he neutralized with his own rifle while ordering the rest of the team to rush past to safety with the wounded. While gallantly continuing his work, he noticed a group of wounded and helpless soldiers some distance away and ran to their rescue although the enemy fire had increased to new fury. As he approached the casualties, he was struck in the head by a shell fragment, but with complete disregard for his gaping wound he continued to his comrades, lifted 1 and carried him on his shoulders 50 yards to safety. He then collapsed and died. By his skilled leadership, indomitable will, and dauntless courage, Pfc. Cicchetti saved the lives of many of his fellow soldiers at the cost of his own.

CLARK, FRANCIS J.

Rank and organization: Technical Sergeant, U.S. Army, Company K, 109th Infantry, 28th Infantry Division. *Place and date:* Near Kalborn, Luxembourg, 12 September 1944; near Sevenig,

Germany, 17 September 1944. *Entered service at:* Salem, N.Y. *Birth:* Whitehall, N.Y. *G.O. No.:* 77, 10 September 1945. *Citation:* He fought gallantly in Luxembourg and Germany. On 12 September 1944, Company K began fording the Our River near Kalborn, Luxembourg, to take high ground on the opposite bank. Covered by early morning fog, the 3d Platoon, in which T/Sgt. Clark was squad leader, successfully negotiated the crossing; but when the 2d Platoon reached the shore, withering automatic and small-arms fire ripped into it, eliminating the platoon leader and platoon sergeant and pinning down the troops in the open. From his comparatively safe position, T/Sgt. Clark crawled alone across a field through a hail of bullets to the stricken troops. He led the platoon to safety and then unhesitatingly returned into the fireswept area to rescue a wounded soldier, carrying him to the American line while hostile gunners tried to cut him down. Later, he led his squad and men of the 2d Platoon in dangerous sorties against strong enemy positions to weaken them by lightning-like jabs. He assaulted an enemy machinegun with handgrenades, killing 2 Germans. He roamed the front and flanks, dashing toward hostile weapons, killing and wounding an undetermined number of the enemy, scattering German patrols and, eventually, forcing the withdrawal of a full company of Germans heavily armed with automatic weapons. On 17 September, near Sevenig, Germany, he advanced alone against an enemy machinegun, killed the gunner and forced the assistant to flee. The Germans counterattacked, and heavy casualties were suffered by Company K. Seeing that 2 platoons lacked leadership, T/Sgt. Clark took over their command and moved among the men to give encouragement. Although wounded on the morning of 18 September, he refused to be evacuated and took up a position in a pillbox when night came. Emerging at daybreak, he killed a German soldier setting up a machinegun not more than 5 yards away. When he located another enemy gun, he moved up unobserved and killed 2 Germans with rifle fire. Later that day he voluntarily braved small-arms fire to take food and water to members of an isolated platoon. T/Sgt. Clark's actions in assuming command when leadership was desperately needed, in launching attacks and beating off counterattacks, in aiding his stranded comrades, and in fearlessly facing powerful enemy fire, were strikingly heroic examples and put fighting heart into the hardpressed men of Company K.

COLALILLO, MIKE

Rank and organization: Private First Class, U.S. Army, Company C, 398th Infantry, 100th Infantry Division. *Place and date:* Near Untergriesheim, Germany, 7 April 1945. *Entered service at:* Duluth, Minn. *Birth:* Hibbing, Minn. *G.O. No.:* 4, 9 January 1946. *Citation:* He was pinned down with other members of his company during an attack against strong enemy positions in the vicinity of Untergriesheim, Germany. Heavy artillery, mortar, and machinegun fire made any move hazardous when he stood up, shouted to the company to follow, and ran forward in the wake of a supporting tank, firing his machine pistol. Inspired by his example, his comrades advanced in the face of savage enemy fire. When his weapon was struck by shrapnel and rendered useless, he climbed to the deck of a friendly tank, manned an exposed machinegun on the turret of the vehicle, and, while bullets rattled about him, fired at an enemy emplacement with such devastating accuracy that he killed or wounded at least 10 hostile soldiers and destroyed their machinegun. Maintaining his extremely dangerous post as the tank forged ahead, he blasted 3 more positions, destroyed another machinegun emplacement and silenced all resistance in his area, killing at least 3 and wounding an undetermined number of riflemen as they fled. His machinegun eventually jammed; so he secured a submachine gun from the tank crew to continue his attack on foot. When our armored forces exhausted their ammunition and the order to withdraw was given, he remained behind to help a seriously wounded comrade over several hundred yards of open terrain rocked by an intense enemy artillery and mortar barrage. By his intrepidity and inspiring courage Pfc. Colalillo gave tremendous impetus to his company's attack, killed or wounded 25 of the enemy in bitter fighting, and assisted a wounded soldier in reaching the American lines at great risk of his own life.

*COLE, DARRELL SAMUEL

Rank and organization: Sergeant, U.S. Marine Corps Reserve. *Born:* 20 July 1920, Flat River, Mo. *Entered service at:* Esther, Mo. *Other Navy award:* Bronze Star Medal. *Citation:* For conspicuous gallantry and intrepidity at the risk of his life above and beyond the call of duty while serving as leader of a Machinegun Section of Company B, 1st Battalion, 23d Marines, 4th Marine Division, in action against enemy Japanese forces during the assault on Iwo Jima in the Volcano Islands, 19 February 1945. Assailed by a tremendous volume of small-arms, mortar and artillery fire as he advanced with 1 squad of his section in the initial assault wave, Sgt. Cole boldly led his men up the sloping beach toward Airfield No. 1 despite the blanketing curtain of flying shrapnel and, personally destroying with handgrenades 2 hostile emplacements which menaced the progress of his unit, continued to move forward until a merciless barrage of fire emanating from 3 Japanese pillboxes halted the advance. Instantly placing his 1 remaining machinegun in action, he delivered a shattering fusillade and succeeded in silencing the nearest and most threatening emplacement before his weapon jammed and the enemy, reopening fire with knee mortars and grenades, pinned down his unit for the second time. Shrewdly gaging the tactical situation and evolving a daring plan of counterattack, Sgt. Cole, armed solely with a pistol and 1 grenade, cooly advanced alone to the hostile pillboxes. Hurling his 1 grenade at the enemy in sudden, swift attack, he quickly withdrew, returned to his own lines for additional grenades and again advanced, attacked, and withdrew. With enemy guns still active, he ran the gauntlet of slashing fire a third time to complete the total destruction of the Japanese strong point and the annihilation of the defending garrison in this final assault. Although instantly killed by an enemy grenade as he returned to his squad, Sgt. Cole had eliminated a formidable Japanese position, thereby enabling his company to storm the remaining fortifications, continue the advance, and seize the objective. By his dauntless initiative, unfaltering courage, and indomitable determination during a critical period of action, Sgt. Cole served as an inspiration to his comrades, and his stouthearted leadership in the face of almost certain death sustained and enhanced the highest tradition of the U.S. Naval Service. He gallantly gave his life for his country.

*COLE, ROBERT G.

Rank and organization: Lieutenant Colonel, U.S. Army, 101st Airborne Division. *Place and date:* Near Carentan, France, 11 June 1944. *Entered service at:* San Antonio, Tex. *Birth:* Fort Sam Houston, Tex. *G.O. No.:* 79, 4 October 1944. *Citation:* For gallantry and intrepidity at the risk of his own life, above and beyond the call of duty on 11 June 1944, in France. Lt. Col. Cole was personally leading his battalion in forcing the last 4 bridges on the road to Carentan when his entire unit was suddenly pinned to the ground by intense and withering enemy rifle, machinegun, mortar, and artillery fire placed upon them from well-prepared and heavily fortified positions within 150 yards of the foremost elements. After the devastating and unceasing enemy fire had for over 1 hour prevented any move and inflicted numerous casualties, Lt. Col. Cole, observing this almost hopeless situation, courageously issued orders to assault the enemy positions with fixed bayonets. With utter disregard for his own safety and completely ignoring the enemy fire, he rose to his feet in front of his battalion and with drawn pistol shouted to his men to follow him in the assault. Catching up a fallen man's rifle and bayonet, he charged on and led the remnants of his battalion across the bullet-swept open ground and into the enemy position. His heroic and valiant action in so inspiring his men resulted in the complete establishment of our bridgehead across the Douve River. The cool fearlessness, personal bravery, and outstanding leadership displayed by Lt. Col. Cole reflect great credit upon himself and are worthy of the highest praise in the military service.

CONNOR, JAMES P.

Rank and organization: Sergeant, U.S. Army, 7th Infantry, 3d Infantry Division. *Place and date:* Cape Cavalaire, southern France, 15 August 1944. *Entered service at:* Wilmington, Del.

Birth: Wilmington, Del. *G.O. No.:* 18, 15 March 1945. *Citation:* For conspicuous gallantry and intrepidity at risk of life above and beyond the call of duty. On 15 August 1944 Sgt. Connor, through sheer grit and determination, led his platoon in clearing an enemy vastly superior in numbers and firepower from strongly entrenched positions on Cape Cavalaire, removing a grave enemy threat to his division during the amphibious landing in southern France, and thereby insured safe and uninterrupted landings for the huge volume of men and materiel which followed. His battle patrol landed on "Red Beach" with the mission of destroying the strongly fortified enemy positions on Cape Cavalaire with utmost speed. From the peninsula the enemy had commanding observation and seriously menaced the vast landing operations taking place. Though knocked down and seriously wounded in the neck by a hanging mine which killed his platoon lieutenant, Sgt. Connor refused medical aid and with his driving spirit practically carried the platoon across several thousand yards of mine-saturated beach through intense fire from mortars, 20-mm. flak guns, machineguns, and snipers. En route to the Cape he personally shot and killed 2 snipers. The platoon sergeant was killed and Sgt. Connor became platoon leader. Receiving a second wound, which lacerated his shoulder and back, he again refused evacuation, expressing determination to carry on until physically unable to continue. He reassured and prodded the hesitating men of his decimated platoon forward through almost impregnable mortar concentrations. Again emphasizing the prevalent urgency of their mission, he impelled his men toward a group of buildings honeycombed with enemy snipers and machineguns. Here he received his third grave wound, this time in the leg, felling him in his tracks. Still resolved to carry on, he relinquished command only after his attempts proved that it was physically impossible to stand. Nevertheless, from his prone position, he gave the orders and directed his men in assaulting the enemy. Infused with Sgt. Connor's dogged determination, the platoon, though reduced to less than one-third of its original 36 men, outflanked and rushed the enemy with such furiousness that they killed 7, captured 40, seized 3 machineguns and considerable other materiel, and took all their assigned objectives, successfully completing their mission. By his repeated examples of tenaciousness and indomitable spirit Sgt. Connor transmitted his heroism to his men until they became a fighting team which could not be stopped.

COOLEY, RAYMOND H.

Rank and organization: Staff Sergeant, U.S. Army, Company B, 27th Infantry, 25th Infantry Division. *Place and date:* Near Lumboy, Luzon, Philippine Islands, 24 February 1945. *Entered service at:* Richard City, Tenn. *Born:* 7 May 1914, Dunlap, Tenn. *G.O. No.:* 77, 10 September 1945. *Citation:* He was a platoon guide in an assault on a camouflaged entrenchment defended by machineguns, rifles, and mortars. When his men were pinned down by 2 enemy machineguns, he voluntarily advanced under heavy fire to within 20 yards of 1 of the guns and attacked it with a handgrenade. The enemy, however, threw the grenade back at him before it could explode. Arming a second grenade, he held it for several seconds of the safe period and then hurled it into the enemy position, where it exploded instantaneously, destroying the gun and crew. He then moved toward the remaining gun, throwing grenades into enemy foxholes as he advanced. Inspired by his actions, 1 squad of his platoon joined him. After he had armed another grenade and was preparing to throw it into the second machinegun position, 6 enemy soldiers rushed at him. Knowing he could not dispose of the armed grenade without injuring his comrades, because of the intermingling in close combat of the men of his platoon and the enemy in the melee which ensued, he deliberately covered the grenade with his body and was severely wounded as it exploded. By his heroic actions, S/Sgt. Cooley not only silenced a machinegun and so inspired his fellow soldiers that they pressed the attack and destroyed the remaining enemy emplacements, but also, in complete disregard of his own safety, accepted certain injury and possible loss of life to avoid wounding his comrades.

COOLIDGE, CHARLES H.

Rank and organization: Technical Sergeant, U.S. Army, Company M, 141st Infantry, 36th Infantry Division. *Place and date:* East of Belmont sur Buttant, France, 24–27 October 1944. *Entered service at:* Signal Mountain, Tenn. *Birth:* Signal Mountain, Tenn. *G.O. No.:* 53, July 1945. *Citation:* Leading a section of heavy machineguns supported by 1 platoon of Company K, he took a position near Hill 623, east of Belmont sur Buttant, France, on 24 October 1944, with the mission of covering the right flank of the 3d Battalion and supporting its action. T/Sgt. Coolidge went forward with a sergeant of Company K to reconnoiter positions for coordinating the fires of the light and heavy machineguns. They ran into an enemy force in the woods estimated to be an infantry company. T/Sgt. Coolidge, attempting to bluff the Germans by a show of assurance and boldness called upon them to surrender, whereupon the enemy opened fire. With his carbine, T/Sgt. Coolidge wounded 2 of them. There being no officer present with the force, T/Sgt. Coolidge at once assumed command. Many of the men were replacements recently arrived; this was their first experience under fire. T/Sgt. Coolidge, unmindful of the enemy fire delivered at close range, walked along the position, calming and encouraging his men and directing their fire. The attack was thrown back. Through 25 and 26 October the enemy launched repeated attacks against the position of this combat group but each was repulsed due to T/Sgt. Coolidge's able leadership. On 27 October, German infantry, supported by 2 tanks, made a determined attack on the position. The area was swept by enemy small-arms, machinegun, and tank fire. T/Sgt. Coolidge armed himself with a bazooka and advanced to within 25 yards of the tanks. His bazooka failed to function and he threw it aside. Securing all the handgrenades he could carry, he crawled forward and inflicted heavy casualties on the advancing enemy. Finally it became apparent that the enemy, in greatly superior force, supported by tanks, would overrun the position. T/Sgt. Coolidge, displaying great coolness and courage, directed and conducted an orderly withdrawal, being himself the last to leave the position. As a result of T/Sgt. Coolidge's heroic and superior leadership, the mission of this combat group was accomplished throughout 4 days of continuous fighting against numerically superior enemy troops in rain and cold and amid dense woods.

*COURTNEY, HENRY ALEXIUS, JR.

Rank and organization: Major, U.S. Marine Corps Reserve. *Born:* 6 January 1916, Duluth, Minn. *Appointed from:* Minnesota. *Citation:* For conspicuous gallantry and intrepidity at the risk of his life above and beyond the call of duty as Executive Officer of the 2d Battalion, 22d Marines, 6th Marine Division, in action against enemy Japanese forces on Okinawa Shima in the Ryukyu Islands, 14 and 15 May 1945. Ordered to hold for the night in static defense behind Sugar Loaf Hill after leading the forward elements of his command in a prolonged fire fight, Maj. Courtney weighed the effect of a hostile night counterattack against the tactical value of an immediate marine assault, resolved to initiate the assault, and promptly obtained permission to advance and seize the forward slope of the hill. Quickly explaining the situation to his small remaining force, he declared his personal intention of moving forward and then proceeded on his way, boldly blasting nearby cave positions and neutralizing enemy guns as he went. Inspired by his courage, every man followed without hesitation, and together the intrepid marines braved a terrific concentration of Japanese gunfire to skirt the hill on the right and reach the reverse slope. Temporarily halting, Maj. Courtney sent guides to the rear for more ammunition and possible replacements. Subsequently reinforced by 26 men and an LVT load of grenades, he determined to storm the crest of the hill and crush any planned counterattack before it could gain sufficient momentum to effect a breakthrough. Leading his men by example rather than by command, he pushed ahead with unrelenting aggressiveness, hurling grenades into cave openings on the slope with devastating effect. Upon reaching the crest and observing large numbers of Japanese forming for action less than 100 yards away, he instantly attacked, waged a furious battle and succeeded in killing many of the enemy and in forcing the remainder to take cover in the caves. Determined to hold, he ordered his men to dig in and, coolly disregarding the continuous hail of flying enemy shrapnel to rally his weary troops, tirelessly aided casualties and assigned his men to more advantageous positions. Although instantly killed by a hostile mortar burst while moving among his men, Maj. Courtney, by his astute military acumen, indomitable leadership and decisive action in the face of overwhelming odds, had contributed essentially to the success of the Okinawa campaign. His great personal valor throughout sustained and enhanced the highest traditions of the U.S. Naval Service. He gallantly gave his life for his country.

*COWAN, RICHARD ELLER

Rank and organization: Private First Class, U.S. Army, Company M, 23d Infantry, 2d Infantry Division. *Place and date:* Near Krinkelter Wald, Belgium, 17 December 1944. *Entered service at:* Wichita, Kans. *Birth:* Lincoln, Nebr. *G.O. No.:* 48, 23 June 1945. *Citation:* He was a heavy machinegunner in a section attached to Company I in the vicinity of Krinkelter Wald, Belgium, 17 December 1944, when that company was attacked by a numerically superior force of German infantry and tanks. The first 6 waves of hostile infantrymen were repulsed with heavy casualties, but a seventh drive with tanks killed or wounded all but 3 of his section, leaving Pvt. Cowan to man his gun, supported by only 15 to 20 riflemen of Company I. He maintained his position, holding off the Germans until the rest of the shattered force had set up a new line along a firebreak. Then, unaided, he moved his machinegun and ammunition to the second position. At the approach of a Royal Tiger tank, he held his fire until about 80 enemy infantrymen supporting the tank appeared at a distance of about 150 yards. His first burst killed or wounded about half of these infantrymen. His position was rocked by an 88-mm. shell when the tank opened fire, but he continued to man his gun, pouring deadly fire into the Germans when they again advanced. He was barely missed by another shell. Fire from three machineguns and innumerable small arms struck all about him; an enemy rocket shook him badly, but did not drive him from his gun. Infiltration by the enemy had by this time made the position untenable, and the order was given to withdraw. Pvt. Cowan was the last man to leave, voluntarily covering the withdrawal of his remaining comrades. His heroic actions were entirely responsible for allowing the remaining men to retire successfully from the scene of their last-ditch stand.

CRAFT, CLARENCE B.

Rank and organization: Private, First Class, U.S. Army, Company G, 382d Infantry, 96th Infantry Division. *Place and date:* Hen Hill, Okinawa, Ryukyu Islands, 31 May 1945. *Entered service at:* Santa Ana, Calif. *Birth:* San Bernardino, Calif. *G.O. No.:* 97, 1 November 1945. *Citation:* He was a rifleman when his platoon spearheaded an attack on Hen Hill, the tactical position on which the entire Naha-Shuri-Yonaburu line of Japanese defense on Okinawa, Ryukyu Islands, was hinged. For 12 days our forces had been stalled, and repeated, heavy assaults by 1 battalion and then another had been thrown back by the enemy with serious casualties. With 5 comrades, Pfc. Craft was dispatched in advance of Company G to feel out the enemy resistance. The group had proceeded only a short distance up the slope when rifle and machinegun fire, coupled with a terrific barrage of grenades, wounded 3 and pinned down the others. Against odds that appeared suicidal, Pfc. Craft launched a remarkable 1-man attack. He stood up in full view of the enemy and began shooting with deadly marksmanship wherever he saw a hostile movement. He steadily advanced up the hill, killing Japanese soldiers with rapid fire, driving others to cover in their strongly disposed trenches, unhesitatingly facing alone the strength that had previously beaten back attacks in battalion strength. He reached the crest of the hill, where he stood silhouetted against the sky while quickly throwing grenades at extremely short range into the enemy positions. His extraordinary assault lifted the pressure from his company for the moment, allowing members of his platoon to comply with his motions to advance and pass him more grenades. With a chain of his comrades supplying him while he stood atop the hill, he furiously hurled a total of 2 cases of grenades into a main trench and other positions on the reverse slope of Hen Hill, meanwhile directing the aim of his fellow soldiers who threw grenades from the slope below him. He left his position, where grenades from both sides were passing over his head and bursting on either slope, to attack the main enemy trench as confusion and panic seized the defenders. Straddling the excavation, he pumped rifle fire into the Japanese at pointblank range, killing many and causing the others to flee down the trench. Pursuing them, he came upon a heavy machinegun which was still creating havoc in the American ranks. With rifle fire and a grenade he wiped out this position. By this time the Japanese were in complete rout and American forces were swarming over the hill. Pfc. Craft continued down the central trench to the mouth of a cave where many of the enemy had taken cover. A satchel charge was brought to him, and he tossed it into the cave. It failed to explode. With great daring, the intrepid fighter retrieved the charge from the cave, relighted the fuse and threw it back, sealing up the Japs in a tomb. In the local action, against tremendously superior forces heavily armed with rifles, machineguns, mortars, and grenades, Pfc. Craft killed at least 25 of the enemy; but his contribution to the campaign on Okinawa was of much more far-reaching consequence for Hen Hill was the key to the entire defense line, which rapidly crumbled after his utterly fearless and heroic attack.

*CRAIG, ROBERT

Rank and organization: Second Lieutenant, U.S. Army, 15th Infantry, 3d Infantry Division. *Place and date:* Near Favoratta, Sicily, 11 July 1943. *Entered service at:* Toledo, Ohio. *Birth:* Scotland. *G.O. No.:* 41, 26 May 1944. *Citation:* For conspicuous gallantry and intrepidity at the risk of life, above and beyond the call of duty, on 11 July 1943, at Favoratta, Sicily. 2d Lt. Craig voluntarily undertook the perilous task of locating and destroying a hidden enemy machinegun which had halted the advance of his company. Attempts by 3 other officers to locate the weapon had resulted in failure, with each officer receiving wounds. 2d Lt. Craig located the gun and snaked his way to a point within 35 yards of the hostile position before being discovered. Charging headlong into the furious automatic fire, he reached the gun, stood over it, and killed the 3 crew members with his carbine. With this obstacle removed, his company continued its advance. Shortly thereafter, while advancing down the forward slope of a ridge, 2d Lt. Craig and his platoon, in a position devoid of cover and concealment, encountered the fire of approximately 100 enemy soldiers. Electing to sacrifice himself so that his platoon might carry on the battle, he ordered his men to withdraw to the cover of the crest while he drew the enemy fire to himself. With no hope of survival, he charged toward the enemy until he was within 25 yards of them. Assuming a kneeling position, he killed 5 and wounded 3 enemy soldiers. While the hostile force concentrated fire on him, his platoon reached the cover of the crest. 2d Lt. Craig was killed by enemy fire, but his intrepid action so inspired his men that they drove the enemy from the area, inflicting heavy casualties on the hostile force.

*CRAIN, MORRIS E.

Rank and organization: Technical Sergeant, U.S. Army, Company E, 141st Infantry, 36th Infantry Division. *Place and date:* Haguenau, France, 13 March 1945. *Entered service at:* Paducah, Ky. *Birth:* Bandana, Ky. *G.O. No.:* 18, 13 February 1946. *Citation:* He led his platoon against powerful German forces during the struggle to enlarge the bridgehead across the Moder River. With great daring and aggressiveness he spearheaded the platoon in killing 10 enemy soldiers, capturing 12 more and securing its objective near an important road junction. Although heavy concentrations of artillery, mortar, and self-propelled gunfire raked the area, he moved about among his men during the day, exhorting them to great efforts and encouraging them to stand firm. He carried ammunition and maintained contact with the company command post, exposing himself to deadly enemy fire. At nightfall the enemy barrage became more intense and tanks entered the fray to cover foot troops while they bombarded our positions with grenades and rockets. As buildings were blasted by the Germans, the Americans fell back from house to house. T/Sgt. Crain deployed another platoon which had been sent to his support and then rushed through murderous tank and small-arms fire to the foremost house, which was being defended by 5 of his men. With the enemy attacking from an adjoining room and a tank firing pointblank at the house, he ordered the men to withdraw while he remained in the face of almost certain death to hold the position. Although shells were crashing through the walls and bullets were hitting all around him, he held his ground and with accurate fire from his submachinegun killed 3 Germans. He was killed when the building was destroyed by the enemy. T/Sgt. Crain's outstanding valor and intrepid leadership enabled his platoon to organize a new defense, repel the attack and preserve the hard-won bridgehead.

*CRAW, DEMAS T.

Rank and organization: Colonel, U.S. Army Air Corps. *Place and date:* Near Port Lyautey, French Morocco, 8 November 1942. *Entered service at:* Michigan. *Born:* 9 April 1900, Traverse City, Mich. *G.O. No.:* 11, 4 March 1943. *Citation:* For conspicuous gallantry and intrepidity in action above and beyond the call of duty. On 8 November 1942, near Port Lyautey, French Morocco, Col. Craw volunteered to accompany the leading wave of assault boats to the shore and pass through the enemy lines to locate the French commander with a view to suspending hostilities. This request was first refused as being too dangerous but upon the officer's insistence that he was qualified to undertake and accomplish the mission he was allowed to go. Encountering heavy fire while in the landing boat and unable to dock in the river because of shell fire from shore batteries, Col. Craw, accompanied by 1 officer and 1 soldier, succeeded in landing on the beach at Mehdia Plage under constant low-level strafing from 3 enemy planes. Riding in a bantam truck toward French headquarters, progress of the party was hindered by fire from our own naval guns. Nearing Port Lyautey, Col. Craw was instantly killed by a sustained burst of machinegun fire at pointblank range from a concealed position near the road.

CRAWFORD, WILLIAM J.

Rank and organization: Private, U.S. Army, 36th Infantry Division. *Place and date:* Near Altavilla, Italy, 13 September 1943. *Entered service at:* Pueblo, Colo. *Birth:* Pueblo, Colo. *G.O. No.:* 57, 20 July 1944. *Citation:* For conspicuous gallantry and intrepidity at risk of life above and beyond the call of duty in action with the enemy near Altavilla, Italy, 13 September 1943. When Company I attacked an enemy-held position on Hill 424, the 3d Platoon, in which Pvt. Crawford was a squad scout, attacked as base platoon for the company. After reaching the crest of the hill, the platoon was pinned down by intense enemy machinegun and small-arms fire. Locating 1 of these guns, which was dug in on a terrace on his immediate front, Pvt. Crawford, without orders and on his own initiative, moved over the hill under enemy fire to a point within a few yards of the gun emplacement and single-handedly destroyed the machinegun and killed 3 of the crew with a handgrenade, thus enabling his platoon to continue its advance. When the platoon, after reaching the crest, was once more delayed by enemy fire, Pvt. Crawford again, in the face of intense fire, advanced directly to the front midway between 2 hostile machinegun nests located on a higher terrace and emplaced in a small ravine. Moving first to the left, with a handgrenade he destroyed 1 gun emplacement and killed the crew; he then worked his way, under continuous fire, to the other and with 1 grenade and the use of his rifle, killed 1 enemy and forced the remainder to flee. Seizing the enemy machinegun, he fired on the withdrawing Germans and facilitated his company's advance.

CREWS, JOHN R.

Rank and organization: Staff Sergeant, U.S. Army, Company F, 253d Infantry, 63d Infantry Division. *Place and date:* Near Lobenbacherhof, Germany, 8 April 1945. *Entered service at:* Bowlegs, Okla. *Birth:* Golden, Okla. *Citation:* He displayed conspicuous gallantry and intrepidity at the risk of his life above and beyond the call of duty on 8 April 1945 near Lobenbacherhof, Germany. As his company was advancing toward the village under heavy fire, an enemy machinegun and automatic rifle with rifle support opened upon it from a hill on the right flank. Seeing that his platoon leader had been wounded by their fire, S/Sgt. Crews, acting on his own initiative, rushed the strongpoint with 2 men of his platoon. Despite the fact that 1 of these men was killed and the other was badly wounded, he continued his advance up the hill in the face of terrific enemy fire. Storming the well-dug-in position singlehandedly, he killed 2 of the crew of the machinegun at pointblank range with his M1 rifle and wrested the gun from the hands of the German whom he had already wounded. He then with his rifle charged the strongly emplaced automatic rifle. Although badly wounded in the thigh by crossfire from the remaining enemy, he kept on and silenced the entire position with his accurate and deadly rifle fire. His actions so unnerved the remaining enemy soldiers that 7 of them surrendered and the others fled. His heroism caused the enemy to concentrate on him and permitted the company to move forward into the village.

*CROMWELL, JOHN PHILIP

Rank and organization: Captain, U.S. Navy. *Born:* 11 September 1901, Henry, Ill. *Appointed from:* Illinois. *Other Navy award:* Legion of Merit. *Citation:* For conspicuous gallantry and intrepidity at the risk of his life above and beyond the call of duty as Commander of a Submarine Coordinated Attack Group with Flag in the U.S.S. *Sculpin,* during the 9th War Patrol of that vessel in enemy-controlled waters off Truk Island, 19 November 1943. Undertaking this patrol prior to the launching of our first large-scale offensive in the Pacific, Capt. Cromwell, alone of the entire Task Group, possessed secret intelligence information of our submarine strategy and tactics, scheduled Fleet movements and specific attack plans. Constantly vigilant and precise in carrying out his secret orders, he moved his underseas flotilla inexorably forward despite savage opposition and established a line of submarines to southeastward of the main Japanese stronghold at Truk. Cool and undaunted as the submarine, rocked and battered by Japanese depth charges, sustained terrific battle damage and sank to an excessive depth, he authorized the *Sculpin* to surface and engage the enemy in a gunfight, thereby providing an opportunity for the crew to abandon ship. Determined to sacrifice himself rather than risk capture and subsequent danger of revealing plans under Japanese torture or use of drugs, he stoically remained aboard the mortally wounded vessel as she plunged to her death. Preserving the security of his mission, at the cost of his own life, he had served his country as he had served the Navy, with deep integrity and an uncompromising devotion to duty. His great moral courage in the face of certain death adds new luster to the traditions of the U.S. Naval Service. He gallantly gave his life for his country.

CURREY, FRANCIS S.

Rank and organization: Sergeant, U.S. Army, Company K, 120th Infantry, 30th Infantry Division: *Place and date:* Malmedy, Belgium, 21 December 1944. *Entered service at:* Hurleyville, N.Y. *Birth:* Loch Sheldrake, N.Y. *G.O. No.:* 69, 17 August 1945. *Citation:* He was an automatic rifleman with the 3d Platoon defending a strong point near Malmedy, Belgium, on 21 December 1944, when the enemy launched a powerful attack. Overrunning tank destroyers and antitank guns located near the strong point, German tanks advanced to the 3d Platoon's position, and, after prolonged fighting, forced the withdrawal of this group to a nearby factory. Sgt. Currey found a bazooka in the building and crossed the street to secure rockets meanwhile enduring intense fire from enemy tanks and hostile infantrymen who had taken up a position at a house a short distance away. In the face of small-arms, machinegun, and artillery fire, he, with a companion, knocked out a tank with 1 shot. Moving to another position, he observed 3 Germans in the doorway of an enemy-held house. He killed or wounded all 3 with his automatic rifle. He emerged from cover and advanced alone to within 50 yards of the house, intent on wrecking it with rockets. Covered by friendly fire, he stood erect, and fired a shot which knocked down half of 1 wall. While in this forward position, he observed 5 Americans who had been pinned down for hours by fire from the house and 3 tanks. Realizing that they could not escape until the enemy tank and infantry guns had been silenced, Sgt. Currey crossed the street to a vehicle, where he procured an armful of antitank grenades. These he launched while under heavy enemy fire, driving the tankmen from the vehicles into the house. He then climbed onto a half-track in full view of the Germans and fired a machinegun at the house. Once again changing his position, he manned another machinegun whose crew had been killed; under his covering fire the 5 soldiers were able to retire to safety. Deprived of tanks and with heavy infantry casualties, the enemy was forced to withdraw. Through his extensive knowledge of weapons and by his heroic and repeated braving of murderous enemy fire, Sgt. Currey was greatly responsible for inflicting heavy losses in men and material on the enemy, for rescuing 5 comrades, 2 of whom were wounded, and for stemming an attack which threatened to flank his battalion's position.

DAHLGREN, EDWARD C.

Rank and organization: Second Lieutenant (then Sergeant), U.S. Army, Company E, 142d Infantry, 36th Infantry Division. *Place and date:* Oberhoffen, France, 11 February 1945. *Entered service at:* Portland, Maine. *Birth:* Perham, Maine. *G.O. No.:* 77, 10 September 1945. *Citation:* He led the 3d Platoon to the rescue of a similar unit which had been surrounded in an enemy counterattack at Oberhoffen, France. As he advanced along a street, he observed several Germans crossing a field about 100 yards away. Running into a barn, he took up a position in a window and swept the hostile troops with submachinegun fire, killing 6, wounding others, and completely disorganizing the group. His platoon then moved forward through intermittent sniper fire and made contact with the beseiged Americans. When the 2 platoons had been reorganized, Sgt. Dahlgren continued to advance along the street until he drew fire from an enemy-held house. In the face of machine-pistol and rifle fire, he ran toward the building, hurled a grenade through the door, and blasted his way inside with his gun. This aggressive attack so rattled the Germans that all 8 men who held the strongpoint immediately surrendered. As

Sgt. Dahlgren started toward the next house, hostile machinegun fire drove him to cover. He secured rifle grenades, stepped to an exposed position, and calmly launched his missiles from a difficult angle until he had destroyed the machinegun and killed its 2 operators. He moved to the rear of the house and suddenly came under the fire of a machinegun emplaced in a barn. Throwing a grenade into the structure, he rushed the position, firing his weapon as he ran; within, he overwhelmed 5 Germans. After reorganizing his unit he advanced to clear hostile riflemen from the building where he had destroyed the machinegun. He entered the house by a window and trapped the Germans in the cellar, where he tossed grenades into their midst, wounding several and forcing 10 more to surrender. While reconnoitering another street with a comrade, he heard German voices in a house. An attack with rifle grenades drove the hostile troops to the cellar. Sgt. Dahlgren entered the building, kicked open the cellar door, and, firing several bursts down the stairway, called for the trapped enemy to surrender. Sixteen soldiers filed out with their hands in the air. The bold leadership and magnificent courage displayed by Sgt. Dahlgren in his heroic attacks were in a large measure responsible for repulsing an enemy counterattack and saving an American platoon from great danger.

DALESSONDRO, PETER J.

Rank and organization: Technical Sergeant, U.S. Army, Company E, 39th Infantry, 9th Infantry Division. *Place and date:* Near Kalterherberg, Germany, 22 December 1944. *Entered service at:* Watervliet, N.Y. *Born:* 19 May 1918, Watervliet, N.Y. *G.O. No.:* 73, 30 August 1945. *Citation:* He was with the 1st Platoon holding an important road junction on high ground near Kalterherberg, Germany, on 22 December 1944. In the early morning hours, the enemy after laying down an intense artillery and mortar barrage, followed through with an all-out attack that threatened to overwhelm the position. T/Sgt. Dalessondro, seeing that his men were becoming disorganized, braved the intense fire to move among them with words of encouragement. Advancing to a fully exposed observation post, he adjusted mortar fire upon the attackers, meanwhile firing upon them with his rifle and encouraging his men in halting and repulsing the attack. Later in the day the enemy launched a second determined attack. Once again, T/Sgt. Dalessondro, in the face of imminent death, rushed to his forward position and immediately called for mortar fire. After exhausting his rifle ammunition, he crawled 30 yards over exposed ground to secure a light machinegun, returned to his position, and fired upon the enemy at almost pointblank range until the gun jammed. He managed to get the gun to fire 1 more burst, which used up his last round, but with these bullets he killed 4 German soldiers who were on the verge of murdering an aid man and 2 wounded soldiers in a nearby foxhole. When the enemy had almost surrounded him, he remained alone, steadfastly facing almost certain death or capture, hurling grenades and calling for mortar fire closer and closer to his outpost as he covered the withdrawal of his platoon to a second line of defense. As the German hordes swarmed about him, he was last heard calling for a barrage, saying, "OK, mortars, let me have it—right in this position!" The gallantry and intrepidity shown by T/Sgt. Dalessondro against an overwhelming enemy attack saved his company from complete rout.

DALY, MICHAEL J.

Rank and organization: Captain (then Lieutenant), U.S. Army, Company A, 15th Infantry, 3d Infantry Division. *Place and date:* Nuremberg, Germany, 18 April 1945. *Entered service at:* Southport, Conn. *Born:* 15 September 1924, New York, N.Y. *G.O. No.:* 77, 10 September 1945. *Citation:* Early in the morning of 18 April 1945, he led his company through the shell-battered, sniper-infested wreckage of Nuremberg, Germany. When blistering machinegun fire caught his unit in an exposed position, he ordered his men to take cover, dashed forward alone, and, as bullets whined about him, shot the 3-man gun-crew with his carbine. Continuing the advance at the head of his company, he located an enemy patrol armed with rocket launchers which threatened friendly armor. He again went forward alone, secured a vantage point and opened fire on the Germans. Immediately he became the target for concentrated machine-pistol and rocket fire, which blasted the rubble about him. Calmly, he continued to shoot at the patrol until he had killed all 6 enemy infantrymen. Continuing boldly far in front of his company, he entered a park, where as his men advanced, a German machinegun opened up on them without warning. With his carbine, he killed the gunner; and then, from a completely exposed position, he directed machinegun fire on the remainder of the crew until all were dead. In a final duel, he wiped out a third machinegun emplacement with rifle fire at a range of 10 yards. By fearlessly engaging in 4 single-handed fire fights with a desperate, powerfully armed enemy, Lt. Daly, voluntarily taking all major risks himself and protecting his men at every opportunity, killed 15 Germans, silenced 3 enemy machineguns and wiped out an entire enemy patrol. His heroism during the lone bitter struggle with fanatical enemy forces was an inspiration to the valiant Americans who took Nuremberg.

*DAMATO, ANTHONY PETER

Rank and organization: Corporal, U.S. Marine Corps. *Born:* 28 March 1922, Shenandoah, Pa. *Accredited to:* Pennsylvania. *Citation:* For conspicuous gallantry and intrepidity at the risk of his life above and beyond the call of duty while serving with an assault company in action against enemy Japanese forces on Engebi Island, Eniwetok Atoll, Marshall Islands, on the night of 19–20 February 1944. Highly vulnerable to sudden attack by small, fanatical groups of Japanese still at large despite the efficient and determined efforts of our forces to clear the area, Cpl. Damato lay with 2 comrades in a large foxhole in his company's defense perimeter which had been dangerously thinned by the forced withdrawal of nearly half of the available men. When 1 of the enemy approached the foxhole undetected and threw in a handgrenade, Cpl. Damato desperately groped for it in the darkness. Realizing the imminent peril to all 3 and fully aware of the consequences of his act, he unhesitatingly flung himself on the grenade and, although instantly killed as his body absorbed the explosion, saved the lives of his 2 companions. Cpl. Damato's splendid initiative, fearless conduct and valiant sacrifice reflect great credit upon himself and the U.S. Naval Service. He gallantly gave his life for his comrades.

*DAVID, ALBERT LeROY

Rank and organization: Lieutenant, Junior Grade, U.S. Navy. *Born:* 18 July 1902, Maryville, Mo. *Accredited to:* Missouri. *Other Navy award:* Navy Cross with Gold Star. *Citation:* For conspicuous gallantry and intrepidity at the risk of his life above and beyond the call of duty while attached to the U.S.S. *Pillsbury* during the capture of an enemy German submarine off French West Africa, 4 June 1944. Taking a vigorous part in the skillfully coordinated attack on the German *U–505* which climaxed a prolonged search by the Task Group, Lt. (then Lt., jg.) David boldly led a party from the *Pillsbury* in boarding the hostile submarine as it circled erratically at 5 or 6 knots on the surface. Fully aware that the U-boat might momentarily sink or be blown up by exploding demolition and scuttling charges, he braved the added danger of enemy gunfire to plunge through the conning tower hatch and, with his small party, exerted every effort to keep the ship afloat and to assist the succeeding and more fully equipped salvage parties in making the *U–505* seaworthy for the long tow across the Atlantic to a U.S. port. By his valiant service during the first successful boarding and capture of an enemy man-o-war on the high seas by the U.S. Navy since 1815, Lt. David contributed materially to the effectiveness of our Battle of the Atlantic and upheld the highest traditions of the U.S. Naval Service.

DAVIS, CHARLES W.

Rank and organization: Major, U.S. Army, 25th Infantry Division. *Place and date:* Guadalcanal Island, 12 January 1943. *Entered service at:* Montgomery, Ala. *Birth:* Gordo, Ala. *G.O. No.:* 40, 17 July 1943. *Citation:* For distinguishing himself conspicuously by gallantry and intrepidity at the risk of his life above and beyond the call of duty in action with the enemy on Guadalcanal Island. On 12 January 1943, Maj. Davis (then Capt.), executive officer of an infantry battalion, volunteered to carry instructions to the leading companies of his battalion which had been caught in crossfire from Japanese machineguns. With complete disregard for his own safety, he made his way to the trapped units, delivered the instructions, supervised their execution, and remained overnight in this exposed position. On the following day, Maj. Davis again volunteered to lead an assault on the Japanese position which was holding up the advance. When his rifle jammed at its first shot, he drew his pistol and, waving his men on, led the assault over the top of the hill. Electrified by this action, another body of soldiers followed and seized the hill. The capture of this position broke Japanese resistance and the battalion was then able to proceed and secure the corps objective. The courage and leadership displayed by Maj. Davis inspired the entire battalion and unquestionably led to the success of its attack.

*DAVIS, GEORGE FLEMING

Rank and organization: Commander, U.S. Navy. *Born:* 23 March 1911, Manila, Philippine Islands. *Accredited to:* Philippine Islands. *Other Navy awards:* Silver Star Medal, Legion of Merit. *Citation:* For conspicuous gallantry and intrepidity at the risk of his life and beyond the call of duty as Commanding Officer of the U.S.S. *Walke* engaged in a detached mission in support of minesweeping operations to clear the waters for entry of our heavy surface and amphibious forces preparatory to the invasion of Lingayen Gulf, Luzon, Philippine Islands, 6 January 1945. Operating without gun support of other surface ships when 4 Japanese suicide planes were detected flying low overland to attack simultaneously, Comdr. Davis boldly took his position in the exposed wings of the bridge and directed control to pick up the leading plane and open fire. Alert and fearless as the *Walke*'s deadly fire sent the first target crashing into the water and caught the second as it passed close over the bridge to plunge into the sea of portside, he remained steadfast in the path of the third plane plunging swiftly to crash the after end of the bridge structure. Seriously wounded when the craft struck, drenched with gasoline and immediately enveloped in flames, he conned the *Walke* in the midst of the wreckage; he rallied his command to heroic efforts; he exhorted his officers and men to save the ship and, still on his feet, saw the barrage from his guns destroy the fourth suicide bomber. With the fires under control and the safety of the ship assured, he consented to be carried below. Succumbing several hours later, Comdr. Davis by his example of valor and his unhesitating self-sacrifice, steeled the fighting spirit of his command into unyielding purpose in completing a vital mission. He gallantly gave his life in the service of his country.

*DEALEY, SAMUEL DAVID

Rank and organization: Commander, U.S. Navy. *Born:* 13 September 1906, Dallas, Tex. *Appointed from:* Texas. *Other Navy awards:* Navy Cross with 3 Gold Stars, Silver Star Medal. *Citation:* For conspicuous gallantry and intrepidity at the risk of his life above and beyond the call of duty as Commanding Officer of the U.S.S. *Harder* during her 5th War Patrol in Japanese-controlled waters. Floodlighted by a bright moon and disclosed to an enemy destroyer escort which bore down with intent to attack, Comdr. Dealey quickly dived to periscope depth and waited for the pursuer to close range, then opened fire, sending the target and all aboard down in flames with his third torpedo. Plunging deep to avoid fierce depth charges, he again surfaced and, within 9 minutes after sighting another destroyer, had sent the enemy down tail first with a hit directly amidship. Evading detection, he penetrated the confined waters off Tawi Tawi with the Japanese Fleet base 6 miles away and scored death blows on 2 patrolling destroyers in quick succession. With his ship heeled over by concussion from the first exploding target and the second vessel nose-diving in a blinding detonation, he cleared the area at high speed. Sighted by a large hostile fleet force on the following day, he swung his bow toward the lead destroyer for another "down-the-throat" shot, fired 3 bow tubes and promptly crash-dived to be terrifically rocked seconds later by the exploding ship as the *Harder* passed beneath. This remarkable record of 5 vital Japanese destroyers sunk in 5 short-range torpedo attacks attests the valiant fighting spirit of Comdr. Dealey and his indomitable command.

DeBLANC, JEFFERSON JOSEPH

Rank and organization: Captain, U.S. Marine Corps Reserve, Marine Fighting Squadron 112. *Place and date:* Off Kolombangara Island in the Solomons group, 31 January 1943. *Entered service at:* Louisiana. *Born:* 15 February 1921, Lockport, La. *Citation:* For conspicuous gallantry and intrepidity at the risk of his life above and beyond the call of duty as leader of a section of 6 fighter planes in Marine Fighting Squadron 112, during aerial operations against enemy Japanese forces off Kolombangara Island in the Solomons group, 31 January 1943. Taking off with his section as escort for a strike force of dive bombers and torpedo planes ordered to attack Japanese surface vessels, 1st Lt. DeBlanc led his flight directly to the target area where, at 14,000 feet, our strike force encountered a large number of Japanese Zeros protecting the enemy's surface craft. In company with the other fighters, 1st Lt. DeBlanc instantly engaged the hostile planes and aggressively countered their repeated attempts to drive off our bombers, persevering in his efforts to protect the diving planes and waging fierce combat until, picking up a call for assistance from the dive bombers, under attack by enemy float planes at 1,000 feet, he broke off his engagement with the Zeros, plunged into the formation of float planes and disrupted the savage attack, enabling our dive bombers and torpedo planes to complete their runs on the Japanese surface disposition and withdraw without further incident. Although his escort mission was fulfilled upon the safe retirement of the bombers, 1st Lt. DeBlanc courageously remained on the scene despite a rapidly diminishing fuel supply and, boldly challenging the enemy's superior number of float planes, fought a valiant battle against terrific odds, seizing the tactical advantage and striking repeatedly to destroy 3 of the hostile aircraft and to disperse the remainder. Prepared to maneuver his damaged plane back to base, he had climbed aloft and set his course when he discovered 2 Zeros closing in behind. Undaunted, he opened fire and blasted both Zeros from the sky in a short, bitterly fought action which resulted in such hopeless damage to his own plane that he was forced to bail out at a perilously low altitude atop the trees on enemy-held Kolombangara. A gallant officer, a superb airman, and an indomitable fighter, 1st Lt. DeBlanc had rendered decisive assistance during a critical stage of operations, and his unwavering fortitude in the face of overwhelming opposition reflects the highest credit upon himself and adds new luster to the traditions of the U.S. Naval Service.

*DeFRANZO, ARTHUR F.

Rank and organization: Staff Sergeant, U.S. Army, 1st Infantry Division. *Place and date:* Near Vaubadon, France, 10 June 1944. *Entered service at:* Saugus, Mass. *Birth:* Saugus, Mass. *G.O. No.:* 1, 4 January 1945. *Citation:* For conspicuous gallantry and intrepidity at the risk of his life, above and beyond the call of duty, on 10 June 1944, near Vaubadon, France. As scouts were advancing across an open field, the enemy suddenly opened fire with several machine-guns and hit 1 of the men. S/Sgt. DeFranzo courageously moved out in the open to the aid of the wounded scout and was himself wounded but brought the man to safety. Refusing aid, S/Sgt. DeFranzo reentered the open field and led the advance upon the enemy. There were always at least 2 machine-guns bringing unrelenting fire upon him, but S/Sgt. DeFranzo kept going forward, firing into the enemy and 1 by 1 the enemy emplacements became silent. While advancing he was again wounded, but continued on until he was within 100 yards of the enemy position and even as he fell, he kept firing his rifle and waving his men forward. When his company came up behind him, S/Sgt. DeFranzo, despite his many severe wounds, suddenly raised himself and once more moved forward in the lead of his men until he was again hit by enemy fire. In a final gesture of indomitable courage, he threw several grenades at the enemy machinegun position and completely destroyed the gun. In this action, S/Sgt. DeFranzo lost his life, but by bearing the brunt of the enemy fire in leading the attack, he prevented a delay in the assault which would have been of considerable benefit to the foe, and he made possible his company's advance with a minimum of casualties. The extraordinary heroism and magnificent devotion to duty displayed by S/Sgt. DeFranzo was a great inspiration to all about him, and is in keeping with the highest traditions of the armed forces.

*DeGLOPPER, CHARLES N.

Rank and organization: Private First Class, U.S. Army, Co. C, 325th Glider Infantry, 82d Airborne Division. *Place and date:* Merderet River at la Fiere, France, 9 June 1944. *Entered service at:* Grand Island, N.Y. *Birth:* Grand Island, N.Y. *G.O. No.:* 22, 28 February 1946. *Citation:* He was a member of Company C, 325th Glider Infantry, on 9 June 1944 advancing with the forward platoon to secure a bridgehead across the Merderet River at La Fiere, France. At dawn the platoon had penetrated an outer line of machineguns and riflemen, but in so doing had become cut off from the rest of the company. Vastly superior forces began a decimation of the stricken unit and put in motion a flanking maneuver which would have completely exposed the American platoon in a shallow roadside ditch where it had taken cover. Detecting this danger, Pfc. DeGlopper volunteered to support his comrades by fire from his automatic rifle while they attempted a withdrawal through a break in a hedgerow 40 yards to the rear. Scorning a concentration of enemy automatic weapons and rifle fire, he walked from the ditch onto the road in full view of the Germans, and sprayed the hostile positions with assault fire. He was wounded, but he continued firing. Struck again, he started to fall; and yet his grim determination and valiant fighting spirit could not be broken. Kneeling in the roadway, weakened by his grievous wounds, he leveled his heavy weapon against the enemy and fired burst after burst until killed outright. He was successful in drawing the enemy action away from his fellow soldiers, who continued the fight from a more advantageous position and established the first bridgehead over the Merderet. In the area where he made his intrepid stand his comrades later found the ground strewn with dead Germans and many machineguns and automatic weapons which he had knocked out of action. Pfc. DeGlopper's gallant sacrifice and unflinching heroism while facing unsurmountable odds were in great measure responsible for a highly important tactical victory in the Normandy Campaign.

*DELEAU, EMILE, Jr.

Rank and organization: Sergeant, U.S. Army, Company A, 142d Infantry, 36th Infantry Division. *Place and date:* Oberhoffen, France, 1–2 February 1945. *Entered service at:* Blaine, Ohio. *Birth:* Lansing, Ohio. *G.O. No.:* 60, 25 July 1945. *Citation:* He led a squad in the night attack on Oberhoffen, France, where fierce house-to-house fighting took place. After clearing 1 building of opposition, he moved his men toward a second house from which heavy machine-gun fire came. He courageously exposed himself to hostile bullets and, firing his submachinegun as he went, advanced steadily toward the enemy position until close enough to hurl grenades through a window, killing 3 Germans and wrecking their gun. His progress was stopped by heavy rifle and machinegun fire from another house. Sgt. Deleau dashed through the door with his gun blazing. Within, he captured 10 Germans. The squad then took up a position for the night and awaited daylight to resume the attack. At dawn of 2 February Sgt. Deleau pressed forward with his unit, killing 2 snipers as he advanced to a point where machinegun fire from a house barred the way. Despite vicious small-arms fire, Sgt. Deleau ran across an open area to reach the rear of the building, where he destroyed 1 machinegun and killed its 2 operators with a grenade. He worked to the front of the structure and located a second machinegun. Finding it impossible to toss a grenade into the house from his protected position, he fearlessly moved away from the building and was about to hurl his explosive when he was instantly killed by a burst from the gun he sought to knock out. With magnificent courage and daring aggressiveness, Sgt. Deleau cleared 4 well-defended houses of Germans, inflicted severe losses on the enemy and at the sacrifice of his own life aided his battalion to reach its objective with a minimum of casualties.

DERVISHIAN, ERNEST H.

Rank and organization: Second Lieutenant, U.S. Army, 34th Infantry Division. *Place and date:* Near Cisterna, Italy, 23 May 1944. *Entered service at:* Richmond, Va. *Birth:* Richmond, Va.

G.O. No.: 3, 8 January 1945. *Citation:* For conspicuous gallantry and intrepidity at risk of life above and beyond the call of duty on 23 May 1944, in the vicinity of Cisterna, Italy. 2d Lt. Dervishian (then Tech. Sgt.) and 4 members of his platoon found themselves far ahead of their company after an aggressive advance in the face of enemy artillery and sniper fire. Approaching a railroad embankment, they observed a force of German soldiers hiding in dugouts. 2d Lt. Dervishian, directing his men to cover him, boldly moved forward and firing his carbine forced 10 Germans to surrender. His men then advanced and captured 15 more Germans occupying adjacent dugouts. The prisoners were returned to the rear to be picked up by advancing units. From the railroad embankment, 2d Lt. Dervishian and his men then observed 9 Germans who were fleeing across a ridge. He and his men opened fire and 3 of the enemy were wounded. As his men were firing, 2d Lt. Dervishian, unnoticed, fearlessly dashed forward alone and captured all of the fleeing enemy before his companions joined him on the ridge. At this point 4 other men joined 2d Lt. Dervishian's group. An attempt was made to send the 4 newly arrived men along the left flank of a large, dense vineyard that lay ahead, but murderous machinegun fire forced them back. Deploying his men, 2d Lt. Dervishian moved to the front of his group and led the advance into the vineyard. He and his men suddenly became pinned down by a machinegun firing at them at a distance of 15 yards. Feigning death while the hostile weapon blazed away at him, 2d Lt. Dervishian assaulted the position during a halt in the firing, using a handgrenade and carbine fire, and forced the 4 German crewmembers to surrender. The 4 men on the left flank were now ordered to enter the vineyard but encountered machinegun fire which killed 1 soldier and wounded another. At this moment the enemy intensified the fight by throwing potato-masher grenades at the valiant band of American soldiers within the vineyard. 2d Lt. Dervishian ordered his men to withdraw; but instead of following, jumped into the machinegun position he had just captured and opened fire with the enemy weapon in the direction of the second hostile machinegun nest. Observing movement in a dugout 2 or 3 yards to the rear, 2d Lt. Dervishian seized a machine-pistol. Simultaneously blazing away at the entrance to the dugout to prevent its occupants from firing and firing his machinegun at the other German nest, he forced 5 Germans in each position to surrender. Determined to rid the area of all Germans, 2d Lt. Dervishian continued his advance alone. Noticing another machinegun position beside a house, he picked up an abandoned machine-pistol and forced 6 more Germans to surrender by spraying their position with fire. Unable to locate additional targets in the vicinity, 2d Lt. Dervishian conducted these prisoners to the rear. The prodigious courage and combat skill exhibited by 2d Lt. Dervishian are exemplary of the finest traditions of the U.S. Armed Forces.

*DIAMOND, JAMES H.

Rank and organization: Private First Class, U.S. Army, Company D, 21st Infantry, 24th Infantry Division. *Place and date:* Mintal, Mindanao, Philippine Islands, 8–14 May 1945. *Entered service at:* Gulfport, Miss. *Birth:* New Orleans, La. *G.O. No.:* 23, 6 March 1946. *Citation:* As a member of the machinegun section, he displayed extreme gallantry and intrepidity above and beyond the call of duty. When a Japanese sniper rose from his foxhole to throw a grenade into their midst, this valiant soldier charged and killed the enemy with a burst from his submachine-gun; then, by delivering sustained fire from his personal arm and simultaneously directing the fire of 105-mm. and .50 caliber weapons upon the enemy pillboxes immobilizing this and another machinegun section, he enabled them to put their guns into action. When 2 infantry companies established a bridgehead, he voluntarily assisted in evacuating the wounded under heavy fire; and then, securing an abandoned vehicle, transported casualties to the rear through mortar and artillery fire so intense as to render the vehicle inoperative and despite the fact he was suffering from a painful wound. The following day he again volunteered, this time for the hazardous job of repairing a bridge under heavy enemy fire. On 14 May 1945, when leading a patrol to evacuate casualties from his battalion, which was cut off, he ran through a virtual hail of Japanese fire to secure an abandoned machinegun. Though mortally wounded as he reached the gun, he succeeded in drawing sufficient fire upon himself so that the remaining members of the patrol could reach safety. Pfc. Diamond's indomitable spirit, constant disregard of danger, and eagerness to assist his comrades, will ever remain a symbol of selflessness and heroic sacrifice to those for whom he gave his life.

*DIETZ, ROBERT H.

Rank and organization: Staff Sergeant, U.S. Army, Company A, 38th Armored Infantry Battalion, 7th Armored Division. *Place and date:* Kirchain, Germany, 29 March 1945. *Entered service at:* Kingston, N.Y. *Birth:* Kingston, N.Y. *G.O. No.:* 119, 17 December 1945. *Citation:* He was a squad leader when the task force to which his unit was attached encountered resistance in its advance on Kirchain, Germany. Between the town's outlying buildings 300 yards distant, and the stalled armored column were a minefield and 2 bridges defended by German rocket-launching teams and riflemen. From the town itself came heavy small-arms fire. Moving forward with his men to protect engineers while they removed the minefield and the demolition charges attached to the bridges, S/Sgt. Dietz came under intense fire. On his own initiative he advanced alone, scorning the bullets which struck all around him, until he was able to kill the bazooka team defending the first bridge. He continued ahead and had killed another bazooka team, bayoneted an enemy soldier armed with a panzerfaust and shot 2 Germans when he was knocked to the ground by another blast of another panzerfaust. He quickly recovered, killed the man who had fired at him and then jumped into waist-deep water under the second bridge to disconnect the demolition charges. His work was completed; but as he stood up to signal that the route was clear he was killed by another enemy volley from the left flank. S/Sgt. Dietz by his intrepidity and valiant effort on his self-imposed mission, singlehandedly opened the road for the capture of Kirchain and left with his comrades an inspiring example of gallantry in the face of formidable odds.

DOOLITTLE, JAMES H. (Air Mission)

Rank and organization: Brigadier General, U.S. Army, Air Corps. *Place and date:* Over Japan. *Entered service at:* Berkeley, Calif. *Birth:* Alameda, Calif. *G.O. No.:* 29, 9 June 1942. *Citation:* For conspicuous leadership above the call of duty, involving personal valor and intrepidity at an extreme hazard to life. With the apparent certainty of being forced to land in enemy territory or to perish at sea, Gen. Doolittle personally led a squadron of Army bombers, manned by volunteer crews, in a highly destructive raid on the Japanese mainland.

DOSS, DESMOND T.

Rank and organization: Private First Class, U.S. Army, Medical Detachment, 307th Infantry, 77th Infantry Division. *Place and date:* Near Urasoe-Mura, Okinawa, Ryukyu Islands, 29 April–21 May 1945. *Entered service at:* Lynchburg, Va. *Birth:* Lynchburg, Va. *G.O. No.:* 97, 1 November 1945. *Citation:* He was a company aid man when the 1st Battalion assaulted a jagged escarpment 400 feet high. As our troops gained the summit, a heavy concentration of artillery, mortar and machinegun fire crashed into them, inflicting approximately 75 casualties and driving the others back. Pfc. Doss refused to seek cover and remained in the fire-swept area with the many stricken, carrying them 1 by 1 to the edge of the escarpment and there lowering them on a rope-supported litter down the face of a cliff to friendly hands. On 2 May, he exposed himself to heavy rifle and mortar fire in rescuing a wounded man 200 yards forward of the lines on the same escarpment; and 2 days later he treated 4 men who had been cut down while assaulting a strongly defended cave, advancing through a shower of grenades to within 8 yards of enemy forces in a cave's mouth, where he dressed his comrades' wounds before making 4 separate trips under fire to evacuate them to safety. On 5 May, he unhesitatingly braved enemy shelling and small-arms fire to assist an artillery officer. He applied bandages, moved his patient to a spot that offered protection from small-arms fire and, while artillery and mortar shells fell close by, painstakingly administered plasma. Later that day, when an American was severely wounded by fire from a cave, Pfc. Doss crawled to him where he had fallen 25 feet from the enemy position, rendered aid, and carried him 100 yards to safety while continually exposed to enemy fire. On 21 May, in a night attack on high ground near Shuri, he remained in exposed territory while the rest of his company took cover, fearlessly risking the chance that he would be mistaken for an infiltrating Japanese and giving aid to the injured until he was himself seriously wounded in the legs by the explosion of a grenade. Rather than call another aid man from cover, he cared for his own injuries and waited 5 hours before litter bearers reached him and started carrying him to cover. The trio was caught in an enemy tank attack and Pfc. Doss, seeing a more critically wounded man nearby, crawled off the litter and directed the bearers to give their first attention to the other man. Awaiting the litter bearers' return, he was again struck, this time suffering a compound fracture of 1 arm. With magnificent fortitude he bound a rifle stock to his shattered arm as a splint and then crawled 300 yards over rough terrain to the aid station. Through his outstanding bravery and unflinching determination in the face of desperately dangerous conditions Pfc. Doss saved the lives of many soldiers. His name became a symbol throughout the 77th Infantry Division for outstanding gallantry far above and beyond the call of duty.

DROWLEY, JESSE R.

Rank and organization: Staff Sergeant, U.S. Army, Americal Infantry Division. *Place and date:* Bougainville, Solomon Islands, 30 January 1944. *Entered service at:* Spokane, Wash. *Birth:* St. Charles, Mich. *G.O. No.:* 73, 6 September 1944. *Citation:* For gallantry and intrepidity at the risk of his life above and beyond the call of duty in action with the enemy at Bougainville, Solomon Islands, 30 January 1944. S/Sgt. Drowley, a squad leader in a platoon whose mission during an attack was to remain under cover while holding the perimeter defense and acting as a reserve for assaulting echelon, saw 3 members of the assault company fall badly wounded. When intense hostile fire prevented aid from reaching the casualties, he fearlessly rushed forward to carry the wounded to cover. After rescuing 2 men, S/Sgt. Drowley discovered an enemy pillbox undetected by assaulting tanks that was inflicting heavy casualties upon the attacking force and was a chief obstacle to the success of the advance. Delegating the rescue of the third man to an assistant, he ran across open terrain to 1 of the tanks. Signaling to the crew, he climbed to the turret, exchanged his weapon for a submachinegun and voluntarily rode the deck of the tank directing it toward the pillbox by tracer fire. The tank, under constant heavy enemy fire, continued to within 20 feet of the pillbox where S/Sgt. Drowley received a severe bullet wound in the chest. Refusing to return for medical treatment, he remained on the tank and continued to direct its progress until the enemy box was definitely located by the crew. At this point he again was wounded by small-arms fire, losing his left eye and falling to the ground. He remained alongside the tank until the pillbox had been completely demolished and another directly behind the first destroyed. S/Sgt. Drowley, his voluntary mission successfully accomplished, returned alone for medical treatment.

DUNHAM, RUSSELL E.

Rank and organization: Technical Sergeant, U.S. Army, Company I, 30th Infantry, 3d Infantry Division. *Place and date:* Near Kayserberg, France, 8 January 1945. *Entered service at:* Brighton, Ill. *Born:* 23 February 1920, East Carondelet, Ill. *G.O. No.:* 37, 11 May 1945. *Citation:* For conspicuous gallantry and intrepidity at risk of life above and beyond the call of duty. At about 1430 hours on 8 January 1945, during an attack on Hill 616, near Kayserberg, France, T/Sgt. Dunham singlehandedly assaulted 3 enemy machineguns. Wearing a white robe made of a mattress cover, carrying 12 carbine magazines and with a dozen handgrenades snagged in his belt, suspenders, and buttonholes, T/Sgt. Dunham advanced in the attack up a snow-covered hill under fire from 2 machineguns and supporting riflemen. His platoon 35 yards behind him, T/Sgt. Dunham crawled 75 yards under heavy direct fire toward the timbered emplacement shielding the left machinegun. As he jumped to his feet 10 yards from the gun and charged forward, machinegun fire tore through his camouflage robe and a rifle bullet seared a 10-inch gash across his back sending him spinning 15 yards down hill into the snow. When the indomitable sergeant sprang to his feet to renew his 1-man assault, a German egg grenade landed beside him. He kicked it aside, and as it exploded 5 yards away, shot and killed the German machinegunner and assistant gunner. His carbine empty, he jumped into the emplacement and hauled out the third member of the gun crew by the collar. Although his back wound was causing him excruciating pain and blood was seeping through his white coat, T/Sgt. Dunham proceeded 50 yards through a storm of automatic and rifle fire to attack the second machinegun. Twenty-five yards from the emplacement he hurled 2 grenades, destroying the gun and its crew; then fired down into the supporting foxholes with his carbine, dispatching and dispersing the enemy riflemen. Although his coat was so thoroughly bloodsoaked that he was a conspicuous target against the white landscape, T/Sgt. Dunham again advanced ahead of his platoon in an assault on enemy positions farther up the hill. Coming under machinegun fire from 65 yards to his front, while rifle grenades exploded 10 yards from his position, he hit the ground and crawled forward. At 15 yards range, he jumped to his feet, staggered a few paces toward the timbered machinegun emplacement and killed the crew with handgrenades. An enemy rifleman fired at pointblank range, but missed him. After killing the rifleman, T/Sgt. Dunham drove others from their foxholes with grenades and carbine fire. Killing 9 Germans—wounding 7 and capturing 2—firing about 175 rounds of carbine ammunition, and expending 11 grenades, T/Sgt. Dunham, despite a painful wound, spearheaded a spectacular and successful diversionary attack.

DUNLAP, ROBERT HUGO

Rank and organization: Captain, U.S. Marine Corps Reserve, Company C, 1st Battalion, 26th Marines, 5th Marine Division. *Place and date:* On Iwo Jima, Volcano Islands, 20 and 21 February 1945. *Entered service at:* Illinois. *Born:* 19 October 1920, Abingdon, Ill. *Citation:* For conspicuous gallantry and intrepidity at the risk of his life above and beyond the call of duty as commanding officer of Company C, 1st Battalion, 26th Marines, 5th Marine Division, in action against enemy Japanese forces during the seizure of Iwo Jima in the Volcano Islands, on 20 and 21 February, 1945. Defying uninterrupted blasts of Japanese artillery, mortar, rifle and machinegun fire, Capt. Dunlap led his troops in a determined advance from low ground uphill toward the steep cliffs from which the enemy poured a devastating rain of shrapnel and bullets, steadily inching forward until the tremendous volume of enemy fire from the caves located high to his front temporarily halted his progress. Determined not to yield, he crawled alone approximately 200 yards forward of his front lines, took observation at the base of the cliff 50 yards from Japanese lines, located the enemy gun positions and returned to his own lines where he relayed the vital information to supporting artillery and naval gunfire units. Persistently disregarding his own personal safety, he then placed himself in an exposed vantage point to direct more accurately the supporting fire and, working without respite for 2 days and 2 nights under constant enemy fire, skillfully directed a smashing bombardment against the almost impregnable Japanese positions despite numerous obstacles and heavy marine casualties. A brilliant leader, Capt. Dunlap inspired his men to heroic efforts during this critical phase of the battle and by his cool decision, indomitable fighting spirit, and daring tactics in the face of fanatic opposition greatly accelerated the final decisive defeat of Japanese countermeasures in his sector and materially furthered the continued advance of his company. His great personal valor and gallant spirit of self-sacrifice throughout the bitter hostilities reflect the highest credit upon Capt. Dunlap and the U.S. Naval Service.

*DUTKO, JOHN W.

Rank and organization: Private First Class, U.S. Army, 3d Infantry Division. *Place and date:* Near Ponte Rotto, Italy, 23 May 1944. *Entered service at:* Riverside, N.J. *Birth:* Dilltown, Pa. *G.O. No.:* 80, 5 October 1944. *Citation:* For conspicuous gallantry and intrepidity at risk of life above and beyond the call of duty, on 23 May 1944, near Ponte Rotto, Italy. Pfc. Dutko left the cover of an abandoned enemy trench at the height of an artillery concentration in a singlehanded attack upon 3 machineguns and an 88-mm. mobile gun. Despite the intense fire of these 4 weapons which were aimed directly at him, Pfc. Dutko ran 100 yards through the impact area, paused momentarily in a shell crater, and then continued his 1-man assault. Although machinegun bullets kicked up the dirt at his heels, and 88-mm. shells exploded within 30 yards of him, Pfc. Dutko nevertheless made his way to a point within 30 yards of the first enemy machinegun and killed both gunners with a handgrenade. Although the second machinegun wounded him, knocking him to the ground, Pfc. Dutko regained his feet and advanced on the 88-mm. gun, firing his Browning automatic rifle from the hip. When he came within 10 yards of this weapon he killed its 5-man crew with 1 long burst of fire. Wheeling on the machinegun which had wounded him, Pfc. Dutko killed the gunner and his assistant. The third German machinegun fired on Pfc. Dutko from a position 20 yards distant wounding him a second time as he proceeded toward the enemy weapon in a half run. He killed both members of its crew with a single burst from his Browning automatic rifle, continued toward the gun and died, his body falling across the dead German crew.

*DYESS, AQUILLA JAMES

Rank and organization: Lieutenant Colonel, U.S. Marine Corps Reserve. *Born:* 11 January 1909, Augusta, Ga. *Appointed from:* Georgia. *Citation:* For conspicuous gallantry and intrepidity at the risk of his life above and beyond the call of duty as Commanding Officer of the 1st Battalion, 24th Marines (Rein), 4th Marine Division, in action against enemy Japanese forces during the assault on Namur Island, Kwajalein Atoll, Marshall Islands, 1 and 2 February 1944. Undaunted by severe fire from automatic Japanese weapons, Lt. Col. Dyess launched a powerful final attack on the second day of the assault, unhesitatingly posting himself between the opposing lines to point out objectives and avenues of approach and personally leading the advancing troops. Alert, and determined to quicken the pace of the offensive against increased enemy fire, he was constantly at the head of advance units, inspiring his men to push forward until the Japanese had been driven back to a small center of resistance and victory assured. While standing on the parapet of an anti-tank trench directing a group of infantry in a flanking attack against the last enemy position, Lt. Col. Dyess was killed by a burst of enemy machinegun fire. His daring and forceful leadership and his valiant fighting spirit in the face of terrific opposition were in keeping with the highest traditions of the U.S. Naval Service. He gallantly gave his life for his country.

EDSON, MERRITT AUSTIN

Rank and organization: Colonel, U.S. Marine Corps. *Born:* 25 April 1897, Rutland, Vt. *Appointed from:* Vermont. *Other Navy awards:* Navy Cross with Gold Star, Silver Star Medal, Legion of Merit with Gold Star. *Citation:* For extraordinary heroism and conspicuous intrepidity above and beyond the call of duty as Commanding Officer of the 1st Marine Raider Battalion, with Parachute Battalion attached, during action against enemy Japanese forces in the Solomon Islands on the night of 13–14 September 1942. After the airfield on Guadalcanal had been seized from the enemy on 8 August, Col. Edson, with a force of 800 men, was assigned to the occupation and defense of a ridge dominating the jungle on either side of the airport. Facing a formidable Japanese attack which, augmented by infiltration, had crashed through our front lines, he, by skillful handling of his troops, successfully withdrew his forward units to a reserve line with minimum casualties. When the enemy, in a subsequent series of violent assaults, engaged our force in desperate hand-to-hand combat with bayonets, rifles, pistols, grenades, and knives, Col. Edson, although continuously exposed to hostile fire throughout the night, personally directed defense of the reserve position against a fanatical foe of greatly superior numbers. By his astute leadership and gallant devotion to duty, he enabled his men, despite severe losses, to cling tenaciously to their position on the vital ridge, thereby retaining command not only of the Guadalcanal airfield, but also of the 1st Division's entire offensive installations in the surrounding area.

EHLERS, WALTER D.

Rank and organization: Staff Sergeant, U.S. Army, 18th Infantry, 1st Infantry Division. *Place and date:* Near Goville, France, 9–10 June 1944. *Entered service at:* Manhattan, Kans. *Birth:* Junction City, Kans. *G.O. No.:* 91, 19 December 1944. *Citation:* For conspicuous gallantry and intrepidity at the risk of his life above and beyond the call of duty on 9–10 June 1944, near Goville, France. S/Sgt. Ehlers, always acting as the spearhead of the attack, repeatedly led his men against heavily defended enemy strong points exposing himself to deadly hostile fire whenever the situation required heroic and courageous leadership. Without waiting for an order, S/Sgt. Ehlers, far ahead of his men, led his squad against a strongly defended enemy strong point, personally killing 4 of an enemy patrol who attacked him en route. Then crawling forward under withering machinegun fire, he pounced upon the guncrew and put it out of action. Turning his attention to 2 mortars protected by the crossfire of 2 machineguns, S/Sgt. Ehlers led his men through this hail of bullets to kill or put to flight the enemy of the mortar section, killing 3 men himself. After mopping up the mortar positions, he again advanced on a machinegun, his progress effectively covered by his squad. When he was almost on top of the gun he leaped to his feet and, although greatly outnumbered, he knocked out the position singlehanded. The next day, having advanced deep into enemy territory, the platoon of which S/Sgt. Ehlers was a member, finding itself in an untenable position as the enemy brought increased mortar, machinegun, and small-arms fire to bear on it, was ordered to withdraw. S/Sgt. Ehlers, after his squad had covered the withdrawal of the remainder of the platoon, stood up and by continuous fire at the semicircle of enemy placements, diverted the bulk of the heavy hostile fire on himself, thus permitting the members of his own squad to withdraw. At this point, though wounded himself, he carried his wounded automatic rifleman to safety and then returned fearlessly over the shell-swept field to retrieve the automatic rifle which he was unable to carry previously. After having his wound treated, he refused to be evacuated, and returned to lead his squad. The intrepid leadership, indomitable courage, and fearless aggressiveness displayed by S/Sgt. Ehlers in the face of overwhelming enemy forces serve as an inspiration to others.

*ELROD, HENRY TALMAGE

Rank and organization: Captain, U.S. Marine Corps. *Born:* 27 September 1905, Rebecca, Ga. *Entered service at:* Ashburn, Ga. *Citation:* For conspicuous gallantry and intrepidity at the risk of his life above and beyond the call of duty while attached to Marine Fighting Squadron 211, during action against enemy Japanese land, surface and aerial units at Wake Island, 8 to 23 December 1941. Engaging vastly superior forces of enemy bombers and warships on 9 and 12 December, Capt. Elrod shot down 2 of a flight of 22 hostile planes and, executing repeated bombing and strafing runs at extremely low altitude and close range, succeeded in inflicting deadly damage upon a large Japanese vessel, thereby sinking the first major warship to be destroyed by small-caliber bombs delivered from a fighter-type aircraft. When his plane was disabled by hostile fire and no other ships were operative, Capt. Elrod assumed command of 1 flank of the line set up in defiance of the enemy landing and, conducting a brilliant defense, enabled his men to hold their positions and repulse intense hostile fusillades to provide covering fire for unarmed ammunition carriers. Capturing an automatic weapon during 1 enemy rush in force, he gave his own firearm to 1 of his men and fought on vigorously against the Japanese. Responsible in a large measure for the strength of his sector's gallant resistance, on 23 December, Capt. Elrod led his men with bold aggressiveness until he fell, mortally wounded. His superb skill as a pilot, daring leadership and unswerving devotion to duty distinguished him among the defenders of Wake Island, and his valiant conduct reflects the highest credit upon himself and the U.S. Naval Service. He gallantly gave his life for his country.

*ENDL, GERALD L.

Rank and organization: Staff Sergeant, U.S. Army, 32d Infantry Division. *Place and date:* Near Anamo, New Guinea, 11 July 1944. *Entered service at:* Janesville, Wis. *Birth:* Ft. Atkinson, Wis. *G.O. No.:* 17, 13 March 1945. *Citation:* For conspicuous gallantry and intrepidity at the risk of his life above and beyond the call of duty near Anamo, New Guinea, on 11 July 1944. S/Sgt. Endl was at the head of the leading platoon of his company advancing along a jungle trail when enemy troops were encountered and a fire fight developed. The enemy attacked in force under heavy rifle, machinegun, and grenade fire. His platoon leader wounded, S/Sgt. Endl immediately assumed command and deployed his platoon on a firing line at the fork in the trail toward which the enemy attack was directed. The dense jungle terrain greatly restricted vision and movement, and he endeavored to penetrate down the trail toward an open clearing of Kunai grass. As he advanced, he detected the enemy, supported by at least 6 light and 2 heavy machineguns, attempting an enveloping movement around both flanks. His commanding officer sent a second platoon to move up on the left flank of the position, but the enemy closed in rapidly, placing our force in imminent danger of being isolated and annihilated. Twelve members of his platoon were wounded, 7 being cut off by the enemy. Realizing that if his platoon were forced farther back, these 7 men would be hopelessly trapped and at the mercy of a vicious enemy, he resolved to advance at all cost, knowing it meant almost certain death, in an effort to rescue his comrades. In the face of extremely heavy fire he went forward alone and for a period of approximately 10 minutes engaged the enemy in a heroic close-range fight, holding them off while his men crawled forward under cover to evacuate the wounded and to withdraw. Courageously refusing to abandon 4 more wounded men who were lying along the trail, 1 by 1 he brought them back to safety. As he was carrying the last man in his arms he was struck by a heavy burst of automatic fire and was killed. By his persistent and daring self-sacrifice and on behalf of his comrades, S/Sgt. Endl made possible the successful evacuation of all but 1 man, and enabled the 2 platoons to withdraw with their wounded and to reorganize with the rest of the company.

*EPPERSON, HAROLD GLENN

Rank and organization: Private First Class, U.S. Marine Corps Reserve. *Born:* 14 July 1923, Akron, Ohio. *Accredited to:* Ohio. *Citation:* For conspicuous gallantry and intrepidity at the risk of his life above and beyond the call of duty while serving with the 1st Battalion, 6th Marines, 2d Marine Division, in action against enemy Japanese forces on the Island of Saipan in the Marianas, on 25 June 1944. With his machinegun emplacement bearing the full brunt of a fanatic assault initiated by the Japanese under cover of predawn darkness, Pfc. Epperson manned his weapon with determined aggressiveness, fighting furiously in the defense of his battalion's position and maintaining a steady stream of devastating fire against rapidly infiltrating hostile troops to aid materially in annihilating several of the enemy and in breaking the abortive attack. Suddenly a Japanese soldier, assumed to be dead, sprang up and hurled a powerful handgrenade into the emplacement. Determined to save his comrades, Pfc. Epperson unhesitatingly chose to sacrifice himself and, diving upon the deadly missile, absorbed the shattering violence of the exploding charge in his own body. Stouthearted and indomitable in the face of certain death, Pfc. Epperson fearlessly yielded his own life that his able comrades might carry on the relentless battle against a ruthless enemy. His superb valor and unfaltering devotion to duty throughout reflect the highest credit upon himself and upon the U.S. Naval Service. He gallantly gave his life for his country.

ERWIN, HENRY E. (Air Mission)

Rank and organization: Staff Sergeant, U.S. Army Air Corps, 52d Bombardment Squadron, 29th Bombardment Group, 20th Air Force. *Place and date:* Koriyama, Japan, 12 April 1945. *Entered service at:* Bessemer, Ala. *Born:* 8 May 1921, Adamsville, Ala. *G.O. No.:* 44, 6 June 1945. *Citation:* He was the radio operator of a B–29 airplane leading a group formation to attack

Koriyama, Japan. He was charged with the additional duty of dropping phosphoresce smoke bombs to aid in assembling the group when the launching point was reached. Upon entering the assembly area, aircraft fire and enemy fighter opposition was encountered. Among the phosphoresce bombs launched by S/Sgt. Erwin, 1 proved faulty, exploding in the launching chute, and shot back into the interior of the aircraft, striking him in the face. The burning phosphoresce obliterated his nose and completely blinded him. Smoke filled the plane, obscuring the vision of the pilot. S/Sgt. Erwin realized that the aircraft and crew would be lost if the burning bomb remained in the plane. Without regard for his own safety, he picked it up and feeling his way, instinctively, crawled around the gun turret and headed for the copilot's window. He found the navigator's table obstructing his passage. Grasping the burning bomb between his forearm and body, he unleashed the spring lock and raised the table. Struggling through the narrow passage he stumbled forward into the smoke-filled pilot's compartment. Groping with his burning hands, he located the window and threw the bomb out. Completely aflame, he fell back upon the floor. The smoke cleared, the pilot, at 300 feet, pulled the plane out of its dive. S/Sgt. Erwin's gallantry and heroism above and beyond the call of duty saved the lives of his comrades.

*EUBANKS, RAY E.

Rank and organization: Sergeant, U.S. Army, Company D, 503d Parachute Infantry. *Place and date:* At Noemfoor Island, Dutch New Guinea, 23 July 1944. *Entered service at:* LaGrange, N.C. *Born:* 6 February 1922, Snow Hill, N.C. *G.O. No.:* 20, 29 March 1945. *Citation:* For conspicuous gallantry and intrepidity at the risk of his life above and beyond the call of duty at Noemfoor Island, Dutch New Guinea, 23 July 1944. While moving to the relief of a platoon isolated by the enemy, his company encountered a strong enemy position supported by machinegun, rifle, and mortar fire. Sgt. Eubanks was ordered to make an attack with 1 squad to neutralize the enemy by fire in order to assist the advance of his company. He maneuvered his squad to within

30 yards of the enemy where heavy fire checked his advance. Directing his men to maintain their fire, he and 2 scouts worked their way forward up a shallow depression to within 25 yards of the enemy. Directing the scouts to remain in place, Sgt. Eubanks armed himself with an automatic rifle and worked himself forward over terrain swept by intense fire to within 15 yards of the enemy position when he opened fire with telling effect. The enemy, having located his position, concentrated their fire with the result that he was wounded and a bullet rendered his rifle useless. In spite of his painful wounds he immediately charged the enemy and using his weapon as a club killed 4 of the enemy before he was himself again hit and killed. Sgt. Eubanks' heroic action, courage, and example in leadership so inspired his men that their advance was successful. They killed 45 of the enemy and drove the remainder from the position, thus effecting the relief of our beleaguered troops.

*EVANS, ERNEST EDWIN

Rank and organization: Commander, U.S. Navy. *Born:* 13 August 1908, Pawnee, Okla. *Accredited to:* Oklahoma. *Other Navy awards:* Navy Cross, Bronze Star Medal. *Citation:* For conspicuous gallantry and intrepidity at the risk of his life above and beyond the call of duty as commanding officer of the U.S.S. *Johnston* in action against major units of the enemy Japanese fleet during the battle off Samar on 25 October 1944. The first to lay a smokescreen and to open fire as an enemy task force, vastly superior in number, firepower and armor, rapidly approached. Comdr. Evans gallantly diverted the powerful blasts of hostile guns from the lightly armed and armored carriers under his protection, launching the first torpedo attack when the *Johnston* came under straddling Japanese shellfire. Undaunted by damage sustained under the terrific volume of fire, he unhesitatingly joined others of his group to provide fire support during subsequent torpedo attacks against the Japanese and, outshooting and outmaneuvering the enemy as he consistently interposed his vessel between the hostile fleet units and our carriers despite the crippling loss of engine power and communications with steering aft, shifted command to the fantail, shouted steering orders through an open hatch to men turning the rudder by hand and battled furiously until the *Johnston,* burning and shuddering from a mortal blow, lay dead in the water after 3 hours of fierce combat. Seriously wounded early in the engagement, Comdr. Evans, by his indomitable courage and brilliant professional skill, aided materially in turning back the enemy during a critical phase of the action. His valiant fighting spirit throughout this historic battle will venture as an inspiration to all who served with him.

EVERHART, FORREST E.

Rank and organization: Technical Sergeant, U.S. Army, Company H, 359th Infantry, 90th Infantry Division. *Place and date:* Near Kerling, France, 12 November 1944. *Entered service at:* Texas City, Tex. *Birth:* Bainbridge, Ohio. *G.O. No.:* 77, 10 September 1945. *Citation:* He commanded a platoon that bore the brunt of a desperate enemy counterattack near Korling, France, before dawn on 12 November 1944. When German tanks and self-propelled guns penetrated his left flank and overwhelming infantry forces threatened to overrun the 1 remaining machinegun in that section, he ran 400 yards through woods churned by artillery and mortar concentrations to strengthen the defense. With the 1 remaining gunner, he directed furious fire into the advancing hordes until they swarmed close to the position. He left the gun, boldly charged the attackers and, after a 15-minute exchange of handgrenades, forced them to withdraw leaving 30 dead behind. He recrossed the fire-swept terrain to his then threatened right flank, exhorted his men and directed murderous fire from the single machinegun at that position. There, in the light of bursting mortar shells, he again closed with the enemy in a handgrenade duel and, after a fierce 30-minute battle, forced the Germans to withdraw leaving another 20 dead. The gallantry and intrepidity of T/Sgt. Everhart in rallying his men and refusing to fall back in the face of terrible odds were highly instrumental in repelling the fanatical enemy counterattack directed at the American bridgehead across the Moselle River.

*FARDY, JOHN PETER

Rank and organization: Corporal, U.S. Marine Corps. *Born:* 8 August 1922, Chicago, Ill. *Accredited to:* Illinois. *Citation:* For conspicuous gallantry and intrepidity at the risk of his life above and beyond the call of duty as a squad leader, serving with Company C, 1st Battalion, 1st Marines, 1st Marine Division, in action against enemy Japanese forces on Okinawa Shima in the Ryukyu Islands, 7 May 1945. When his squad was suddenly assailed by extremely heavy small-arms fire from the front during a determined advance against strongly fortified, fiercely defended Japanese positions, Cpl. Fardy temporarily deployed his men along a nearby drainage ditch. Shortly thereafter, an enemy grenade fell among the marines in the ditch. Instantly throwing himself upon the deadly missile, Cpl. Fardy absorbed the exploding blast in his own body, thereby protecting his comrades from certain and perhaps fatal injuries. Concerned solely for the welfare of his men, he willingly relinquished his own hope of survival that his fellow marines might live to carry on the fight against a fanatic enemy. A stouthearted leader and indomitable fighter, Cpl. Fardy, by his prompt decision and resolute spirit of self-sacrifice in the face of certain death, had rendered valiant service, and his conduct throughout reflects the highest credit upon himself and the U.S. Naval Service. He gallantly gave his life for his country.

*FEMOYER, ROBERT E. (Air Mission)

Rank and organization: Second Lieutenant, 711th Bombing Squadron, 447th Bomber Group, U.S. Army Air Corps. *Place and date:* Over Merseburg, Germany, 2 November 1944. *Entered service at:* Jacksonville, Fla. *Born:* 31 October 1921, Huntington, W. Va. *G.O. No.:* 35, 9 May 1945. *Citation:* For conspicuous gallantry and intrepidity at the risk of his life above and beyond the call of duty near Merseburg, Germany, on 2 November 1944. While on a mission, the bomber, of which 2d Lt. Femoyer was the navigator, was struck by 3 enemy antiaircraft shells. The plane suffered serious damage and 2d Lt. Femoyer was severely wounded in the side and back by shell fragments which penetrated his body. In spite of extreme pain and great loss of blood he refused an offered injection of morphine. He was determined to keep his mental faculties clear in order that he might direct his plane out of danger and so save his comrades. Not being able to arise from the floor, he asked to be propped up in order to enable him to see his charts and instruments. He successfully directed the navigation of his lone bomber for 2½ hours so well it avoided enemy flak and returned to the field without further damage. Only when the plane had arrived in the safe area over the English Channel did he feel that he had accomplished his objective; then, and only then, he permitted an injection of a sedative. He died shortly after being removed from the plane. The heroism and self-sacrifice of 2d Lt. Femoyer are in keeping with the highest traditions of the U.S. Army.

FIELDS, JAMES H.

Rank and organization: First Lieutenant, U.S. Army, 10th Armored Infantry, 4th Armored Division. *Place and date:* Rechicourt, France, 27 September 1944. *Entered service at:* Houston, Tex. *Birth:* Caddo, Tex. *G.O. No.:* 13, 27 February 1945. *Citation:* For conspicuous gallantry and intrepidity at risk of life above and beyond the call of duty, at Rechicourt, France. On 27 September 1944, during a sharp action with the enemy infantry and tank forces, 1st Lt. Fields personally led his platoon in a counterattack on the enemy position. Although his platoon had been seriously depleted, the zeal and fervor of his leadership was such as to inspire his small force to accomplish their mission in the face of overwhelming enemy opposition. Seeing that 1 of the men had been wounded, he left his slit trench and with complete disregard for his personal safety attended the wounded man and administered first aid. While returning to his slit trench he was seriously wounded by a shell burst, the fragments of which cut through his face and head, tearing his teeth, gums, and nasal passage. Although rendered speechless by his wounds, 1st Lt. Fields refused to be evacuated and continued to lead his platoon by the use of hand signals. On 1 occasion, when 2 enemy machineguns had a portion of his unit under deadly crossfire, he left his hole, wounded as he was, ran to a light machinegun, whose crew had been knocked out, picked up the gun, and fired it from his hip with such deadly accuracy that both the enemy gun positions were silenced. His action so impressed his men that they found new courage to take up the fire fight, increasing their firepower, and exposing themselves more than ever to harass the enemy with additional bazooka and machinegun fire. Only when his objective had been taken and the enemy scattered did 1st Lt. Fields consent to be evacuated to the battalion command post. At this point he refused to move further back until he had explained to his battalion commander by drawing on paper the position of his men and the disposition of the enemy forces. The dauntless and gallant heroism displayed by 1st Lt. Fields were largely responsible for the repulse of the enemy forces and contributed in a large measure to the successful capture of his battalion objective during this action. His eagerness and determination to close with the enemy and to destroy him was an inspiration to the entire command, and are in the highest traditions of the U.S. Armed Forces.

FINN, JOHN WILLIAM

Rank and organization: Lieutenant, U.S. Navy. *Place and date:* Naval Air Station, Kaneohe Bay, Territory of Hawaii, 7 December 1941. *Entered service at:* California. *Born:* 23 July 1909, Los Angeles, Calif. *Citation:* For extraordinary heroism, distinguished service, and devotion above and beyond the call of duty. During the first attack by Japanese airplanes on the Naval Air Station, Kaneohe Bay, on 7 December 1941, Lt. Finn promptly secured and manned a .50-caliber machinegun mounted on an instruction stand in a completely exposed section of the parking ramp, which was under heavy enemy machinegun strafing fire. Although painfully wounded many times, he continued to man this gun and to return the enemy's fire vigorously and with telling effect throughout the enemy strafing and bombing attacks and with complete disregard for his own personal safety. It was only by specific orders that he was persuaded to leave his post to seek medical attention. Following first-aid treatment, although obviously suffering much pain and moving with great difficulty, he returned to the squadron area and actively supervised the rearming of returning planes. His extraordinary heroism and conduct in this action were in keeping with the highest traditions of the U.S. Naval Service.

FISHER, ALMOND E.

Rank and organization: Second Lieutenant, U.S. Army, Company E, 157th Infantry, 45th Infantry Division. *Place and date:* Near Grammont, Fance, 12–13 September 1944. *Entered service at:* Brooklyn, N.Y. *Birth:* Hume, N.Y. *G.O. No.:* 32, 23 April 1945. *Citation:* For conspicuous gallantry and intrepidity at the risk of his life above and beyond the call of duty on the night of 12–13 September 1944, near Grammont, France. In the darkness of early morning, 2d Lt. Fisher was leading a platoon of Company E, 157th Infantry, in single column to the attack of a strongly defended hill position. At 2:30 A.M., the forward elements were brought under enemy machinegun fire from a distance of not more than 20 yards. Working his way alone to within 20 feet of the gun emplacement, he opened fire with his carbine and killed the entire guncrew. A few minutes after the advance was resumed, heavy machinegun fire was encountered from the left flank. Again crawling forward alone under withering fire, he blasted the gun and crew from their positions with handgrenades. After a halt to replenish ammunition, the advance was again resumed and continued for 1 hour before being stopped by intense machinegun and rifle fire. Through the courageous and skillful leadership of 2d Lt. Fisher, the pocket of determined enemy resistance was rapidly obliterated. Spotting an emplaced machine pistol a short time later, with 1 of his men he moved forward and destroyed the position. As the advance continued the fire fight became more intense. When a bypassed German climbed from his foxhole and attempted to tear an M1 rifle from the hands of 1 of his men, 2d Lt. Fisher whirled and killed the enemy with a burst from his carbine. About 30 minutes later the platoon came under the heavy fire of machineguns from across an open field. 2d Lt. Fisher, disregarding the terrific fire, moved across the field with no cover or concealment to within range, knocked the gun from the position and killed or wounded the crew. Still under heavy fire he returned to his platoon and continued the advance. Once again heavy fire was encountered from a machinegun directly in front. Calling for handgrenades, he found only 2 remaining in the entire platoon. Pulling the pins and carrying a grenade in each hand, he crawled toward the gun emplacement, moving across areas devoid of cover and under intense fire to within 15 yards when he threw the grenades, demolished the gun and killed the guncrew. With ammunition low and daybreak near, he ordered his men to dig in and hold the ground already won. Under constant fire from the front and from both flanks, he moved among them directing the preparations for the defense. Shortly after the ammunition supply was replenished, the Germans launched a last determined effort against the depleted group. Attacked by superior numbers from the front, right, and left flank, and even from the rear, the platoon, in bitter hand-to-hand engagements drove back the enemy at every point. Wounded in both feet by close-range machine pistol fire early in the battle, 2d Lt. Fisher refused medical attention. Unable to walk, he crawled from man to man encouraging them and checking each position. Only after the fighting had subsided did 2d Lt. Fisher crawl 300 yards to the aid station from which he was evacuated. His extraordinary heroism, magnificent valor, and aggressive determination in the face of pointblank enemy fire is an inspiration to his organization and reflects the finest traditions of the U.S. Armed Forces.

*FLAHERTY, FRANCIS C.

Rank and organization: Ensign, U.S. Naval Reserve. *Born:* 15 March 1919, Charlotte, Mich. *Accredited to:* Michigan. *Citation:* For conspicuous devotion to duty and extraordinary courage and complete disregard of his own life, above and beyond the call of duty, during the attack on the Fleet in Pearl Harbor, by Japanese forces on 7 December 1941. When it was seen that the U.S.S. *Oklahoma* was going to capsize and the order was given to abandon ship, Ens. Flaherty remained in a turret, holding a flashlight so the remainder of the turret crew could see to escape, thereby sacrificing his own life.

*FLEMING, RICHARD E.

Rank and organization: Captain, U.S. Marine Corps Reserve. *Born:* 2 November 1917, St. Paul, Minn. *Appointed from:* Minnesota. *Citation:* For extraordinary heroism and conspicuous intrepidity above and beyond the call of duty as Flight Officer, Marine Scout-Bombing Squadron 241, during action against enemy Japanese forces in the battle of Midway on 4 and 5 June 1942. When his Squadron Commander was shot down during the initial attack upon an enemy aircraft carrier, Capt. Fleming led the remainder of the division with such fearless determination that he dived his own plane to the perilously low altitude of 400 feet before releasing his bomb. Although his craft was riddled by 179 hits in the blistering hail of fire that burst upon him from Japanese fighter guns and antiaircraft batteries, he pulled out with only 2 minor wounds inflicted upon himself. On the night of 4 June, when the squadron commander lost his way and became separated from the others, Capt. Fleming brought his own plane in for a safe landing at its base despite hazardous weather conditions and total darkness. The following day, after less than 4 hours' sleep, he led the second division of his squadron in a coordinated glide-bombing and dive-bombing assault upon a Japanese battleship. Undeterred by a fateful approach glide, during which his ship was struck and set afire, he grimly pressed home his attack to an altitude of 500 feet, released his bomb to score a near miss on the stern of his target, then crashed to the sea in flames. His dauntless perseverance and unyielding devotion to duty were in keeping with the highest traditions of the U.S. Naval Service.

FLUCKEY, EUGENE BENNETT

Rank and organization: Commander, U.S. Navy, Commanding U.S.S. *Barb. Place and date:* Along coast of China, 19 December 1944 to 15 February 1945. *Entered service at:* Illinois. *Born:* 5 October 1913, Washington, D.C. *Other Navy award:* Navy Cross with 3 Gold Stars. *Citation:* For conspicuous gallantry and intrepidity at the risk of his life above and beyond the call of duty as commanding officer of the U.S.S. *Barb* during her 11th war patrol along the east coast of China from 19 December 1944 to 15 February 1945. After sinking a large enemy ammunition ship and damaging additional tonnage during a running 2-hour night battle on 8 January, Comdr. Fluckey, in an exceptional feat of brilliant deduction and bold tracking on 25 January, located a concentration of more than 30 enemy ships in the lower reaches of Nankuan Chiang (Mamkwan Harbor). Fully aware that a safe retirement would necessitate an hour's run at full speed through the uncharted, mined, and rock-obstructed waters, he bravely ordered, "Battle station—torpedoes!" In a daring penetration of the heavy enemy screen, and riding in 5 fathoms of water, he launched the *Barb's* last forward torpedoes at 3,000-yard range. Quickly bringing the ship's stern tubes to bear, he turned loose 4 more torpedoes into the enemy, obtaining 8 direct hits on 6 of the main targets to explode a large ammunition ship and cause inestimable damage by the resultant flying shells and other pyrotechnics. Clearing the treacherous area at high speed, he brought the *Barb* through to safety and 4 days later sank a large Japanese freighter to complete a record of heroic combat achievement, reflecting the highest credit upon Comdr. Fluckey, his gallant officers and men, and the U.S. Naval Service.

FOSS, JOSEPH JACOB

Rank and organization: Captain, U.S. Marine Corps Reserve, Marine Fighting Squadron 121, 1st Marine Aircraft Wing. *Place and date:* Over Guadalcanal, 9 October to 19 November 1942, 15 and 23 January 1943. *Entered service at:* South Dakota. *Born:* 17 April 1915, Sioux Falls, S. Dak. *Citation:* For outstanding heroism and courage above and beyond the call of duty as executive officer of Marine Fighting Squadron 121, 1st Marine Aircraft Wing, at Guadalcanal. Engaging in almost daily combat with the enemy from 9 October to 19 November 1942, Capt. Foss personally shot down 23 Japanese planes and damaged others so severely that their destruction was extremely probable. In addition, during this period, he successfully led a large number of escort missions, skillfully covering reconnaissance, bombing, and photographic planes as well as surface craft. On 15 January 1943, he added 3 more enemy planes to his already brilliant successes for a record of aerial combat achievement unsurpassed in this war. Boldly searching out an approaching enemy force on 25 January, Capt. Foss led his 8 F4F Marine planes and 4 Army P-38's into action and, undaunted by tremendously superior numbers, intercepted and struck with such force that 4 Japanese fighters were shot down and the bombers were turned back without releasing a single bomb. His remarkable flying skill, inspiring leadership, and indomitable fighting spirit were distinctive factors in the defense of strategic American positions on Guadalcanal.

*FOSTER, WILLIAM ADELBERT

Rank and organization: Private First Class, U.S. Marine Corps Reserve. *Born:* 17 February 1915, Cleveland, Ohio. *Accredited to:* Ohio. *Citation:* For conspicuous gallantry and intrepidity at the risk of his life above and beyond the call of duty while serving as a rifleman with the 3d Battalion, 1st Marines, 1st Marine Division, in action against enemy Japanese forces on Okinawa Shima in the Ryukyu Chain 2 May 1945. Dug in with another marine on the point of the perimeter defense after waging a furious assault against a strongly fortified Japanese position, Pfc. Foster and his comrade engaged in a fierce handgrenade duel with infiltrating enemy soldiers. Suddenly an enemy grenade landed beyond reach in the foxhole. Instantly diving on the deadly missile, Pfc. Foster absorbed the exploding charge in his own body, thereby protecting the other marine from serious injury. Although mortally wounded as a result of his heroic action, he quickly rallied, handed his own remaining 2 grenades to his comrade and said, "Make them count." Stouthearted and indomitable, he had unhesitatingly relinquished his own chance of survival that his fellow marine might carry on the relentless fight against a fanatic enemy, and his dauntless determination, cool decision and valiant spirit of self-sacrifice in the face of certain death reflect the highest credit upon Pfc. Foster and upon the U.S. Naval Service. He gallantly gave his life in the service of his country.

*FOURNIER, WILLIAM G.

Rank and organization: Sergeant, U.S. Army, Company M, 35th Infantry, 25th Infantry Division. *Place and date:* Mount Austen, Guadalcanal, Solomon Islands, 10 January 1943. *Entered service at:* Winterport, Maine. *Born:* Norwich, Conn. *G.O. No.:* 28, 5 June 1943. *Citation:* For gallantry and intrepidity above and beyond the call of duty. As leader of a machinegun section charged with the protection of other battalion units, his group was attacked by a superior number of Japanese, his gunner killed, his assistant gunner wounded, and an adjoining guncrew put out of action. Ordered to withdraw from this hazardous position, Sgt. Fournier refused to retire but rushed forward to the idle gun and, with the aid of another soldier who joined him, held up the machinegun by the tripod to increase its field action. They opened fire and inflicted heavy casualties upon the enemy. While so engaged both these gallant soldiers were killed, but their sturdy defensive was a decisive factor in the following success of the attacking battalion.

*FOWLER, THOMAS W.

Rank and organization: Second Lieutenant, U.S. Army, 1st Armored Division. *Place and date:* Near Carano, Italy, 23 May 1944. *Entered service at:* Wichita Falls, Tex. *Birth:* Wichita Falls, Tex. *G.O. No.:* 84, 28 October, 1944. *Citation:* For conspicuous gallantry and intrepidity at risk of life above and beyond the call of duty, on 23 May 1944, in the vicinity of Carano, Italy. In the midst of a full-scale armored-infantry attack, 2d Lt. Fowler, while on foot, came upon 2 completely disorganized infantry platoons held up in their advance by an enemy minefield. Although a tank officer, he immediately reorganized the infantry. He then made a personal reconnaissance through the minefield, clearing a path as he went, by lifting the antipersonnel mines out of the ground with his hands. After he had gone through the 75-yard belt of deadly explosives, he returned to the infantry and led them through the minefield, a squad at a time. As they deployed, 2d Lt. Fowler, despite small-arms fire and the constant danger of antipersonnel mines, made a reconnaissance into enemy territory in search of a route to continue the advance. He then returned through the minefield and, on foot, he led the tanks through the mines into a position from which they could best support the infantry. Acting as scout 300 yards in front of the infantry, he led the 2 platoons forward until he had gained his objective, where he came upon several dug-in enemy infantrymen. Having taken them by surprise, 2d Lt. Fowler dragged them out of their foxholes and sent them to the rear; twice, when they resisted, he threw handgrenades into their dugouts. Realizing that a dangerous gap existed between his company and the unit to his right, 2d Lt. Fowler decided to continue his advance until the gap was filled. He reconnoitered to his front, brought the infantry into position where they dug in and, under heavy mortar and small-arms fire, brought his tanks forward. A few minutes later, the enemy began an armored counterattack. Several Mark VI tanks fired their cannons directly on 2d Lt. Fowler's position. One of his tanks was set afire. With utter disregard for his own life, with shells bursting near him, he ran directly into the enemy tank fire to reach the burning vehicle. For a half-hour, under intense strafing from the advancing tanks, although all other elements had withdrawn, he remained in his forward position, attempting to save the lives of the wounded tank crew. Only when the enemy tanks had almost overrun him, did he withdraw a short distance where he personally rendered first aid to 9 wounded infantrymen in the midst of the relentless incoming fire. 2d Lt. Fowler's courage, his ability to estimate the situation and to recognize his full responsibility as an officer in the Army of the United States, exemplify the high traditions of the military service for which he later gave his life.

*FRYAR, ELMER E.

Rank and organization: Private, U.S. Army, Company E, 511th Parachute Infantry, 11th Airborne Division. *Place and date:* Leyte, Philippine Islands, 8 December 1944. *Entered service at:* Denver, Colo. *Birth:* Denver, Colo. *G.O. No.:* 35, 9 May 1945. *Citation:* For conspicuous gallantry and intrepidity at the risk of his life above and beyond the call of duty. Pvt. Fryar's battalion encountered the enemy strongly entrenched in a position supported by mortars and automatic weapons. The battalion attacked, but in spite of repeated efforts was unable to take the position. Pvt. Fryar's company was ordered to cover the battalion's withdrawal to a more suitable point from which to attack, but the enemy launched a strong counterattack which threatened to cut off the company. Seeing an enemy platoon moving to outflank his company, he moved to higher ground and opened heavy and accurate fire. He was hit, and wounded, but continuing his attack he drove the enemy back with a loss of 27 killed. While withdrawing to overtake his squad, he found a seriously wounded comrade, helped him to the rear, and soon overtook his platoon leader, who was assisting another wounded. While these 4 were moving to rejoin their platoon, an enemy sniper appeared and aimed his weapon at the platoon leader. Pvt. Fryar instantly sprang forward, received the full burst of automatic fire in his own body and fell mortally wounded. With his remaining strength he threw a handgrenade and killed the sniper. Pvt. Fryar's indomitable fighting spirit and extraordinary gallantry above and beyond the call of duty contributed outstandingly to the success of the battalion's withdrawal and its subsequent attack and defeat of the enemy. His heroic action in unhesitatingly giving his own life for his comrade in arms exemplifies the highest tradition of the U.S. Armed Forces.

FUNK, LEONARD A., JR.

Rank and organization: First Sergeant, U.S. Army, Company C, 508th Parachute Infantry, 82d Airborne Division. *Place and date:* Holzheim, Belgium, 29 January 1945. *Entered service at:* Wilkinsburg, Pa. *Birth:* Braddock Township, Pa. *G.O. No.:* 75, 5 September 1945. *Citation:* He distinguished himself by gallant, intrepid actions against the enemy. After advancing 15 miles in a driving snowstorm, the American force prepared to attack through waist-deep drifts. The company executive officer became a casualty, and 1st Sgt. Funk immediately assumed his duties, forming headquarters soldiers into a combat unit for an assault in the face of direct artillery shelling and harassing fire from the right flank. Under his skillful and courageous leadership, this miscellaneous group and the 3d Platoon attacked 15 houses, cleared them, and took 30 prisoners without suffering a casualty. The fierce drive of Company C quickly overran Holzheim, netting some 80 prisoners, who were placed under a 4-man guard, all that could be spared, while the rest of the understrength unit went about mopping up isolated points of resistance. An enemy patrol, by means of a ruse, succeeded in capturing the guards and freeing the prisoners, and had begun preparations to attack Company C from the rear when 1st Sgt. Funk walked around the building and into their midst. He was ordered to surrender by a German officer who pushed a machine pistol into his stomach. Although overwhelmingly outnumbered and facing almost certain death, 1st Sgt. Funk, pretending to comply with the order, began slowly to unsling his submachinegun from his shoulder and then, with lightning motion, brought the muzzle into line and riddled the German officer. He turned upon the other Germans, firing and shouting to the other Americans to seize the enemy's weapons. In the ensuing fight 21 Germans were killed, many wounded, and the remainder captured. 1st Sgt. Funk's bold action and heroic disregard for his own safety were directly responsible for the recapture of a vastly superior enemy force, which, if allowed to remain free, could have taken the widespread units of Company C by surprise and endangered the entire attack plan.

FUQUA, SAMUEL GLENN

Rank and organization: Captain, U.S. Navy, U.S.S. *Arizona. Place and date:* Pearl Harbor, Territory of Hawaii, 7 December 1941. *Entered service at:* Laddonia, Mo. *Born:* 15 October 1899, Laddonia, Mo. *Citation:* For distinguished conduct in action, outstanding heroism, and utter disregard of his own safety above and beyond the call of duty during the attack on the Fleet in Pearl

Harbor, by Japanese forces on 7 December 1941. Upon the commencement of the attack, Lt. Comdr. Fuqua rushed to the quarterdeck of the U.S.S. *Arizona* to which he was attached where he was stunned and knocked down by the explosion of a large bomb which hit the quarterdeck, penetrated several decks, and started a severe fire. Upon regaining consciousness, he began to direct the fighting of the fire and the rescue of wounded and injured personnel. Almost immediately there was a tremendous explosion forward, which made the ship appear to rise out of the water, shudder, and settle down by the bow rapidly. The whole forward part of the ship was enveloped in flames which were spreading rapidly, and wounded and burned men were pouring out of the ship to the quarterdeck. Despite these conditions, his harrowing experience, and severe enemy bombing and strafing, at the time, Lt. Comdr. Fuqua continued to direct the fighting of fires in order to check them while the wounded and burned could be taken from the ship and supervised the rescue of these men in such an amazingly calm and cool manner and with such excellent judgment that it inspired everyone who saw him and undoubtedly resulted in the saving of many lives. After realizing the ship could not be saved and that he was the senior surviving officer aboard, he directed it to be abandoned, but continued to remain on the quarterdeck and directed abandoning ship and rescue of personnel until satisfied that all personnel that could be had been saved, after which he left his ship with the boatload. The conduct of Lt. Comdr. Fuqua was not only in keeping with the highest traditions of the naval service but characterizes him as an outstanding leader of men.

GALER, ROBERT EDWARD

Rank and organization: Major, U.S. Marine Corps, Marine Fighter Sqdn. 244. *Place:* Solomon Islands Area. *Entered service at:* Washington. *Born:* 23 October 1913, Seattle, Wash. *Other Navy awards:* Navy Cross, Distinguished Flying Cross. *Citation:* For conspicuous heroism and courage above and beyond the call of duty as leader of a marine fighter squadron in aerial combat with enemy Japanese forces in the Solomon Islands area. Leading his squadron repeatedly in daring and aggressive raids against Japanese aerial forces, vastly superior in numbers, Maj. Galer availed himself of every favorable attack opportunity, individually shooting down 11 enemy bomber and fighter aircraft over a period of 29 days. Though suffering the extreme physical strain attendant upon protracted fighter operations at an altitude above 25,000 feet, the squadron under his zealous and inspiring leadership shot down a total of 27 Japanese planes. His superb airmanship, his outstanding skill and personal valor reflect great credit upon Maj. Galer's gallant fighting spirit and upon the U.S. Naval Service.

*GALT, WILLIAM WYLIE

Rank and organization: Captain, U.S. Army, 168th Infantry, 34th Infantry Division. *Place and date:* At Villa Crocetta, Italy, 29 May 1944. *Entered service at:* Stanford, Mont. *Birth:* Geyser, Mont. *G.O. No.:* 7, 1 February 1945. *Citation:* For conspicuous gallantry and intrepidity above and beyond the call of duty. Capt. Galt, Battalion S-3, at a particularly critical period following 2 unsuccessful attacks by his battalion, of his own volition went forward and ascertained just how critical the situation was. He volunteered, at the risk of his life, personally to lead the battalion against the objective. When the lone remaining tank destroyer refused to go forward, Capt. Galt jumped on the tank destroyer and ordered it to precede the attack. As the tank destroyer moved forward, followed by a company of riflemen, Capt. Galt manned the .30-caliber machinegun in the turret of the tank destroyer, located and directed fire on an enemy 77-mm. antitank gun, and destroyed it. Nearing the enemy positions, Capt. Galt stood fully exposed in the turret, ceaselessly firing his machinegun and tossing handgrenades into the enemy zigzag series of trenches despite the hail of sniper and machinegun bullets ricocheting off the tank destroyer. As the tank destroyer moved, Capt. Galt so maneuvered it that 40 of the enemy were trapped in one trench. When they refused to surrender, Capt. Galt pressed the trigger of the machinegun and dispatched every one of them. A few minutes later an 88-mm. shell struck the tank destroyer and Capt. Galt fell mortally wounded across his machinegun. He had personally killed 40 Germans and wounded many more. Capt. Galt pitted his judgment and superb courage against overwhelming odds, exemplifying the highest measure of devotion to his country and the finest traditions of the U.S. Army.

*GAMMON, ARCHER T.

Rank and organization: Staff Sergeant, U.S. Army, Company A, 9th Armored Infantry Battalion, 6th Armored Division. *Place and date:* Near Bastogne, Belgium, 11 January 1945. *Entered service at:* Roanoke, Va. *Born:* 11 September 1918, Chatham, Va. *G.O. No.:* 18, 13 February 1946. *Citation:* He charged 30 yards through hip-deep snow to knock out a machinegun and its 3-man crew with grenades, saving his platoon from being decimated and allowing it to continue its advance from an open field into some nearby woods. The platoon's advance through the woods had only begun when a machinegun supported by riflemen opened fire and a Tiger Royal tank sent 88-mm. shells screaming at the unit from the left flank. S/Sgt. Gammon, disregarding all thoughts of personal safety, rushed forward, then cut to the left, crossing the width of the platoon's skirmish line in an attempt to get within grenade range of the tank and its protecting foot troops. Intense fire was concentrated on him by riflemen and the machinegun emplaced near the tank. He charged the automatic weapon, wiped out its crew of 4 with grenades, and, with supreme daring, advanced to within 25 yards of the armored vehicle, killing 2 hostile infantrymen with rifle fire as he moved forward. The tank had started to withdraw, backing a short distance, then firing, backing some more, and then stopping to blast out another round, when the man whose singlehanded relentless attack had put the ponderous machine on the defensive was struck and instantly killed by a direct hit from the Tiger Royal's heavy gun. By his intrepidity and extreme devotion to the task of driving the enemy back no matter what the odds, S/Sgt. Gammon cleared the woods of German forces, for the tank continued to withdraw, leaving open the path for the gallant squad leader's platoon.

GARCIA, MARCARIO

Rank and organization: Staff Sergeant, U.S. Army, Company B, 22d Infantry, 4th Infantry Division. *Place and date:* Near Grosshau, Germany, 27 November 1944. *Entered service at:* Sugarland, Tex. *Born:* 20 January 1920, Villa de Castano, Mexico. *G.O. No.:* 74, 1 September 1945. *Citation:* While an acting squad leader of Company B, 22d Infantry, on 27 November 1944, near Grosshau, Germany, he singlehandedly assaulted 2 enemy machinegun emplacements. Attacking prepared positions on a wooded hill, which could be approached only through meager cover, his company was pinned down by intense machinegun fire and subjected to a concentrated artillery and mortar barrage. Although painfully wounded, he refused to be evacuated and on his own initiative crawled forward alone until he reached a position near an enemy emplacement. Hurling grenades, he boldly assaulted the position, destroyed the gun, and with his rifle killed 3 of the enemy who attempted to escape. When he rejoined his company, a second machinegun opened fire and again the intrepid soldier went forward, utterly disregarding his own safety. He stormed the position and destroyed the gun, killed 3 more Germans, and captured 4 prisoners. He fought on with his unit until the objective was taken and only then did he permit himself to be removed for medical care. S/Sgt. (then private) Garcia's conspicuous heroism, his inspiring, courageous conduct, and his complete disregard for his personal safety wiped out 2 enemy emplacements and enabled his company to advance and secure its objective.

GARMAN, HAROLD A.

Rank and organization: Private, U.S. Army, Company B, 5th Medical Battalion, 5th Infantry Division. *Place and date:* Near Montereau, France, 25 August 1944. *Entered service at:* Albion, Ill. *Born:* 26 February 1918, Fairfield, Ill. *G.O. No.:* 20, 29 March 1945. *Citation:* For conspicuous gallantry and intrepidity at the risk of his life above and beyond the call of duty. On 25 August 1944, in the vicinity of Montereau, France, the enemy was sharply contesting any enlargement of the bridgehead which our forces had established on the northern bank of the Seine River in this sector. Casualties were being evacuated to the southern shore in assault boats paddled by litter bearers from a medical battalion. Pvt. Garman, also a litter bearer in this battalion, was working on the friendly shore carrying the wounded from the boats to waiting ambulances. As 1 boatload of wounded reached midstream, a German machinegun suddenly opened fire upon it from a commanding position on the northern bank 100 yards away. All of the men in the boat immediately took to the water except 1 man who was so badly wounded he could not rise from his litter. Two other patients who were unable to swim because of their wounds clung to the sides of the boat. Seeing the extreme danger of these patients, Pvt. Garman without a moment's hesitation plunged into the Seine. Swimming directly into a hail of machinegun bullets, he rapidly reached the assault boat and then while still under accurately aimed fire towed the boat with great effort to the southern shore. This soldier's moving heroism not only saved the lives of the three patients but so inspired his comrades that additional assault boats were immediately procured and the evacuation of the wounded resumed. Pvt. Garman's great courage and his heroic devotion to the highest tenets of the Medical Corps may be written with great pride in the annals of the corps.

GARY, DONALD ARTHUR

Rank and organization: Lieutenant, Junior Grade, U.S. Navy, U.S.S. *Franklin. Place and date:* Japanese Home Islands near Kobe, Japan, 19 March 1945. *Entered service at:* Ohio. *Born:* 23 July 1903, Findlay, Ohio. *Citation:* For conspicuous gallantry and intrepidity at the risk of his life above and beyond the call of duty as an engineering officer attached to the U.S.S. *Franklin* when that vessel was fiercely attacked by enemy aircraft during the operations against the Japanese Home Islands near Kobe, Japan, 19 March 1945. Stationed on the third deck when the ship was rocked by a series of violent explosions set off in her own ready bombs, rockets, and ammunition by the hostile attack, Lt. (jg.) Gary unhesitatingly risked his life to assist several hundred men trapped in a messing compartment filled with smoke, and with no apparent egress. As the imperiled men below decks became increasingly panic stricken under the raging fury of incessant explosions, he confidently assured them he would find a means of effecting their release and, groping through the dark, debris-filled corridors, ultimately discovered an escapeway. Stanchly determined, he struggled back to the messing compartment 3 times despite menacing flames, flooding water, and the ominous threat of sudden additional explosions, on each occasion calmly leading his men through the blanketing pall of smoke until the last one had been saved. Selfless in his concern for his ship and his fellows, he constantly rallied others about him, repeatedly organized and led firefighting parties into the blazing inferno on the flight deck and, when firerooms 1 and 2 were found to be inoperable, entered the No. 3 fireroom and directed the raising of steam in 1 boiler in the face of extreme difficulty and hazard. An inspiring and courageous leader, Lt. (jg.) Gary rendered self-sacrificing service under the most perilous conditions and, by his heroic initiative, fortitude, and valor, was responsible for the saving of several hundred lives. His conduct throughout reflects the highest credit upon himself and upon the U.S. Naval Service.

GERSTUNG, ROBERT E.

Rank and organization: Technical Sergeant, U.S. Army, Company H, 313th Infantry, 79th Infantry Division. *Place and date:* Siegfried Line near Berg, Germany, 19 December 1944. *Entered service at:* Chicago, Ill. *Born:* 6 August 1915, Chicago, Ill. *G.O. No.:* 75, 5 September 1945. *Citation:* On 19 December 1944 he was ordered with his heavy machinegun squad to the support of an infantry company attacking the outer defense of the Siegfried Line near Berg, Germany. For 8 hours he maintained a position made almost untenable by the density of artillery and mortar fire concentrated upon it and the proximity of enemy troops who threw handgrenades into the emplacement. While all other members of his squad became casualties, he remained at his gun. When he ran out of ammunition, he fearlessly dashed across bullet-swept, open terrain to secure a new supply from a disabled friendly tank. A fierce barrage pierced the water jacket of his gun, but he continued to fire until the weapon overheated and jammed. Instead of withdrawing, he crawled 50 yards across coverless ground to another of his company's machineguns which had been silenced when its entire crew was killed. He continued to man this gun, giving support vitally needed by the infantry. At one time he came under direct fire from a hostile tank, which shot the glove from his hand with an armor-piercing shell but could not drive him from his position or stop his shooting. When the American forces were ordered to retire to their original positions, he remained at his gun, giving the only covering fire. Finally withdrawing, he cradled the heavy weapon in his left arm, slung a belt of ammunition over his shoulder, and walked to the rear, loosing small bursts at the enemy as he went. One hundred yards from safety, he was struck in the leg by a mortar shell; but, with a supreme effort, he crawled the remaining distance, dragging along the gun which had served him and his comrades so well. By his remarkable perseverance, indomitable courage, and heroic devotion to his task in the face of devastating fire, T/Sgt. Gerstung gave his fellow soldiers powerful support in their encounter with formidable enemy forces.

*GIBSON, ERIC G.

Rank and organization: Technician Fifth Grade, U.S. Army, 3d Infantry Division. *Place and date:* Near Isola Bella, Italy, 28 January 1944. *Entered service at:* Chicago, Ill. *Birth:* Nysund, Sweden. *G.O. No.:* 74, 11 September 1944. *Citation:* For conspicuous gallantry and intrepidity at risk of life above and beyond the call of duty. On 28 January 1944, near Isola Bella, Italy, Tech. 5th Grade Gibson, company cook, led a squad of replacements through their initial baptism of fire, destroyed four enemy positions, killed 5 and captured 2 German soldiers, and secured the left flank of his company during an attack on a strongpoint. Placing himself 50 yards in front of his new men, Gibson advanced down the wide stream ditch known as the Fossa Femminamorta, keeping pace with the advance of his company. An enemy soldier allowed Tech. 5th Grade Gibson to come within 20 yards of his concealed position and then opened fire on him with a machine pistol. Despite the stream of automatic fire which barely missed him, Gibson charged the position, firing his submachinegun every few steps. Reaching the position, Gibson fired point-blank at his opponent, killing him. An artillery concentration fell in and around the ditch; the concussion from one shell knocked him flat. As he got to his feet Gibson was fired on by two soldiers armed with a machine pistol and a rifle from a position only 75 yards distant. Gibson immediately raced toward the foe. Halfway to the position a machinegun opened fire on him. Bullets came within inches of his body, yet Gibson never paused in his forward movement. He killed one and captured the other soldier. Shortly after, when he was fired upon by a heavy machinegun 200 yards down the ditch, Gibson crawled back to his squad and ordered it to lay down a base of fire while he flanked the emplacement. Despite all warning, Gibson crawled 125 yards through an artillery concentration and the cross fire of 2 machineguns which showered dirt over his body, threw 2 handgrenades into the emplacement and charged it with his submachinegun, killing 2 of the enemy and capturing a third. Before leading his men around a bend in the stream ditch, Gibson went forward alone to reconnoiter. Hearing an exchange of machine pistol and submachinegun fire, Gibson's squad went forward to find that its leader had run 35 yards toward an outpost, killed the machine pistol man, and had himself been killed while firing at the Germans.

*GILMORE, HOWARD WALTER

Rank and organization: Commander, U.S. Navy. *Born:* 29 September 1902, Selma, Ala. *Appointed from:* Louisiana. *Other Navy award:* Navy Cross with one gold star. *Citation:* For distinguished gallantry and valor above and beyond the call of duty as commanding officer of the U.S.S. *Growler* during her Fourth War Patrol in the Southwest Pacific from 10 January to 7 February 1943. Boldly striking at the enemy in spite of continuous hostile air and anti-submarine patrols, Comdr. Gilmore sank one Japanese freighter and damaged another by torpedo fire, successfully evading severe depth charges following each attack. In the darkness of night on 7 February, an enemy gunboat closed range and prepared to ram the *Growler*. Comdr. Gilmore daringly maneuvered to avoid the crash and rammed the attacker instead, ripping into her port side at 17 knots and bursting wide her plates. In the terrific fire of the sinking gunboat's heavy machineguns, Comdr. Gilmore calmly gave the order to clear the bridge, and refusing safety for himself, remained on deck while his men preceded him below. Struck down by the fusillade of bullets and having done his utmost against the enemy, in his final living moments, Comdr. Gilmore gave his last order to the officer of the deck, "Take her down." The *Growler* dived; seriously damaged but under control, she was brought safely to port by her well-trained crew inspired by the courageous fighting spirit of their dead captain.

*GONSALVES, HAROLD

Rank and organization: Private First Class, U.S. Marine Corps Reserve. *Born:* 28 January 1926, Alameda, Calif. *Accredited to:* California. *Citation:* For conspicuous gallantry and intrepidity at the risk of his life above and beyond the call of duty while serving as Acting Scout Sergeant with the 4th Battalion, 15th Marines, 6th Marine Division, during action against enemy Japanese forces on Okinawa Shima in the Ryukyu Chain, 15 April 1945. Undaunted by the powerfully organized opposition encountered on Motobu Peninsula during the fierce assault waged by his battalion against the Japanese stronghold at Mount Yaetake, Pfc. Gonsalves repeatedly braved the terrific enemy bombardment to aid his forward observation team in directing well-placed artillery fire. When his commanding officer determined to move into the front lines in order to register a more effective bombardment in the enemy's defensive position, he unhesitatingly advanced uphill with the officer and another Marine despite a slashing barrage of enemy mortar and rifle fire. As they reached the front and a Japanese grenade fell close within the group, instantly Pfc. Gonsalves dived on the deadly missile, absorbing the exploding charge in his own body and thereby protecting the others from serious and perhaps fatal wounds. Stouthearted and indomitable,

Pfc. Gonsalves readily yielded his own chances of survival that his fellow marines might carry on the relentless battle against a fanatic enemy and his cool decision, prompt action and valiant spirit of self-sacrifice in the face of certain death reflect the highest credit upon himself and upon the U.S. Naval Service.

*GONZALES, DAVID M.

Rank and organization: Private First Class, U.S. Army, Company A, 127th Infantry, 32d Infantry Division. *Place and date:* Villa Verde Trail, Luzon, Philippine Islands, 25 April 1945. *Entered service at:* Pacoima, Calif. *Birth:* Pacoima, Calif. *G.O. No.:* 115, 8 December 1945. *Citation:* He was pinned down with his company. As enemy fire swept the area, making any movement extremely hazardous, a 500-pound bomb smashed into the company's perimeter, burying 5 men with its explosion. Pfc. Gonzales, without hesitation, seized an entrenching tool and under a hail of fire crawled 15 yards to his entombed comrades, where his commanding officer, who had also rushed forward, was beginning to dig the men out. Nearing his goal, he saw the officer struck and instantly killed by machinegun fire. Undismayed, he set to work swiftly and surely with his hands and the entrenching tool while enemy sniper and machinegun bullets struck all about him. He succeeded in digging one of the men out of the pile of rock and sand. To dig faster he stood up regardless of the greater danger from so exposing himself. He extricated a second man, and then another. As he completed the liberation of the third, he was hit and mortally wounded, but the comrades for whom he so gallantly gave his life were safely evacuated. Pfc. Gonzales' valiant and intrepid conduct exemplifies the highest tradition of the military service.

GORDON, NATHAN GREEN

Rank and organization: Lieutenant, U.S. Navy, commander of Catalina patrol plane. *Place and date:* Bismarck Sea, 15 February 1944. *Entered service at:* Arkansas. *Born:* 4 September 1916, Morrilton, Ark. *Citation:* For extraordinary heroism above and beyond the call of duty as commander of a Catalina patrol plane in rescuing personnel of the U.S. Army 5th Air Force shot down in combat over Kavieng Harbor in the Bismarck Sea, 15 February 1944. On air alert in the vicinity of Vitu Islands, Lt. (then Lt. jg.) Gordon unhesitatingly responded to a report of the crash and flew boldly into the harbor, defying close-range fire from enemy shore guns to make 3 separate landings in full view of the Japanese and pick up 9 men, several of them injured. With his cumbersome flying boat dangerously overloaded, he made a brilliant takeoff despite heavy swells and almost total absence of wind and set a course for base, only to receive the report of another group stranded in a rubber liferaft 600 yards from the enemy shore. Promptly turning back, he again risked his life to set his plane down under direct fire of the heaviest defenses of Kavieng and take aboard 6 more survivors, coolly making his fourth dexterous takeoff with 15 rescued officers and men. By his exceptional daring, personal valor, and incomparable airmanship under most perilous conditions, Lt. Gordon prevented certain death or capture of our airmen by the Japanese.

*GOTT, DONALD J. (Air Mission)

Rank and organization: First Lieutenant, U.S. Army Air Corps, 729th Bomber Squadron, 452d Bombardment Group. *Place and date:* Saarbrucken, Germany, 9 November 1944. *Entered service at:* Arnett, Okla. *Born:* 3 June 1923, Arnett, Okla. *G.O. No.:* 38, 16 May 1945. *Citation:* On a bombing run upon the marshaling yards at Saarbrucken a B–17 aircraft piloted by 1st. Lt. Gott was seriously damaged by antiaircraft fire. Three of the aircraft's engines were damaged beyond control and on fire; dangerous flames from the No. 4 engine were leaping back as far as the tail assembly. Flares in the cockpit were ignited and a fire raged therein, which was further increased by free-flowing fluid from damaged hydraulic lines. The interphone system was rendered useless. In addition to these serious mechanical difficulties the engineer was wounded in the leg and the radio operator's arm was severed below the elbow. Suffering from intense pain, despite the application of a tourniquet, the radio operator fell unconscious. Faced with the imminent explosion of his aircraft, and death to his entire crew, mere seconds before bombs away on the target, 1st. Lt. Gott and his copilot conferred. Something had to be done immediately to save the life of the wounded radio operator. The lack of a static line and the thought that his unconscious body striking the ground in unknown territory would not bring immediate medical attention forced a quick decision. 1st. Lt. Gott and his copilot decided to fly the flaming aircraft to friendly territory and then attempt to crash land. Bombs were released on the target and the crippled aircraft proceeded alone to Allied-controlled territory. When that had been reached, 1st. Lt. Gott had the copilot personally inform all crewmembers to bail out. The copilot chose to remain with 1st. Lt. Gott in order to assist in landing the bomber. With only one normally functioning engine, and with the danger of explosion much greater, the aircraft banked into an open field, and when it was at an altitude of 100 feet it exploded, crashed, exploded again and then disintegrated. All 3 crewmembers were instantly killed. 1st. Lt. Gott's loyalty to his crew, his determination to accomplish the task set forth to him, and his deed of knowingly performing what may have been his last service to his country was an example of valor at its highest.

*GRABIARZ, WILLIAM J.

Rank and organization: Private First Class, U.S. Army, Troop E, 5th Cavalry, 1st Cavalry Division. *Place and date:* Manila, Luzon, Philippine Islands, 23 February 1945. *Entered service at:* Buffalo, N.Y. *Birth:* Buffalo, N.Y. *G.O. No.:* 115, 8 December 1945. *Citation:* He was a scout when the unit advanced with tanks along a street in Manila, Luzon, Philippine Islands. Without warning, enemy machinegun and rifle fire from concealed positions in the Customs building swept the street, striking down the troop commander and driving his men to cover. As the officer lay in the open road, unable to move and completely exposed to the point-blank enemy fire, Pfc. Grabiarz voluntarily ran from behind a tank to carry him to safety, but was himself wounded in the shoulder. Ignoring both the pain in his injured useless arm and his comrades' shouts to seek the cover which was only a few yards distant, the valiant rescuer continued his efforts to drag his commander out of range. Finding this impossible, he rejected the opportunity to save himself and deliberately covered the officer with his own body to form a human shield, calling as he did so for a tank to maneuver into position between him and the hostile emplacement. The enemy riddled him with concentrated fire before the tank could interpose itself. Our troops found that he had been successful in preventing bullets from striking his leader, who survived. Through his magnificent sacrifice in gallantly giving his life to save that of his commander, Pfc. Grabiarz provided an outstanding and lasting inspiration to his fellow soldiers.

*GRAY, ROSS FRANKLIN

Rank and organization: Sergeant, U.S. Marine Corps Reserve. *Born:* 1 August 1920, Marvel Valley, Ala. *Accredited to:* Alabama. *Citation:* For conspicuous gallantry and intrepidity at the risk of his life above and beyond the call of duty as a Platoon Sergeant attached to Company A, 1st Battalion, 25th Marines, 4th Marine Division, in action against enemy Japanese forces on Iwo Jima, Volcano Islands, 21 February 1945. Shrewdly gaging the tactical situation when his platoon was held up by a sudden barrage of hostile grenades while advancing toward the high ground northeast of Airfield No. 1, Sgt. Gray promptly organized the withdrawal of his men from enemy grenade range, quickly moved forward alone to reconnoiter and discovered a heavily mined area extending along the front of a strong network of emplacements joined by covered trenches. Although assailed by furious gunfire, he cleared a path leading through the minefield to one of the fortifications, then returned to the platoon position and, informing his leader of the serious situation, volunteered to initiate an attack under cover of 3 fellow marines. Alone and unarmed but carrying a huge satchel charge, he crept up on the Japanese emplacement, boldly hurled the short-fused explosive and sealed the entrance. Instantly taken under machinegun fire from a second entrance to the same position, he unhesitatingly braved the increasingly vicious fusillades to crawl back for another charge, returned to his objective and blasted the second opening, thereby demolishing the position. Repeatedly covering the ground between the savagely defended enemy fortifications and his platoon area, he systematically approached, attacked and withdrew under blanketing fire to destroy a total of 6 Japanese positions, more than 25 troops and a quantity of vital ordnance gear and ammunition. Stouthearted and indomitable, Sgt. Gray had singlehandedly overcome a strong enemy garrison and had completely disarmed a large minefield before finally rejoining his unit. By his great personal valor, daring tactics and tenacious perseverance in the face of extreme peril, he had contributed materially to the fulfillment of his company mission. His gallant conduct throughout enhanced and sustained the highest traditions of the U.S. Naval Service.

GREGG, STEPHEN R.

Rank and organization: Second Lieutenant, U.S. Army, 143d Infantry, 36th Infantry Division. *Place and date:* Near Montelimar, France, 27 August 1944. *Entered service at:* Bayonne, N.J. *Birth:* New York, N.Y. *G.O. No.:* 31, 17 April 1945. *Citation:* For conspicuous gallantry and intrepidity at risk of life above and beyond the call of duty on 27 August 1944, in the vicinity of Montelimar, France. As his platoon advanced upon the enemy positions, the leading scout was fired upon and 2d Lt. Gregg (then a Tech. Sgt.) immediately put his machineguns into action to cover the advance of the riflemen. The Germans, who were at close range, threw handgrenades at the riflemen, killing some and wounding 7. Each time a medical aid man attempted to reach the wounded, the Germans fired at him. Realizing the seriousness of the situation, 2d Lt. Gregg took 1 of the light .30 caliber machineguns, and firing from the hip, started boldly up the hill with the medical aid man following him. Although the enemy was throwing handgrenades at him, 2d Lt. Gregg remained and fired into the enemy positions while the medical aid man removed the 7 wounded men to safety. When 2d Lt. Gregg had expended all his ammunition, he was covered by 4 Germans who ordered him to surrender. Since the attention of most of the Germans had been diverted by watching this action, friendly riflemen were able to maneuver into firing positions. One, seeing 2d Lt. Gregg's situation, opened fire on his captors. The 4 Germans hit the ground and thereupon 2d Lt. Gregg recovered a machine pistol from one of the Germans and managed to escape to his other machinegun positions. He manned a gun, firing at his captors, killed 1 of them and wounded the other. This action so discouraged the Germans that the platoon was able to continue its advance up the hill to achieve its objective. The following morning, just prior to daybreak, the Germans launched a strong attack, supported by tanks, in an attempt to drive Company L from the hill. As these tanks moved along the valley and their foot troops advanced up the hill, 2d Lt. Gregg immediately ordered his mortars into action. During the day, by careful observation, he was able to direct effective fire on the enemy, inflicting heavy casualties. By late afternoon he had directed 600 rounds when his communication to the mortars was knocked out. Without hesitation he started checking his wires, although the area was under heavy enemy small-arms and artillery fire. When he was within 100 yards of his mortar position, 1 of his men informed him that the section had been captured and the Germans were using the mortars to fire on the company. 2d Lt. Gregg with this man and another nearby rifleman started for the gun position where he could see 5 Germans firing his mortars. He ordered the 2 men to cover him, crawled up, threw a handgrenade into the position, and then charged it. The handgrenade killed 1, injured 2; 2d Lt. Gregg took the other 2 prisoners, and put his mortars back into action.

*GRUENNERT, KENNETH E.

Rank and organization: Sergeant, U.S. Army, Company L, 127th Infantry, 32d Infantry Division. *Place and date:* Near Buna, New Guinea, 24 December 1942. *Entered service at:* Helenville, Wis. *Birth:* Helenville, Wis. *G.O. No.:* 66, 11 October 1943. *Citation:* For conspicuous gallantry and intrepidity in action above and beyond the call of duty. On 24 December 1942, near Buna, New Guinea, Sgt. Gruennert was second in command of a platoon with a mission to drive through the enemy lines to the beach 600 yards ahead. Within 150 yards of the objective, the platoon encountered 2 hostile pillboxes. Sgt. Gruennert advanced alone on the first and put it out of action with handgrenades and rifle fire, killing 3 of the enemy. Seriously wounded in the shoulder, he bandaged his wound under cover of the pillbox, refusing to withdraw to the aid station and leave his men. He then, with undiminished daring, and under extremely heavy fire, attacked the second pillbox. As he neared it he threw grenades which forced the enemy out where they were easy targets for his platoon. Before the leading elements of his platoon could reach him he was shot by enemy snipers. His inspiring valor cleared the way for his platoon which was the first to attain the beach in this successful effort to split the enemy position.

*GURKE, HENRY

Rank and organization: Private First Class, U.S. Marine Corps. *Born:* 6 November 1922, Neche, N. Dak. *Accredited to:* North Dakota. *Citation:* For extraordinary heroism and courage above and beyond the call of duty while attached to the 3d Marine Raider Battalion during action against enemy Japanese forces in the Solomon Islands area on 9 November 1943. While his platoon was engaged in the defense of a vital road block near Empress Augusta Bay on Bougainville Island, Pfc. Gurke, in company with another Marine, was delivering a fierce stream of fire against the main vanguard of the Japanese. Concluding from the increasing ferocity of grenade barrages that the enemy was determined to annihilate their small, 2-man foxhole, he resorted to a bold and desperate measure for holding out despite the torrential hail of shells. When a Japanese grenade dropped squarely into the foxhole, Pfc. Gurke, mindful that his companion manned an automatic weapon of superior fire power and therefore could provide more effective resistance, thrust him roughly aside and flung his own body over the missile to smother the explosion. With unswerving devotion to duty and superb valor, Pfc. Gurke sacrificed himself in order that his comrade might live to carry on the fight. He gallantly gave his life in the service of his country.

HALL, GEORGE J.

Rank and organization: Staff Sergeant, U.S. Army, 135th Infantry, 34th Infantry Division. *Place and date:* Near Anzio, Italy, 23 May 1944. *Entered service at:* Boston, Mass. *Born:* 9 January 1921, Stoneham, Mass. *G.O. No.:* 24, 6 April 1945. *Citation:* For conspicuous gallantry and intrepidity at risk of life above and beyond the call of duty. Attacking across flat, open terrain under direct enemy observation, S/Sgt. Hall's company was pinned down by grazing fire from 3 enemy machineguns and harassing sniper fire. S/Sgt. Hall volunteered to eliminate these obstacles in the path of advance. Crawling along a plowed furrow through furious machinegun fire, he made his way to a point within handgrenade range of 1 of the enemy positions. He pounded the enemy with 4 handgrenades, and when the smoke had died away, S/Sgt. Hall and 2 dead Germans occupied the position, while 4 of the enemy were crawling back to our lines as prisoners. Discovering a quantity of German potato-masher grenades in the position, S/Sgt. Hall engaged the second enemy nest in a deadly exchange of grenades. Each time he exposed himself to throw a grenade the Germans fired machinegun bursts at him. The vicious duel finally ended in S/Sgt. Hall's favor with 5 of the enemy surrendered and 5 others lay dead. Turning his attention to the third machinegun, S/Sgt. Hall left his position and crawled along a furrow, the enemy firing frantically in an effort to halt him. As he neared his final objective, an enemy artillery concentration fell on the area, and S/Sgt. Hall's right leg was severed by a shellburst. With 2 enemy machineguns eliminated, his company was able to flank the third and continue its advance without incurring excessive casualties. S/Sgt. Hall's fearlessness, his determined fighting spirit, and his prodigious combat skill exemplify the heroic tradition of the American Infantryman.

*HALL, LEWIS

Rank and organization: Technician Fifth Grade, U.S. Army, Company M, 35th Infantry, 25th Infantry Division. *Place and date:* Mount Austen, Guadalcanal, Solomon Islands, 10 January

1943. *Entered service at:* Obetz, Rural Station 7, Columbus, Ohio. *Born:* 1895, Bloom, Ohio. *G.O. No.:* 28, 5 June 1943. *Citation:* For gallantry and intrepidity above and beyond the call of duty. As leader of a machinegun squad charged with the protection of other battalion units, his group was attacked by a superior number of Japanese, his gunner killed, his assistant gunner wounded, and an adjoining guncrew put out of action. Ordered to withdraw from his hazardous position, he refused to retire but rushed forward to the idle gun and with the aid of another soldier who joined him and held up the machinegun by the tripod to increase its field of action he opened fire and inflicted heavy casualties upon the enemy. While so engaged both these gallant soldiers were killed, but their sturdy defense was a decisive factor in the following success of the attacking battalion.

HALL, WILLIAM E.

Rank and organization: Lieutenant, Junior Grade, U.S. Naval Reserve. *Place and date:* Coral Sea, 7 and 8 May 1942. *Entered service at:* Utah. *Born:* 31 October 1913, Storrs, Utah. *Citation:* For extreme courage and conspicuous heroism in combat above and beyond the call of duty as pilot of a scouting plane in action against enemy Japanese forces in the Coral Sea on 7 and 8 May 1942. In a resolute and determined attack on 7 May, Lt. (jg.) Hall dived his plane at an enemy Japanese aircraft carrier, contributing materially to the destruction of that vessel. On 8 May, facing heavy and fierce fighter opposition, he again displayed extraordinary skill as an airman and the aggressive spirit of a fighter in repeated and effectively executed counterattacks against a superior number of enemy planes in which 3 enemy aircraft were destroyed. Though seriously wounded in this engagement, Lt. (jg.) Hall, maintaining the fearless and indomitable tactics pursued throughout these actions, succeeded in landing his plane safe.

*HALLMAN, SHERWOOD H.

Rank and organization: Staff Sergeant, U.S. Army, 175th Infantry, 29th Infantry Division. *Place and date:* Brest, Brittany, France, 13 September 1944. *Entered service at:* Spring City, Pa. *Birth:* Spring City, Pa. *G.O. No.:* 31, 17 April 1945. *Citation:* For conspicuous gallantry and intrepidity at risk of his life above and beyond the call of duty. On 13 September 1944, in Brittany, France, the 2d Battalion in its attack on the fortified city of Brest was held up by a strongly defended enemy position which had prevented its advance despite repeated attacks extending over a 3-day period. Finally, Company F advanced to within several hundred yards of the enemy position but was again halted by intense fire. Realizing that the position must be neutralized without delay, S/Sgt. Hallman ordered his squad to cover his movements with fire while he advanced alone to a point from which he could make the assault. Without hesitating, S/Sgt. Hallman leaped over a hedgerow into a sunken road, the central point of the German defenses which was known to contain an enemy machinegun position and at least 30 enemy riflemen. Firing his carbine and hurling grenades, S/Sgt. Hallman, unassisted, killed or wounded 4 of the enemy, then ordered the remainder to surrender. Immediately, 12 of the enemy surrendered and the position was shortly secured by the remainder of his company. Seeing the surrender of this position, about 75 of the enemy in the vicinity surrendered, yielding a defensive organization which the battalion with heavy supporting fires had been unable to take. This single heroic act on the part of S/Sgt. Hallman resulted in the immediate advance of the entire battalion for a distance of 2,000 yards to a position from which Fort Keranroux was captured later the same day. S/Sgt. Hallman's fighting determination and intrepidity in battle exemplify the highest tradition of the U.S. Armed Forces.

*HALYBURTON, WILLIAM DAVID, Jr.

Rank and organization: Pharmacist's Mate Second Class, U.S. Naval Reserve. *Born:* 2 August 1924, Canton, N.C. *Accredited to:*

North Carolina. *Citation:* For conspicuous gallantry and intrepidity at the risk of his life above and beyond the call of duty while serving with a Marine Rifle Company in the 2d Battalion, 5th Marines, 1st Marine Division, during action against enemy Japanese forces on Okinawa Shima in the Ryukyu Chain, 10 May 1945. Undaunted by the deadly accuracy of Japanese counterfire as his unit pushed the attack through a strategically important draw, Halyburton unhesitatingly dashed across the draw and up the hill into an open fireswept field where the company advance squad was suddenly pinned down under a terrific concentration of mortar, machinegun and sniper fire with resultant severe casualties. Moving steadily forward despite the enemy's merciless barrage, he reached the wounded marine who lay farthest away and was rendering first aid when his patient was struck for the second time by a Japanese bullet. Instantly placing himself in the direct line of fire, he shielded the fallen fighter with his own body and staunchly continued his ministrations although constantly menaced by the slashing fury of shrapnel and bullets falling on all sides. Alert, determined and completely unselfish in his concern for the helpless marine, he persevered in his efforts until he himself sustained mortal wounds and collapsed, heroically sacrificing himself that his comrade might live. By his outstanding valor and unwavering devotion to duty in the face of tremendous odds, Halyburton sustained and enhanced the highest traditions of the U.S. Naval Service. He gallantly gave his life in the service of his country.

HAMILTON, PIERPONT M.

Rank and organization: Major, U.S. Army Air Corps. *Place and date:* Near Port Lyautey, French Morocco, 8 November 1942. *Entered service at:* New York, N.Y. *Born:* 3 August 1898, Tuxedo Park, N.Y. *G.O. No.:* 4, 23 January 1943. *Citation:* For conspicuous gallantry and intrepidity in action above and beyond the call of duty. On 8 November 1942, near Port Lyautey, French Morocco, Lt. Col. Hamilton volunteered to accompany Col. Demas Craw on a dangerous mission to the French commander, designed to bring about a cessation of hostilities. Driven away from the mouth of the Sebou River by heavy shelling from all sides, the landing boat was finally beached at Mehdia Plage despite continuous machinegun fire from 3 low-flying hostile planes. Driven in a light truck toward French headquarters, this courageous mission encountered intermittent firing, and as it neared Port Lyautey a heavy burst of machinegun fire was delivered upon the truck from pointblank range, killing Col. Craw instantly. Although captured immediately, after this incident, Lt. Col. Hamilton completed the mission.

*HAMMERBERG, OWEN FRANCIS PATRICK

Rank and organization: Boatswain's Mate Second Class, U.S. Navy. *Born:* 31 May 1920, Daggett, Mich. *Accredited to:* Michigan. *Citation:* For conspicuous gallantry and intrepidity at the risk of his life above and beyond the call of duty as a diver engaged in rescue operations at West Loch, Pearl Harbor, 17 February 1945. Aware of the danger when 2 fellow divers were hopelessly trapped in a cave-in of steel wreckage while tunneling with jet nozzels under an LST sunk in 40 feet of water and 20 feet of mud. Hammerberg unhesitatingly went overboard in a valiant attempt to effect their rescue despite the certain hazard of additional cave-ins and the risk of fouling his lifeline on jagged pieces of steel imbedded in the shifting mud. Washing a passage through the original excavation, he reached the first of the trapped men, freed him from the wreckage and, working desperately in pitch-black darkness, finally effected his release from fouled lines, thereby enabling him to reach the surface. Wearied but undaunted after several hours of arduous labor, Hammerberg resolved to continue his struggle to wash through the oozing submarine, subterranean mud in a determined effort to save the second diver. Venturing still farther under the buried hulk, he held tenaciously to his purpose, reaching a place immediately above the other man just as another cave-in occurred and a heavy piece of steel pinned him crosswise over his shipmate in a position which protected the man beneath from further injury while placing the full brunt of terrific pressure on himself. Although he succumbed in agony 18 hours after he had gone to the aid of his fellow divers, Hammerberg, by his cool judgment, unfaltering professional skill and consistent disregard of all personal danger in the face of tremendous odds, had contributed effectively to the saving of his 2 comrades. His heroic spirit of self-sacrifice throughout enhanced and sustained the highest traditions of the U.S. Naval Service. He gallantly gave his life in the service of his country.

*HANSEN, DALE MERLIN

Rank and organization: Private, U.S. Marine Corps. *Born:* 13 December 1922, Wisner, Nebr. *Accredited to:* Nebraska. *Citation:* For conspicuous gallantry and intrepidity at the risk of his life above and beyond the call of duty while serving with Company E, 2d Battalion, 1st Marines, 1st Marine Division, in action against enemy Japanese forces on Okinawa Shima in the Ryukyu Chain, 7 May 1945. Cool and courageous in combat, Pvt. Hansen unhesitatingly took the initiative during a critical stage of the action and, armed with a rocket launcher, crawled to an exposed position where he attacked and destroyed a strategically located hostile pillbox. With his weapon subsequently destroyed by enemy fire, he seized a rifle and continued his 1-man assault. Reaching the crest of a ridge, he leaped across, opened fire on 6 Japanese and killed 4 before his rifle jammed. Attacked by the remaining 2 Japanese, he beat them off with the butt of his rifle and then climbed back to cover. Promptly returning with another weapon and supply of grenades, he fearlessly advanced, destroyed a strong mortar position and annihilated 8 more of the enemy. In the forefront of battle throughout this bitterly waged engagement, Pvt. Hansen, by his indomitable determination, bold tactics and complete disregard of all personal danger, contributed essentially to the success of his company's mission and to the ultimate capture of this fiercely defended outpost of the Japanese Empire. His great personal valor in the face of extreme peril reflects the highest credit upon himself and the U.S. Naval Service.

*HANSON, ROBERT MURRAY

Rank and organization: First Lieutenant, U.S. Marine Corps Reserve. *Born:* 4 February 1920, Lucknow, India. *Accredited to:* Massachusetts. *Other Navy awards:* Navy Cross, Air Medal. *Citation:* For conspicuous gallantry and intrepidity at the risk of his life and above and beyond the call of duty as fighter pilot attached to Marine Fighting Squadron 215 in action against enemy Japanese forces at Bougainville Island, 1 November 1943; and New Britain Island, 24 January 1944. Undeterred by fierce opposition, and fearless in the face of overwhelming odds, 1st Lt. Hanson fought the Japanese boldly and with daring aggressiveness. On 1 November, while flying cover for our landing operations at Empress Augusta Bay, he dauntlessly attacked 6 enemy torpedo bombers, forcing them to jettison their bombs and destroying 1 Japanese plane during the action. Cut off from his division while deep in enemy territory during a high cover flight over Simpson Harbor on 24 January, 1st Lt. Hanson waged a lone and gallant battle against hostile interceptors as they were orbiting to attack our bombers and, striking with devastating fury, brought down 4 Zeroes and probably a fifth. Handling his plane superbly in both pursuit and attack measures, he was a master of individual air combat, accounting for a total of 25 Japanese aircraft in this theater of war. His great personal valor and invincible fighting spirit were in keeping with the highest traditions of the U.S. Naval Service.

*HARMON, ROY W.

Rank and organization: Sergeant, U.S. Army, Company C, 362d Infantry, 91st Infantry Division. *Place and date:* Near Casaglia, Italy, 12 July 1944. *Entered service at:* Pixley, Calif. *Birth:* Talala, Okla. *G.O. No.:* 83, 2 October 1945. *Citation:* He was an acting squad leader when heavy machinegun fire from enemy positions, well dug in on commanding ground and camouflaged by haystacks, stopped his company's advance and pinned down 1 platoon where it was exposed to almost certain annihilation. Ordered to rescue the beleaguered platoon by neutralizing the German automatic fire, he led his squad forward along a draw to the right of the trapped unit against 3 key positions which poured murderous fire into his helpless comrades. When within range, his squad fired tracer bullets in an attempt to set fire to the 3 haystacks which were strung out in a loose line directly to the front, 75, 150, and 250 yards away. Realizing that this attack was ineffective, Sgt. Harmon ordered his squad to hold their position and voluntarily began a 1-man assault. Carrying white phosphorus grenades and a submachinegun, he skillfully took advantage of what little cover the terrain afforded and crept to within 25 yards of the first position. He set the haystack afire with a grenade, and when 2 of the enemy attempted to flee from the inferno, he killed them with his submachinegun. Crawling toward the second machinegun emplacement, he attracted fire and was wounded; but he continued to advance and destroyed the position with handgrenades, killing the occupants. He then attacked the third machinegun, running to a small knoll, then crawling over ground which offered no concealment or cover. About halfway to his objective, he was again wounded. But he struggled ahead until within 20 yards of the machinegun nest, where he raised himself to his knees to throw a grenade. He was knocked down by direct enemy fire. With a final, magnificent effort, he again arose, hurled the grenade and fell dead, riddled by bullets. His missile fired the third position, destroying it. Sgt. Harmon's extraordinary heroism, gallantry, and self-sacrifice saved a platoon from being wiped out, and made it possible for his company to advance against powerful enemy resistance.

*HARR, HARRY R.

Rank and organization: Corporal, U.S. Army, Company D, 124th Infantry, 31st Infantry Division. *Place and date:* Near Maglamin, Mindanao, Philippine Islands, 5 June 1945. *Entered service at:* East Freedom, Pa. *Born:* Pine Croft, Pa. *G.O. No.:* 28, 28 March 1946. *Citation:* He displayed conspicuous gallantry and intrepidity. In a fierce counterattack, the Japanese closed in on his machinegun emplacement, hurling handgrenades, 1 of which exploded under the gun, putting it out of action and wounding 2 of the crew. While the remaining gunners were desperately attempting to repair their weapon another grenade landed squarely in the emplacement. Quickly realizing he could not safely throw the unexploded missile from the crowded position, Cpl. Harr unhesitatingly covered it with his body to smother the blast. His supremely courageous act, which cost him his life, saved 4 of his comrades and enabled them to continue their mission.

HARRELL, WILLIAM GEORGE

Rank and organization: Sergeant, U.S. Marine Corps, 1st Battalion, 28th Marines, 5th Marine Division. *Place and date:* Iwo Jima, Volcano Islands, 3 March 1945. *Entered service at:* Mercedes, Tex. *Born:* 26 June 1922, Rio Grande City, Tex. *Citation:* For conspicuous gallantry and intrepidity at the risk of his life above and beyond the call of duty as leader of an assault group attached to the 1st Battalion, 28th Marines, 5th Marine Division during hand-to-hand combat with enemy Japanese at Iwo Jima, Volcano Islands, on 3 March 1945. Standing watch alternately with another marine in a terrain studded with caves and ravines, Sgt. Harrell was holding a position in a perimeter defense around the company command post when Japanese troops infiltrated our lines in the early hours of dawn. Awakened by a sudden attack, he quickly opened fire with his carbine and killed 2 of the enemy as they emerged from a ravine in the light of a star shellburst. Unmindful of his danger as hostile grenades fell closer, he waged a fierce lone battle until an exploding missile tore off his left hand and fractured his thigh. He was vainly attempting to reload the carbine when his companion returned from the command post with another weapon. Wounded again by a Japanese who rushed the foxhole wielding a saber in the darkness, Sgt. Harrell succeeded in drawing his pistol and killing his opponent and then ordered his wounded companion to a place of safety. Exhausted by profuse bleeding but still unbeaten, he fearlessly met the challenge of 2 more enemy troops who charged his position and placed a grenade near his head. Killing 1 man with his pistol, he grasped the sputtering grenade with his good right hand, and, pushing it painfully toward the crouching soldier, saw his remaining assailant destroyed but his own hand severed in the explosion. At dawn Sgt. Harrell was evacuated from a position hedged by the bodies of 12 dead Japanese, at least 5 of whom he had personally destroyed in his self-sacrificing defense of the command post. His grim fortitude, exceptional valor, and indomitable fighting spirit against almost insurmountable odds reflect the highest credit upon himself and enhance the finest traditions of the U.S. Naval Service.

*HARRIS, JAMES L.

Rank and organization: Second Lieutenant, U.S. Army, 756th Tank Battalion. *Place and date:* At Vagney, France, 7 October 1944. *Entered service at:* Hillsboro, Tex. *Birth:* Hillsboro, Tex. *G.O. No.:* 32, 23 April 1945. *Citation:* For conspicuous gallantry and intrepidity at risk of life above and beyond the call of duty on 7 October 1944, in Vagney, France. At 9 p.m. an enemy raiding party, comprising a tank and 2 platoons of infantry, infiltrated through the lines under cover of mist and darkness and attacked an infantry battalion command post with handgrenades, retiring a short distance to an ambush position on hearing the approach of the M4 tank commanded by 2d Lt. Harris. Realizing the need for bold aggressive action, 2d Lt. Harris ordered his tank to halt while he proceeded on foot, fully 10 yards ahead of his 6-man patrol and armed only with a service pistol, to probe the darkness for the enemy. Although struck down and mortally wounded by machinegun bullets which penetrated his solar plexus, he crawled back to his tank, leaving a trail of blood behind him, and, too weak to climb inside it, issued fire orders while lying on the road between the 2 contending armored vehicles. Although the tank which he commanded was destroyed in the course of the fire fight, he stood the enemy off until friendly tanks, preparing to come to his aid, caused the enemy to withdraw and thereby lose an opportunity to kill or capture the entire battalion command personnel. Suffering a second wound, which severed his leg at the hip, in the course of this tank duel, 2d Lt. Harris refused aid until after a wounded member of his crew had been carried to safety. He died before he could be given medical attention.

*HASTINGS, JOE R.

Rank and organization: Private First Class, U.S. Army, Company C, 386th Infantry, 97th Infantry Division. *Place and date:* Drabenderhohe, Germany, 12 April 1945. *Entered service at:* Magnolia, Ohio. *Birth:* Malvern, Ohio. *G.O. No.:* 101, 8 November 1945. *Citation:* He fought gallantly during an attack against strong enemy forces defending Drabenderhohe, Germany, from the dug-in positions on commanding ground. As squad leader of a light machinegun section supporting the advance of the 1st and 3d Platoons, he braved direct rifle, machinegun, 20-mm., and mortar fire, some of which repeatedly missed him only by inches, and rushed forward over 350 yards of open, rolling fields to reach a position from which he could fire on the enemy troops. From this vantage point he killed the crews of a 20-mm. gun and a machinegun, drove several enemy riflemen from their positions, and so successfully shielded the 1st Platoon, that it had time to reorganize and remove its wounded to safety. Observing that the 3d Platoon to his right was being met by very heavy 40-mm. and machinegun fire, he ran 150 yards with his gun to the leading elements of that unit, where he killed the crew of the 40-mm. gun. As spearhead of the 3d Platoon's attack, he advanced, firing his gun held at hip height, disregarding the bullets that whipped past him, until the assault had carried 175 yards to the objective. In this charge he and the riflemen he led killed or wounded many of the fanatical enemy and put 2 machineguns out of action. Pfc. Hastings, by his intrepidity, outstanding leadership, and unrelenting determination to wipe out the formidable German opposition, cleared the path for his company's advance into Drabenderhohe. He was killed 4 days later while again supporting the 3d Platoon.

*HAUGE, LOUIS JAMES, Jr.

Rank and organization: Corporal, U.S. Marine Corps Reserve. *Born:* 12 December 1924, Ada, Minn. *Accredited to:* Minnesota. *Citation:* For conspicuous gallantry and intrepidity at the risk of his life above and beyond the call of duty as leader of a machinegun squad serving with Company C, 1st Battalion, 1st Marines, 1st Marine Division, in action against enemy Japanese forces on Okinawa Shima in the Ryukyu Chain on 14 May 1945. Alert and aggressive during a determined assault against a strongly fortified Japanese hill position, Cpl. Hauge boldly took the initiative when his company's left flank was pinned down under a heavy machinegun and mortar barrage with resultant severe casualties and, quickly locating the 2 machineguns which were delivering the uninterrupted stream of enfilade fire, ordered his squad to maintain a covering barrage as he rushed across an exposed area toward the furiously blazing enemy weapons. Although painfully wounded as he charged the first machinegun, he launched a vigorous singlehanded grenade attack, destroyed the entire hostile gun position and move relentlessly forward toward the other emplacement despite his wounds and the increasingly heavy Japanese fire. Undaunted by the savage opposition, he again hurled his deadly grenades with unerring aim and succeeded in demolishing the second enemy gun before he fell under the slashing fury of Japanese sniper fire. By his ready grasp of the critical situation and his heroic 1-man assault tactics, Cpl. Hauge had eliminated 2 strategically placed enemy weapons, thereby releasing the besieged troops from an overwhelming volume of hostile fire and enabling his company to advance. His indomitable fighting spirit and decisive valor in the face of almost certain death reflect the highest credit upon Cpl. Hauge and the U.S. Naval Service. He gallantly gave his life in the service of his country.

HAWK, JOHN D.

Rank and organization: Sergeant, U.S. Army, Company E, 359th Infantry, 90th Infantry Division. *Place and date:* Near Chambois, France, 20 August 1944. *Entered service at:* Bremerton, Wash. *Born:* 30 May 1924, San Francisco, Calif. *G.O. No.:* 55, 13 July 1945. *Citation:* He manned a light machinegun on 20 August 1944, near Chambois, France, a key point in the encirclement which created the Falaise Pocket. During an enemy counterattack, his position was menaced by a strong force of tanks and infantry. His fire forced the infantry to withdraw, but an artillery shell knocked out his gun and wounded him in the right thigh. Securing a bazooka, he and another man stalked the tanks and forced them to retire to a wooded section. In the lull which followed, Sgt. Hawk reorganized 2 machinegun squads and, in the face of intense enemy fire, directed the assembly of 1 workable weapon from 2 damaged guns. When another enemy assault developed, he was forced to pull back from the pressure of spearheading armor. Two of our tank destroyers were brought up. Their shots were ineffective because of the terrain until Sgt. Hawk, despite his wound, boldly climbed to an exposed position on a knoll where, unmoved by fusillades from the enemy, he became a human aiming stake for the destroyers. Realizing that his shouted fire directions could not be heard above the noise of battle, he ran back to the destroyers through a concentration of bullets and shrapnel to correct the range. He returned to his exposed position, repeating this performance until 2 of the tanks were knocked out and a third driven off. Still at great risk, he continued to direct the destroyers' fire into the Germans' wooded position until the enemy came out and surrendered. Sgt. Hawk's fearless initiative and heroic conduct, even while suffering from a painful wound, was in large measure responsible for crushing 2 desperate attempts of the enemy to escape from the Falaise Picket and for taking more than 500 prisoners.

*HAWKINS, WILLIAM DEAN

Rank and organization: First Lieutenant, U.S. Marine Corps. *Born:* 19 April 1914, Fort Scott, Kans. *Appointed from:* El Paso, Tex. *Citation:* For valorous and gallant conduct above and beyond the call of duty as commanding officer of a Scout Sniper Platoon attached to the Assault Regiment in action against Japanese-held Tarawa in the Gilbert Island, 20 and 21 November 1943. The first to disembark from the jeep lighter, 1st Lt. Hawkins unhesitatingly moved forward under heavy enemy fire at the end of the Betio Pier, neutralizing emplacements in coverage of troops assaulting the main beach positions. Fearlessly leading his men on to join the forces fighting desperately to gain a beachhead, he repeatedly risked his life throughout the day and night to direct and lead attacks on pillboxes and installations with grenades and demolitions. At dawn on the following day, 1st Lt. Hawkins resumed the dangerous mission of clearing the limited beachhead of Japanese resistance, personally initiating an assault on a hostile position fortified by 5 enemy machineguns, and, crawling forward in the face of withering fire, boldly fired point-blank into the loopholes and completed the destruction with grenades. Refusing to withdraw after being seriously wounded in the chest during this skirmish, 1st Lt. Hawkins steadfastly carried the fight to the enemy, destroying 3 more pillboxes before he was caught in a burst of Japanese shellfire and mortally wounded. His relentless fighting spirit in the face of formidable opposition and his exceptionally daring tactics served as an inspiration to his comrades during the most crucial phase of the battle and reflect the highest credit upon the U.S. Naval Service. He gallantly gave his life for his country.

HAWKS, LLOYD C.

Rank and organization: Private First Class, U.S. Army, Medical Detachment, 30th Infantry, 3d Infantry Division. *Place and date:* Near Carano, Italy, 30 January 1944. *Entered service at:* Park Rapids, Minn. *Born:* 13 January 1911, Becker, Minn. *G.O. No.:* 5, 15 January 1945. *Citation:* For gallantry and intrepidity at risk of life above and beyond the call of duty. On 30 January 1944, at 3 p.m., near Carano, Italy, Pfc. Hawks braved an enemy counterattack in order to rescue 2 wounded men who, unable to move, were lying in an exposed position within 30 yards of the enemy. Two riflemen, attempting the rescue, had been forced to return to their fighting holes by extremely severe enemy machinegun fire, after crawling only 10 yards toward the casualties. An aid man, whom the enemy could plainly identify as such, had been critically wounded in a similar attempt. Pfc. Hawks, nevertheless, crawled 50 yards through a veritable hail of machinegun bullets and flying mortar fragments to a small ditch, administered first aid to his fellow aid man who had sought cover therein, and continued toward the 2 wounded men 50 yards distant. An enemy machinegun bullet penetrated his helmet, knocking it from his head, momentarily stunning him. Thirteen bullets passed through his helmet as it lay on the ground within 6 inches of his body. Pfc. Hawks crawled to the casualties, administered first aid to the more seriously wounded man and dragged him to a covered position 25 yards distant. Despite continuous automatic fire from positions only 30 yards away and shells which exploded within 25 yards, Pfc. Hawks returned to the second man and administered first aid to him. As he raised himself to obtain bandages from his medical kit his right hip was shattered by a burst of machinegun fire and a second burst splintered his left forearm. Displaying dogged determination and extreme self-control, Pfc. Hawks, despite severe pain and his dangling left arm, completed the task of bandaging the remaining casualty and with superhuman effort dragged him to the same depression to which he had brought the first man. Finding insufficient cover for 3 men at this point, Pfc. Hawks crawled 75 yards in an effort to regain his company, reaching the ditch in which his fellow aid man was lying.

*HEDRICK, CLINTON M.

Rank and organization: Technical Sergeant, U.S. Army, Company I, 194th Glider Infantry, 17th Airborne Division. *Place and date:* Near Lembeck, Germany, 27–28 March 1945. *Entered service at:* Riverton, W. Va. *Birth:* Cherrygrove, W. Va. *G.O. No.:* 89, 19 October 1945. *Citation:* He displayed extraordinary heroism and gallantry in action on 27–28 March 1945, in Germany. Following an airborne landing near Wesel, his unit was assigned as the assault platoon for the assault on Lembeck. Three times the landing elements were pinned down by intense automatic weapons fire from strongly defended positions. Each time, T/Sgt. Hedrick fearlessly charged through heavy fire, shooting his automatic rifle from his hip. His courageous action so inspired his men that they reduced the enemy positions in rapid succession. When 6 of the enemy attempted a surprise, flanking movement, he quickly turned and killed the entire party with a burst of fire. Later, the enemy withdrew across the moat into Lembeck Castle. T/Sgt. Hedrick, with utter disregard for his own safety, plunged across the drawbridge alone in pursuit. When a German soldier, with hands upraised, declared the garrison wished to surrender, he entered the castle yard with 4 of his men to accept the capitulation. The group moved through a sally port, and was met by fire from a German self-propelled gun. Although mortally wounded, T/Sgt. Hedrick fired at the enemy gun and covered the withdrawal of his comrades. He died while being evacuated after the castle was taken. His great personal courage and heroic leadership contributed in large measure to the speedy capture of Lembeck and provided an inspiring example to his comrades.

HENDRIX, JAMES R.

Rank and organization: Private, U.S. Army, Company C, 53d Armored Infantry Battalion, 4th Armored Division. *Place and date:* Near Assenois, Belgium, 26 December 1944. *Entered service at:* Lepanto, Ark. *Birth:* Lepanto, Ark. *G.O. No.:* 74, 1 September 1945. *Citation:* On the night of 26 December 1944, near Assenois, Belgium, he was with the leading element engaged in the final thrust to break through to the besieged garrison at Bastogne when halted by a fierce combination of artillery and small-arms fire. He dismounted from his halftrack and advanced against two 88-mm. guns, and, by the ferocity of his rifle fire, compelled the guncrews to take cover and then to surrender. Later in the attack he again left his vehicle, voluntarily, to aid 2 wounded soldiers, helpless and exposed to intense machinegun fire. Effectively silencing 2 hostile machineguns, he held off the enemy by his own fire until the wounded men were evacuated. Pvt. Hendrix again distinguished himself when he hastened to the aid of still another soldier who was trapped in a burning halftrack. Braving enemy sniper fire and exploding mines and ammunition in the vehicle, he extricated the wounded man and extinguished his flaming clothing, thereby saving the life of his fellow soldier. Pvt. Hendrix, by his superb courage and heroism, exemplified the highest traditions of the military service.

*HENRY, ROBERT T.

Rank and organization: Private, U.S. Army, 16th Infantry, 1st Infantry Division. *Place and date:* Luchem, Germany, 3 December 1944. *Entered service at:* Greenville, Miss. *Birth:* Greenville, Miss. *G.O. No.:* 45, 12 June 1945. *Citation:* Near Luchem, Germany, he volunteered to attempt the destruction of a nest of 5 enemy machineguns located in a bunker 150 yards to the flank which had stopped the advance of his platoon. Stripping off his pack, overshoes, helmet, and overcoat, he sprinted alone with his rifle and handgrenades across the open terrain toward the enemy emplacement. Before he had gone half the distance he was hit by a burst of machinegun fire. Dropping his rifle, he continued to stagger forward until he fell mortally wounded only 10 yards from the enemy emplacement. His singlehanded attack forced the enemy to leave the machineguns. During this break in hostile fire the platoon moved forward and overran the position. Pvt. Henry, by his gallantry and intrepidity and utter disregard for his own life, enabled his company to reach its objective, capturing this key defense and 70 German prisoners.

HERRERA, SILVESTRE S.

Rank and organization: Private First Class, U.S. Army, Company E, 142d Infantry, 36th Infantry Division. *Place and date:* Near Mertzwiller, France, 15 March 1945. *Entered service at:* Phoenix, Ariz. *Birth:* El Paso, Tex. *G.O. No.:* 75, 5 September 1945. *Citation:* He advanced with a platoon along a wooded road until stopped by heavy enemy machinegun fire. As the rest of the unit took cover, he made a 1-man frontal assault on a strongpoint and captured 8 enemy soldiers. When the platoon resumed its advance and was subjected to fire from a second emplacement beyond an extensive minefield, Pvt. Herrera again moved forward, disregarding the danger of exploding mines, to attack the position. He stepped on a mine and had both feet severed; but, despite intense pain and unchecked loss of blood, he pinned down the enemy with accurate rifle fire while a friendly squad captured the enemy gun by skirting the minefield and rushing in from the flank. The magnificent courage, extraordinary heroism, and willing self-sacrifice displayed by Pvt. Herrera resulted in the capture of 2 enemy strongpoints and the taking of 8 prisoners.

HERRING, RUFUS G.

Rank and organization: Lieutenant, U.S. Naval Reserve, LCI (G) 449. *Place and date:* Iwo Jima, 17 February 1945. *Entered service at:* North Carolina. *Born:* 11 June 1921, Roseboro, N.C. *Citation:* For conspicuous gallantry and intrepidity at the risk of his life above and beyond the call of duty as commanding officer of LCI (G) *449* operating as a unit of LCI (G) Group 8, during the pre-invasion attack on Iwo Jima on 17 February 1945. Boldly closing the strongly fortified shores under the devastating fire of Japanese coastal defense guns, Lt. (then Lt. (j.g.)) Herring directed shattering barrages of 40-mm. and 20-mm. gunfire against hostile beaches until struck down by the enemy's savage counterfire which blasted the *449*'s heavy guns and whipped her decks into sheets of flame. Regaining consciousness despite profuse bleeding he was again critically wounded when a Japanese mortar crashed the conning station, instantly killing or fatally wounding most of the officers and leaving the ship wallowing without navigational control. Upon recovering the second time, Lt. Herring resolutely climbed down to the pilothouse and, fighting against his rapidly waning strength, took over the helm, established communication with the engineroom, and carried on valiantly until relief could be obtained. When no longer able to stand, he propped himself against empty shell cases and rallied his men to the aid of the wounded; he maintained position in the firing line with his 20-mm. guns in action in the face of sustained enemy fire, and conned his crippled ship to safety. His unwavering fortitude, aggressive perseverance, and indomitable spirit against terrific odds reflect the highest credit upon Lt. Herring and uphold the highest traditions of the U.S. Naval Service.

*HILL, EDWIN JOSEPH

Rank and organization: Chief Boatswain, U.S. Navy. *Born:* 4 October 1894, Philadelphia, Pa. *Accredited to:* Pennsylvania. *Citation:* For distinguished conduct in the line of his profession, extraordinary courage, and disregard of his own safety during the attack on the Fleet in Pearl Harbor, by Japanese forces on 7 December 1941. During the height of the strafing and bombing, Chief Boatswain Hill led his men of the line-handling details of the U.S.S. *Nevada* to the quays, cast off the lines and swam back to his ship. Later, while on the forecastle, attempting to let go the anchors, he was blown overboard and killed by the explosion of several bombs.

HORNER, FREEMAN V.

Rank and organization: Staff Sergeant, U.S. Army, Company K, 119th Infantry, 30th Infantry Division. *Place and date:* Wurselen, Germany, 16 November 1944. *Entered service at:* Shamokin, Pa. *Birth:* Mount Carmel, Pa. *G.O. No.:* 95, 30 October 1945. *Citation:* S/Sgt. Horner and other members of his company were attacking Wurselen, Germany, against stubborn resistance on 16 November 1944, when machinegun fire from houses on the edge of the town pinned the attackers in flat, open terrain 100 yards from their objective. As they lay in the field, enemy artillery observers directed fire upon them, causing serious casualties. Realizing that the machineguns must be eliminated in order to permit the company to advance from its precarious position, S/Sgt. Horner voluntarily stood up with his submachinegun and rushed into the teeth of concentrated fire, burdened by a heavy load of ammunition and handgrenades. Just as he reached a position of seeming safety, he was fired on by a machinegun which had remained silent up until that time. He coolly wheeled in his fully exposed position while bullets barely missed him and killed 2 hostile gunners with a single, devastating burst. He turned to face the fire of the other 2 machineguns, and dodging fire as he ran, charged the 2 positions 50 yards away. Demoralized by their inability to hit the intrepid infantryman, the enemy abandoned their guns and took cover in the cellar of the house they occupied. S/Sgt. Horner burst into the building, hurled 2 grenades down the cellar stairs, and called for the Germans to surrender. Four men gave up to him. By his extraordinary courage, S/Sgt. Horner destroyed 3 enemy machinegun positions, killed or captured 7 enemy, and cleared the path for his company's successful assault on Wurselen.

HOWARD, JAMES H. (Air Mission)

Rank and organization: Lieutenant Colonel, U.S. Army Air Corps. *Place and date:* Over Oschersleben, Germany, 11 January 1944. *Entered service at:* St. Louis, Mo. *Birth:* Canton, China. *G.O. No.:* 45, 5 June 1944. *Citation:* For conspicuous gallantry and intrepidity above and beyond the call of duty in action with the enemy near Oschersleben, Germany, on 11 January 1944. On that day Col. Howard was the leader of a group of P–51 aircraft providing support for a heavy bomber formation on a long-range mission deep in enemy territory. As Col. Howard's group met the bombers in the target area the bomber force was attacked by numerous enemy fighters. Col. Howard, with his group, and at once engaged the enemy and himself destroyed a German ME. 110. As a result of this attack Col. Howard lost contact with his group, and at once returned to the level of the bomber formation. He then saw that the bombers were being heavily attacked by enemy airplanes and that no other friendly fighters were at hand. While Col. Howard could have waited to attempt to assemble his group before engaging the enemy, he chose instead to attack singlehanded a formation of more than 30 German airplanes. With utter disregard for his own safety he immediately pressed home determined attacks for some 30 minutes, during which time he destroyed 3 enemy airplanes and probably destroyed and damaged others. Toward the end of this engagement 3 of his guns went out of action and his fuel supply was becoming dangerously low. Despite these handicaps and the almost insuperable odds against him, Col. Howard continued his aggressive action in an attempt to protect the bombers from the numerous fighters. His skill, courage, and intrepidity on this occasion set an example of heroism which will be an inspiration to the U.S. Armed Forces.

HUFF, PAUL B.

Rank and organization: Corporal, U.S. Army, 509th Parachute Infantry Battalion. *Place and date:* Near Carano, Italy, 8 February 1944. *Entered service at:* Cleveland, Tenn. *Birth:* Cleveland, Tenn. *G.O. No.:* 41, 26 May 1944. *Citation:* For conspicuous gallantry and intrepidity at risk of life above and beyond the call of duty, in action on 8 February 1944, near Carano, Italy. Cpl. Huff volunterred to lead a 6-man patrol with the mission of determining the location and strength of an enemy unit which was delivering fire on the exposed right flank of his company. The terrain over which he had to travel consisted of exposed, rolling ground, affording the enemy excellent visibility. As the patrol advanced, its members were subjected to small arms and machinegun fire and a concentration of mortar fire, shells bursting within 5 to 10 yards of them and bullets striking the ground at their feet. Moving ahead of his patrol, Cpl. Huff drew fire from 3 enemy machineguns and a 20-mm. weapon. Realizing the danger confronting his patrol, he advanced alone under deadly fire through a minefield and arrived at a point within 75 yards of the nearest machinegun position. Under direct fire from the rear machinegun, he crawled the remaining 75 yards to the closest emplacement, killed the crew with his submachinegun and destroyed the gun. During this act he fired from a kneeling position which drew fire from other positions, enabling him to estimate correctly the strength and location of the enemy. Still under concentrated fire, he returned to his patrol and led his men to safety. As a result of the information he gained, a patrol in strength sent out that afternoon, 1 group under the leadership of Cpl. Huff, succeeded in routing an enemy company of 125 men, killing 27 Germans and capturing 21 others, with a loss of only 3 patrol members. Cpl. Huff's intrepid leadership and daring combat skill reflect the finest traditions of the American infantryman.

*HUGHES, LLOYD H. (Air Mission)

Rank and organization: Second Lieutenant, U.S. Army Air Corps, 564th Bomber Squadron, 389th Bomber Group, 9th Air Force. *Place and date:* Ploesti Raid, Rumania. 1 August 1943. *Entered service at:* San Antonio, Tex. *Born:* 12 July 1921, Alexandria, La. *G.O. No.:* 17, 26 February 1944. *Citation:* For conspicuous gallantry in action and intrepidity at the risk of his life above and beyond the call of duty. On 1 August 1943, 2d Lt. Hughes served in the capacity of pilot of a heavy bombardment aircraft participating in a long and hazardous minimum-altitude attack against the Axis oil refineries of Ploesti, Rumania, launched from the northern shores of Africa. Flying in the last formation to attack the target, he arrived in the target area after previous flights had thoroughly alerted the enemy defenses. Approaching the target through intense and accurate antiaircraft fire and dense balloon barrages at dangerously low altitude, his plane received several direct hits from both large and small caliber antiaircraft guns which seriously damaged his aircraft, causing sheets of escaping gasoline to stream from the bomb bay and from the left wing. This damage was inflicted at a time prior to reaching the target when 2d Lt. Hughes could have made a forced landing in any of the grain fields readily available at that time. The target area was blazing with burning oil tanks and damaged refinery installations from which flames leaped high above the bombing level of the formation. With full knowledge of the consequences of entering this blazing inferno when his airplane was profusely leaking gasoline in two separate locations, 2d Lt. Hughes, motivated only by his high conception of duty which called for the destruction of his assigned target at any cost, did not elect to make a forced landing or turn back from the attack. Instead, rather than jeopardize the formation and the success of the attack, he unhesitatingly entered the blazing area and dropped his bomb load with great precision. After successfully bombing the objective, his aircraft emerged from the conflagration with the left wing aflame. Only then did he attempt a forced landing, but because of the advanced stage of the fire enveloping his aircraft the plane crashed and was consumed. By 2d Lt. Hughes' heroic decision to complete his mission regardless of the consequences in utter disregard for his own life, and by his gallant and valorous execution of this decision, he has rendered a service to our country in the defeat of our enemies which will everlastingly be outstanding in the annals of our Nation's history.

*HUTCHINS, JOHNNIE DAVID

Rank and organization: Seaman First Class, U.S. Naval Reserve. *Born:* 4 August 1922, Weimer, Tex. *Accredited to:* Texas. *Citation:* For extraordinary heroism and conspicuous valor above and beyond the call of duty while serving on board a Landing Ship, Tank, during the assault on Lae, New Guinea, 4 September 1943. As the ship on which Hutchins was stationed approached the enemy-occupied beach under a veritable hail of fire from Japanese shore batteries and aerial bombardment, a hostile torpedo pierced the surf and bore down upon the vessel with deadly accuracy. In the tense split seconds before the helmsman could steer clear of the threatening missile, a bomb struck the pilot house, dislodged him from his station, and left the stricken ship helplessly exposed. Fully aware of the dire peril of the situation, Hutchins, although mortally wounded by the shattering explosion, quickly grasped the wheel and exhausted the last of his strength in maneuvering the vessel clear of the advancing torpedo. Still clinging to the helm, he eventually succumbed to his injuries, his final thoughts concerned only with the safety of his ship, his final efforts expended toward the security of his mission. He gallantly gave his life in the service of his country.

*JACHMAN, ISADORE S.

Rank and organization: Staff Sergeant, U.S. Army, Company B, 513th Parachute Infantry Regiment. *Place and date:* Flamierge, Belgium, 4 January 1945. *Entered service at:* Baltimore, Md. *Birth:* Berlin, Germany. *G.O. No.:* 25, 9 June 1950. *Citation:* For conspicuous gallantry and intrepidity above and beyond the call of duty at Flamierge, Belgium, on 4 January 1945, when his company was pinned down by enemy artillery, mortar, and small-arms fire, 2 hostile tanks attacked the unit, inflicting heavy casualties. S/Sgt. Jachman, seeing the desperate plight of his comrades, left his place of cover and with total disregard for his own safety dashed across open ground through a hail of fire and seizing a bazooka from a fallen comrade advanced on the tanks, which concentrated their fire on him. Firing the weapon alone, he damaged one and forced both to retire. S/Sgt. Jachman's heroic action, in which he suffered fatal wounds, disrupted the entire enemy attack, reflecting the highest credit upon himself and the parachute infantry.

JACKSON, ARTHUR J.

Rank and organization: Private First Class, U.S. Marine Corps, 3d Battalion, 7th Marines, 1st Marine Division. *Place and date:* Island of Peleliu in the Palau group, 18 September 1944. *Entered service at:* Oregon. *Born:* 18 October 1924, Cleveland, Ohio. *Citation:* For conspicuous gallantry and intrepidity at the risk of his life above and beyond the call of duty while serving with the 3d Battalion, 7th Marines, 1st Marine Division, in action against enemy Japanese forces on the Island of Peleliu in the Palau group, 18 September 1944. Boldly taking the initiative when his platoon's left flank advance was held up by the fire of Japanese troops concealed in strongly fortified positions, Pfc. Jackson unhesitatingly proceeded forward of our lines and, courageously defying the heavy barrages, charged a large pillbox housing approximately 35 enemy soldiers. Pouring his automatic fire into the opening of the fixed installation to trap the occupying troops, he hurled white phosphorus grenades and explosive charges brought up by a fellow marine, demolishing the pillbox and killing all of the enemy. Advancing alone under the continuous fire from other hostile emplacements, he employed similar means to smash 2 smaller positions in the immediate vicinity. Determined to crush the entire pocket of resistance although harassed on all sides by the shattering blasts of Japanese weapons and covered only by small rifle parties, he stormed 1 gun position after another, dealing death and destruction to the savagely fighting enemy in his inexorable drive against the remaining defenses, and succeeded in wiping out a total of 12 pillboxes and 50 Japanese soldiers. Stouthearted and indomitable despite the terrific odds, Pfc. Jackson resolutely maintained control of the platoon's left flank movement throughout his valiant 1-man assault and, by his cool decision and relentless fighting spirit during a critical situation, contributed essentially to the complete annihilation of the enemy in the southern sector of the island. His gallant initiative and heroic conduct in the face of extreme peril reflect the highest credit upon Pfc. Jackson and the U.S. Naval Service.

JACOBSON, DOUGLAS THOMAS

Rank and organization: Private First Class, U.S. Marine Corps Reserve, 3d Battalion, 23d Marines, 4th Marine Division. *Place and date:* Iwo Jima, Volcano Islands, 26 February 1945. *Entered service at:* New York. *Born:* 25 November 1925, Rochester, N.Y. *Citation:* For conspicuous gallantry and intrepidity at the risk of his life above and beyond the call of duty while serving with the 3d Battalion, 23d Marines, 4th Marine Division, in combat against enemy Japanese forces during the seizure of Iwo Jima in the Volcano Island, 26 February 1945. Promptly destroying a stubborn 20-mm. antiaircraft gun and its crew after assuming the duties of a bazooka man who had been killed, Pfc. Jacobson waged a relentless battle as his unit fought desperately toward the summit of Hill 382 in an effort to penetrate the heart of Japanese cross-island defense. Employing his weapon with ready accuracy when his platoon was halted by overwhelming enemy fire on 26 February, he first destroyed 2 hostile machinegun positions, then attacked a large blockhouse, completely neutralizing the fortification before dispatching the 5-man crew of a second pillbox and exploding the installation with a terrific demolitions blast. Moving steadily forward, he wiped out an earth-covered rifle emplacement and, confronted by a cluster of similar emplacements which constituted the perimeter of enemy defenses in his assigned sector, fearlessly advanced, quickly reduced all 6 positions to a shambles, killed 10 of the enemy, and enabled our forces to occupy the strong point. Determined to widen the breach thus forced, he volunteered his services to an adjacent assault company, neutralized a pillbox holding up its advance, opened fire on a Japanese tank pouring a steady stream of bullets on 1 of our supporting tanks, and smashed the enemy tank's gun turret in a brief but furious action culminating in a singlehanded assault against still another blockhouse and the subsequent neutralization of its firepower. By his dauntless skill and valor, Pfc. Jacobson destroyed a total of 16 enemy positions and annihilated approximately 75 Japanese, thereby contributing essentially to the success of his division's operations against this fanatically defended outpost of the Japanese Empire. His gallant conduct in the face of tremendous odds enhanced and sustained the highest traditions of the U.S. Naval Service.

*JERSTAD, JOHN L. (Air Mission)

Rank and organization: Major, U.S. Army Air Corps, 9th Air Force. *Place and date:* Ploesti Raid, Rumania, 1 August 1943. *Entered service at:* Racine, Wis. *Born:* 12 February 1918, Racine, Wis. *G.O. No.:* 72, 28 October 1943. *Citation:* For conspicuous gallantry and intrepidity above and beyond the call of duty. On 1 August 1943, he served as pilot of the lead aircraft in his group in a daring low-level attack against enemy oil refineries and installations at Ploesti, Rumania. Although he had completed more than his share of missions and was no longer connected with this group, so high was his conception of duty that he volunteered to lead the formation in the correct belief that his participation would contribute materially to success in this attack. Maj. Jerstad led the formation into attack with full realization of the extreme hazards involved and despite withering fire from heavy and light antiaircraft guns. Three miles from the target his airplane was hit, badly damaged, and set on fire. Ignoring the fact that he was flying over a field suitable for a forced landing, he kept on the course. After the bombs of his aircraft were released on the target, the fire in his ship became so intense as to make further progress impossible and he crashed into the target area. By his voluntary acceptance of a mission he knew was extremely hazardous, and his assumption of an intrepid course of action at the risk of life over and above the call of duty, Maj. Jerstad set an example of heroism which will be an inspiration to the U.S. Armed Forces.

*JOHNSON, ELDEN H.

Rank and organization: Private, U.S. Army, 15th Infantry, 3d Infantry Division. *Place and date:* Near Valmontone, Italy, 3 June 1944. *Entered service at:* East Weymouth, Mass. *Birth:* Bivalue, N.J. *G.O. No.:* 38, 16 May 1945. *Citation:* For conspicuous gallantry and intrepidity at risk of life above and beyond the call of duty. Pvt. Johnson elected to sacrifice his life in order that his comrades might extricate themselves from an ambush. Braving the massed fire of about 60 riflemen, 3 machineguns, and 3 tanks from positions only 25 yards distant, he stood erect and signaled his patrol leader to withdraw. The whole area was brightly illuminated by enemy flares. Then, despite 20-mm. machineguns, machine pistol, and rifle fire directed at him, Pvt. Johnson advanced beyond the enemy in a slow deliberate walk. Firing his automatic rifle from the hip, he succeeded in distracting the enemy and enabled his 12 comrades to escape. Advancing to within 5 yards of a machinegun, emptying his weapon, Pvt. Johnson killed its crew. Standing in full view of the enemy he reloaded and turned on the riflemen to the left, firing directly into their positions. He either killed or wounded 4 of them. A burst of machinegun fire tore into Pvt. Johnson and he dropped to his knees. Fighting to the very last, he steadied himself on his knees and sent a final burst of fire crashing into another German. With that he slumped forward dead. Pvt. Johnson had willingly given his life in order that his comrades might live. These acts on the part of Pvt. Johnson were an inspiration to the entire command and are in keeping with the highest traditions of the armed forces.

JOHNSON, LEON W. (Air Mission)

Rank and organization: Colonel, U.S. Army Air Corps, 44th Bomber Group, 9th Air Force. *Place and date:* Ploesti Raid, Rumania, 1 August 1943. *Entered service at:* Moline, Kans. *Born:* 13

September 1904, Columbia, Mo. *G.O. No.:* 54, 7 September 1943. *Citation:* For conspicuous gallantry in action and intrepidity at the risk of his life above and beyond the call of duty on 1 August 1943. Col. Johnson, as commanding officer of a heavy bombardment group, let the formation of the aircraft of his organization constituting the fourth element of the mass low-level bombing attack of the 9th U.S. Air Force against the vitally important enemy target of the Ploesti oil refineries. While proceeding to the target on this 2,400-mile flight, his element became separated from the leading elements of the mass formation in maintaining the formation of the unit while avoiding dangerous cumulous cloud conditions encountered over mountainous territory. Though temporarily lost, he reestablished contact with the third element and continued on the mission with this reduced force to the prearranged point of attack, where it was discovered that the target assigned to Col. Johnson's group had been attacked and damaged by a preceding element. Though having lost the element of surprise upon which the safety and success of such a daring form of mission in heavy bombardment aircraft so strongly depended, Col. Johnson elected to carry out his planned low-level attack despite the thoroughly alerted defenses, the destructive antiaircraft fire, enemy fighter airplanes, the imminent danger of exploding delayed action bombs from the previous element, of oil fires and explosions, and of intense smoke obscuring the target. By his gallant courage, brilliant leadership, and superior flying skill, Col. Johnson so led his formation as to destroy totally the important refining plants and installations which were the object of his mission. Col. Johnson's personal contribution to the success of this historic raid, and the conspicuous gallantry in action, and intrepidity at the risk of his life above and beyond the call of duty demonstrated by him on this occasion constitute such deeds of valor and distinguished service as have during our Nation's history formed the finest traditions of our Armed Forces.

*JOHNSON, LEROY

Rank and organization: Sergeant, U.S. Army, Company K, 126th Infantry, 32d Infantry Division. *Place and date:* Near Limon, Leyte, Philippine Islands, 15 December 1944. *Entered service at:* Oakdale, La. *Birth:* Caney Creek, La. *G.O. No.:* 83, 2 October 1945. *Citation:* He was squad leader of a 9-man patrol sent to reconnoiter a ridge held by a well-entrenched enemy force. Seeing an enemy machinegun position, he ordered his men to remain behind while he crawled to within 6 yards of the gun. One of the enemy crew jumped up and prepared to man the weapon. Quickly withdrawing, Sgt. Johnson rejoined his patrol and reported the situation to his commanding officer. Ordered to destroy the gun, which covered the approaches to several other enemy positions, he chose 3 other men, armed them with hand grenades, and led them to a point near the objective. After taking partial cover behind a log, the men had knocked out the gun and begun an assault when hostile troops on the flank hurled several grenades. As he started for cover, Sgt. Johnson saw 2 unexploded grenades which had fallen near his men. Knowing that his comrades would be wounded or killed by the explosion, he deliberately threw himself on the grenades and received their full charge in his body. Fatally wounded by the blast, he died soon afterward. Through his outstanding gallantry in sacrificing his life for his comrades, Sgt. Johnson provided a shining example of the highest traditions of the U.S. Army.

JOHNSON, OSCAR G.

Rank and organization: Sergeant, U.S. Army, Company B, 363d Infantry, 91st Infantry Division. *Place and date:* Near Scarperia, Italy, 16–18 September 1944. *Entered service at:* Foster City, Mich. *Birth:* Foster City, Mich. *G.O. No.:* 58, 19 July 1945. *Citation:* (then Pfc.) He practically singlehanded protected the left flank of his company's position in the offensive to break the German's gothic line. Company B was the extreme left assault unit of the corps. The advance was stopped by heavy fire from Monticelli Ridge, and the company took cover behind an embankment. Sgt. Johnson, a mortar gunner, having expended his ammunition, assumed the duties of a rifleman. As leader of a squad of 7 men he was ordered to establish a combat post 50 yards to the left of the company to cover its exposed flank. Repeated enemy counterattacks, supported by artillery, mortar, and machinegun fire from the high ground to his front, had by the afternoon of 16 September killed or wounded all his men. Collecting weapons and ammunition from his fallen comrades, in the face of hostile fire, he held his exposed position and inflicted heavy casualties upon the enemy, who several times came close enough to throw handgrenades. On the night of 16–17 September, the enemy launched his heaviest attack on Company B, putting his greatest pressure against the lone defender of the left flank. In spite of mortar fire which crashed about him and machine-gun bullets which whipped the crest of his shallow trench, Sgt. Johnson stood erect and repulsed the attack with grenades and small-arms fire. He remained awake and on the alert throughout the night, frustrating all attempts at infiltration. On 17 September, 25 German soldiers surrendered to him. Two men, sent to reinforce him that afternoon, were caught in a devastating mortar and artillery barrage. With no thought of his own safety, Sgt. Johnson rushed to the shellhole where they lay half buried and seriously wounded, covered their position by his fire, and assisted a Medical Corpsman in rendering aid. That night he secured their removal to the rear and remained on watch until his company was relieved. Five companies of a German paratroop regiment had been repeatedly committed to the attack on Company B without success. Twenty dead Germans were found in front of his position. By his heroic stand and utter disregard for personal safety, Sgt. Johnson was in a large measure responsible for defeating the enemy's attempts to turn the exposed left flank.

JOHNSTON, WILLIAM J.

Rank and organization: Private First Class, U.S. Army, Company G, 180th Infantry, 45th Infantry Division. *Place and date:* Near Padiglione, Italy, 17–19 February 1944. *Entered service at:* Colchester, Conn. *Birth:* Trenton, N.J. *G.O. No.:* 73, 6 September 1944. *Citation:* For conspicuous gallantry and intrepidity at risk of life above and beyond the call of duty in action against the enemy. On 17 February 1944, near Padiglione, Italy, he observed and fired upon an attacking force of approximately 80 Germans, causing at least 25 casualties and forcing withdrawal of the remainder. All that day he manned his gun without relief, subject to mortar, artillery, and sniper fire. Two Germans individually worked so close to his position that his machinegun was ineffective, whereupon he killed 1 with his pistol, the second with a rifle taken from another soldier. When a rifleman protecting his gun position was killed by a sniper, he immediately moved the body and relocated the machinegun in that spot in order to obtain a better field of fire. He volunteered to cover the platoon's withdrawal and was the last man to leave that night. In his new position he maintained an all-night vigil, the next day causing 7 German casualties. On the afternoon of the 18th, the organization on the left flank having been forced to withdraw, he again covered the withdrawal of his own organization. Shortly thereafter, he was seriously wounded over the heart, and a passing soldier saw him trying to crawl up the embankment. The soldier aided him to resume his position behind the machinegun which was soon heard in action for about 10 minutes. Though reported killed, Pfc. Johnston was seen returning to the American lines on the morning of 19 February slowly and painfully working his way back from his overrun position through enemy lines. He gave valuable information of new enemy dispositions. His heroic determination to destroy the enemy and his disregard of his own safety aided immeasurably in halting a strong enemy attack, caused an enormous amount of enemy casualties, and so inspired his fellow soldiers that they fought for and held a vitally important position against greatly superior forces.

*JONES, HERBERT CHARPOIT

Rank and organization: Ensign, U.S. Naval Reserve. *Born:* 1 December 1918, Los Angeles, Calif. *Accredited to:* California. *Citation:* For conspicuous devotion to duty, extraordinary courage, and complete disregard of his own life, above and beyond the call of duty, during the attack on the Fleet in Pearl Harbor, by Japanese forces on 7 December 1941. Ens. Jones organized and led a party, which was supplying ammunition to the antiaircraft battery of the U.S.S. *California* after the mechanical hoists were put out of action when he was fatally wounded by a bomb explosion. When 2 men attempted to take him from the area which was on fire, he refused to let them do so, saying in words to the effect, "Leave me alone! I am done for. Get out of here before the magazines go off."

*JULIAN, JOSEPH RODOLPH

Rank and organization: Platoon Sergeant, U.S. Marine Corps Reserve. *Born:* 3 April 1918, Sturbridge, Mass. *Accredited to:* Massachusetts. *Citation:* For conspicuous gallantry and intrepidity at the risk of his life above and beyond the call of duty as a P/Sgt. serving with the 1st Battalion, 27th Marines, 5th Marine Division, in action against enemy Japanese forces during the seizure of Iwo Jima in the Volcano Islands, 9 March 1945. Determined to force a breakthrough when Japanese troops occupying trenches and fortified positions on the left front laid down a terrific machinegun and mortar barrage in a desperate effort to halt his company's advance, P/Sgt. Julian quickly established his platoon's guns in strategic supporting positions, and then, acting on his own initiative, fearlessly moved forward to execute a 1-man assault on the nearest pillbox. Advancing alone, he hurled deadly demolitions and white phosphorus grenades into the emplacement, killing 2 of the enemy and driving the remaining 5 out into the adjoining trench system. Seizing a discarded rifle, he jumped into the trench and dispatched the 5 before they could make an escape. Intent on wiping out all resistance, he obtained more explosives and, accompanied by another marine, again charged the hostile fortifications and knocked out 2 more cave positions. Immediately thereafter, he launched a bazooka attack unassisted, firing 4 rounds into the 1 remaining pillbox and completely destroying it before he fell, mortally wounded by a vicious burst of enemy fire. Stouthearted and indomitable, P/Sgt. Julian consistently disregarded all personal danger and, by his bold decision, daring tactics, and relentless fighting spirit during a critical phase of the battle, contributed materially to the continued advance of his company and to the success of his division's operations in the sustained drive toward the conquest of this fiercely defended outpost of the Japanese Empire. His outstanding valor and unfaltering spirit of self-sacrifice throughout the bitter conflict sustained and enhanced the highest traditions of the U.S. Naval Service. He gallantly gave his life for his country.

*KANDLE, VICTOR L.

Rank and organization: First Lieutenant, U.S. Army, 15th Infantry, 3d Infantry Division. *Place and date:* Near La Forge, France, 9 October 1944. *Entered service at:* Redwood City, Calif. *Birth:* Roy, Wash. *G.O. No.:* 37, 11 May 1945. *Citation:* For conspicuous gallantry and intrepidity at risk of his life above and beyond the call of duty. On 9 October 1944, at about noon, near La Forge, France, 1st Lt. Kandle, while leading a reconnaissance patrol into enemy territory, engaged in a duel at pointblank range with a German field officer and killed him. Having already taken 5 enemy prisoners that morning, he led a skeleton platoon of 16 men, reinforced with a light machinegun squad, through fog and over precipitous mountain terrain to fall on the rear of a German quarry stronghold which had checked the advance of an infantry battalion for 2 days. Rushing forward, several yards ahead of his assault elements, 1st Lt. Kandle fought his way into the heart of the enemy strongpoint, and, by his boldness and audacity, forced the Germans to surrender. Harassed by machinegun fire from a position which he had bypassed in the dense fog, he moved to within 15 yards of the enemy, killed a German machinegunner with accurate rifle fire and led his men in the destruction of another machinegun crew and its rifle security elements. Finally, he led his small force against a fortified house held by 2 German officers and 30 enlisted men. After establishing a base of fire, he rushed forward alone through an open clearing in full view of the enemy, smashed through a barricaded door, and forced all 32 Germans to surrender. His intrepidity and bold leadership resulted in the capture or killing of 3 enemy officers and 54 enlisted men, the destruction of 3 enemy strongpoints, and the seizure of enemy positions which had halted a battalion attack.

KANE, JOHN R. (Air Mission)

Rank and organization: Colonel, U.S. Army Air Corps, 9th Air Force. *Place and date:* Ploesti Raid, Rumania, 1 August 1943. *Entered service at:* Shreveport, La. *Birth:* McGregor, Tex. *G.O. No.:* 54, 9 August 1943. *Citation:* For conspicuous gallantry in action and intrepidity at the risk of his life above and beyond the call of duty on 1 August 1943. On this date he led the third element of heavy bombardment aircraft in a mass low-level bombing attack against the vitally important enemy target of the Ploesti oil refineries. En route to the target, which necessitated a round-trip flight of over 2,400 miles, Col. Kane's element became separated from the leading portion of the massed formation in avoiding dense and dangerous cumulous cloud conditions over mountainous terrain. Rather than turn back from such a vital mission he elected to proceed to his target. Upon arrival at the target area it was discovered that another group had apparently missed its target and had previously attacked and damaged the target assigned to Col. Kane's element. Despite the thoroughly warned defenses, the intensive antiaircraft fire, enemy fighter airplanes, extreme hazards on a low-level attack of exploding delayed action bombs from the previous element, of oil fires and explosions and dense smoke over the target area, Col. Kane elected to lead his formation into the attack. By his gallant courage, brilliant leadership, and superior flying skill, he and the formation under his command successfully attacked this vast refinery so essential to our enemies' war effort. Through his conspicuous gallantry in this most hazardous action against the enemy, and by his intrepidity at the risk of his life above and beyond the call of duty, Col. Kane personally contributed vitally to the success of this daring mission and thereby rendered most distinguished service in the furtherance of the defeat of our enemies.

KEARBY, NEEL E. (Air Mission)

Rank and organization: Colonel, U.S. Army Air Corps. *Place and date:* Near Wewak, New Guinea, 11 October 1943. *Entered service at:* Dallas, Tex. *Birth:* Wichita Falls, Tex. *G.O. No.:* 3, 6 January 1944. *Citation:* For conspicuous gallantry and intrepidity above and beyond the call of duty in action with the enemy, Col. Kearby volunteered to lead a flight of 4 fighters to reconnoiter the strongly defended enemy base at Wewak. Having observed enemy installations and reinforcements at 4 airfields, and secured important tactical information, he saw an enemy fighter below him, made a diving attack and shot it down in flames. The small formation then sighted approximately 12 enemy bombers accompanied by 36 fighters. Although his mission had been completed, his fuel was running low, and the numerical odds were 12 to 1, he gave the signal to attack. Diving into the midst of the enemy airplanes he shot down 3 in quick succession. Observing 1 of his comrades with 2 enemy fighters in pursuit, he destroyed both enemy aircraft. The enemy broke off in large numbers to make a multiple attack on his airplane but despite his peril he made one more pass before seeking cloud protection. Coming into the clear, he called his flight together and led them to a friendly base. Col. Kearby brought down 6 enemy aircraft in this action, undertaken with superb daring after his mission was completed.

*KEATHLEY, GEORGE D.

Rank and organization: Staff Sergeant, U.S. Army, 85th Infantry Division. *Place and date:* Mt. Altuzzo, Italy, 14 September 1944. *Entered service at:* Lamesa, Tex. *Birth:* Olney, Tex. *G.O. No.:* 20, 29 March 1945. *Citation:* For conspicuous gallantry and intrepidity at risk of life above and beyond the call of duty, in action on the western ridge of Mount Altuzzo, Italy. After bitter fighting his company had advanced to within 50 yards of the objective, where it was held up due to intense enemy sniper, automatic, small-arms, and mortar fire. The enemy launched 3 desperate counterattacks in an effort to regain their former positions, but all 3 were repulsed with heavy casualties on both sides. All officers and noncommissioned officers of the 2d and 3d platoons of Company B had become casualties, and S/Sgt. Keathley, guide of the 1st platoon, moved up and assumed command of both the 2d and 3d platoons, reduced to 20 men. The remnants of the 2 platoons were dangerously low on ammunition, so S/Sgt. Keathley, under deadly small-arms and mortar fire, crawled from 1 casualty to another, collecting their ammunition and administering first aid. He then visited each man of his 2 platoons, issuing the precious ammunition he had collected from the dead and wounded, and giving them words of encouragement. The enemy now delivered their fourth counterattack, which was approximately 2 companies in strength. In a furious charge they attacked from the front and both flanks, throwing handgrenades, firing automatic weapons, and assisted by a terrific mortar barrage. So strong was the enemy counterattack that the company was given up for lost. The remnants of the 2d and 3d platoons of Company B were now looking to S/Sgt. Keathley for leadership. He shouted his orders precisely and with determination and the men responded with all that was in them. Time after time the enemy tried to drive a wedge into S/Sgt. Keathley's position and each time they were driven back, suffering huge casualties. Suddenly an enemy handgrenade hit and exploded near S/Sgt. Keathley, inflicting a mortal wound in his left side. However, hurling defiance at the enemy, he rose to his feet. Taking his left hand away from his wound and using it to steady his rifle, he fired and killed an attacking enemy soldier, and continued shouting orders to his men. His heroic and intrepid action so inspired his men that they fought with incomparable determination and viciousness. For 15 minutes S/Sgt. Keathley continued leading his men and effectively firing his rifle. He could have sought a sheltered spot and perhaps saved his life, but instead he elected to set an example for his men and make every possible effort to hold his position. Finally, friendly artillery fire helped to force the enemy to withdraw, leaving behind many of their number either dead or seriously wounded. S/Sgt. Keathley died a few moments later. Had it not been for his indomitable courage and incomparable heroism, the remnants of 3 rifle platoons of Company B might well have been annihilated by the overwhelming enemy attacking force. His actions were in keeping with the highest traditions of the military service.

*KEFURT, GUS

Rank and organization: Staff Sergeant, U.S. Army, Company K, 15th Infantry, 3d Infantry Division. *Place and date:* Near Bennwihr, France, 23–24 December 1944. *Entered service at:* Youngstown, Ohio. *Birth:* Greenville, Pa. *Citation:* He distinguished himself by conspicuous gallantry and intrepidity above and beyond the call of duty on 23 and 24 December 1944, near Bennwihr, France. Early in the attack S/Sgt. Kefurt jumped through an opening in a wall to be confronted by about 15 Germans. Although outnumbered he opened fire, killing 10 and capturing the others. During a seesaw battle which developed he effectively adjusted artillery fire on an enemy tank close to his position although exposed to small-arms fire. When night fell he maintained a 3-man outpost in the center of the town in the middle of the German positions and successfully fought off several hostile patrols attempting to penetrate our lines. Assuming command of his platoon the following morning he led it in hand-to-hand fighting through the town until blocked by a tank. Using rifle grenades he forced surrender of its crew and some supporting infantry. He then continued his attack from house to house against heavy machinegun and rifle fire. Advancing against a strongpoint that was holding up the company, his platoon was subjected to a strong counterattack and infiltration to its rear. Suffering heavy casualties in their exposed position the men remained there due to S/Sgt. Kefurt's personal example of bravery, determination and leadership. He constantly exposed himself to fire by going from man to man to direct fire. During this time he killed approximately 15 of the enemy at close range. Although severely wounded in the leg he refused first aid and immediately resumed fighting. When the forces to his rear were pushed back 3 hours later, he refused to be evacuated, but, during several more counterattacks moved painfully about under intense small-arms and mortar fire, stiffening the resistance of his platoon by encouraging individual men and by his own fire until he was killed. As a result of S/Sgt. Kefurt's gallantry the position was maintained.

*KELLEY, JONAH E.

Rank and organization: Staff Sergeant, U.S. Army, 311th Infantry, 78th Infantry Division. *Place and date:* Kesternich, Germany, 30–31 January 1945. *Entered service at:* Keyser, W. Va. *Birth:* Roda, W. Va. *G.O. No.:* 77, 10 September 1945. *Citation:* In charge of the leading squad of Company E, he heroically spearheaded the attack in furious house-to-house fighting. Early on 30 January, he led his men through intense mortar and small-arms fire in repeated assaults on barricaded houses. Although twice wounded, once when struck in the back, the second time when a mortar shell fragment passed through his left hand and rendered it practically useless, he refused to withdraw and continued to lead his squad after hasty dressings had been applied. His serious wounds forced him to fire his rifle with 1 hand, resting it on rubble or over his left forearm. To blast his way forward with handgrenades, he set aside his rifle to pull the pins with his teeth while grasping the missiles with his good hand. Despite these handicaps, he created tremendous havoc in the enemy ranks. He rushed 1 house, killing 3 of the enemy and clearing the way for his squad to advance. On approaching the next house, he was fired upon from an upstairs window. He killed the sniper with a single shot and similarly accounted for another enemy soldier who ran from the cellar of the house. As darkness came, he assigned his men to defensive positions, never leaving them to seek medical attention. At dawn the next day, the squad resumed the attack, advancing to a point where heavy automatic and small-arms fire stalled them. Despite his wounds, S/Sgt. Kelley moved out alone, located an enemy gunner dug in under a haystack and killed him with rifle fire. He returned to his men and found that a German machinegun, from a well-protected position in a neighboring house, still held up the advance. Ordering the squad to remain in comparatively safe positions, he valiantly dashed into the open and attacked the position singlehandedly through a hail of bullets. He was hit several times and fell to his knees when within 25 yards of his objective; but he summoned his waning strength and emptied his rifle into the machinegun nest, silencing the weapon before he died. The superb courage, aggressiveness, and utter disregard for his own safety displayed by S/Sgt. Kelley inspired the men he led and enabled them to penetrate the last line of defense held by the enemy in the village of Kesternich.

*KELLEY, OVA A.

Rank and organization: Private, U.S. Army, Company A, 382d Infantry, 96th Infantry Division. *Place and date:* Leyte, Philippine Islands, 8 December 1944. *Entered service at:* Norwood, Mo. *Birth:* Norwood, Mo. *G.O. No.:* 89, 19 October 1945. *Citation:* For conspicuous gallantry and intrepidity at the risk of his life above and beyond the call of duty. Before dawn, near the edge of the enemy-held Buri airstrip, the company was immobilized by heavy, accurate rifle and machinegun fire from hostile troops entrenched in bomb craters and a ditch less than 100 yards distant. The company commander ordered a mortar concentration which destroyed 1 machinegun but failed to dislodge the main body of the enemy. At this critical moment Pvt. Kelley, on his own initiative, left his shallow foxhole with an armload of handgrenades and began a 1-man assault on the foe. Throwing his missiles with great accuracy, he moved forward, killed or wounded 5 men, and forced the remainder to flee in a disorganized route. He picked up a M1 rifle and emptied its clip at the running Japanese, killing 3. Discarding this weapon, he took a carbine and killed 3 more of the enemy. Inspired by his example, his comrades followed him in a charge which destroyed the entire enemy force of 34 enlisted men and 2 officers and captured 2 heavy and 1 light machineguns. Pvt. Kelley continued to press the attack on to an airstrip, where sniper fire wounded him so grievously that he died 2 days later. His outstanding courage, aggressiveness, and initiative in the face of grave danger was an inspiration to his entire company and led to the success of the attack.

KELLY, CHARLES E.

Rank and organization: Corporal, U.S. Army, Company L, 143d Infantry, 36th Infantry Division. *Place and date:* Near Altavilla, Italy, 13 September 1943. *Entered service at:* Pittsburgh, Pa. *Birth:* Pittsburgh, Pa. *G.O. No.:* 13, 18 February 1944. *Citation:* For conspicuous gallantry and intrepidity at risk of life above and beyond the call of duty. On 13 September 1943, near Altavilla, Italy, Cpl. Kelly voluntarily joined a patrol which located and neutralized enemy machinegun positions. After this hazardous duty he volunteered to establish contact with a battalion of U.S. infantry which was believed to be located on Hill 315, a mile distant. He traveled over a route commanded by enemy observation and under sniper, mortar, and artillery fire; and later he returned with the correct information that the enemy occupied Hill 315 in organized positions. Immediately thereafter Cpl. Kelly, again a volunteer patrol member, assisted materially in the destruction of 2 enemy machinegun nests under conditions requiring great skill and courage. Having effectively fired his weapon until all the ammunition was exhausted, he secured permission to obtain more at an ammunition dump. Arriving at the dump, which was located near a storehouse on the extreme flank of his regiment's position, Cpl. Kelly found that the Germans were attacking ferociously at this point. He obtained his ammunition and was given the mission of protecting the rear of the storehouse. He held his position throughout the night. The following morning the enemy attack was resumed. Cpl. Kelly took a position at an open window of the storehouse. One machinegunner had been killed at this position and several other soldiers wounded. Cpl. Kelly delivered continuous aimed and effective fire upon the enemy with his automatic rifle until the weapon locked from overheating. Finding another automatic rifle, he again directed effective fire upon the enemy until this weapon also locked. At this critical point, with the enemy threatening to overrun the position, Cpl. Kelly picked up 60-mm. mortar shells, pulled the safety pins, and used the shells as grenades, killing at least 5 of the enemy. When it became imperative that the house be evacuated, Cpl. Kelly, despite his sergeant's injunctions, volunteered to hold the position until the remainder of the detachment could withdraw. As the detachment moved out, Cpl. Kelly was observed deliberately loading and firing a rocket launcher from the window. He was successful in covering the withdrawal of the unit, and later in joining his own organization. Cpl. Kelly's fighting determination and intrepidity in battle exemplify the highest traditions of the U.S. Armed Forces.

*KELLY, JOHN D.

Rank and organization: Technical Sergeant (then Corporal), U.S. Army, Company E, 314th Infantry, 79th Infantry Division. *Place and date:* Fort du Roule, Cherbourg, France, 25 June 1944. *Entered service at:* Cambridge Springs, Pa. *Birth:* Venango Township, Pa. *G.O. No.:* 6, 24 January 1945. *Citation:* For conspicuous gallantry and intrepidity at the risk of his life above and beyond the call of duty. On 25 June 1944, in the vicinity of Fort du Roule, Cherbourg, France, when Cpl. Kelly's unit was pinned down by heavy enemy machinegun fire emanating from a deeply entrenched strongpoint on the slope leading up to the fort, Cpl. Kelly volunteered to attempt to neutralize the strongpoint. Arming himself with a pole charge about 10 feet long and with 15 pounds of explosive affixed, he climbed the slope under a withering blast of machinegun fire and placed the charge at the strongpoint's base. The subsequent blast was ineffective, and again, alone and unhesitatingly, he braved the slope to repeat the operation. This second blast blew off the ends of the enemy guns. Cpl. Kelly then climbed the slope a third time to place a pole charge at the strongpoint's rear entrance. When this had been blown open he hurled handgrenades inside the position, forcing survivors of the enemy guncrews to come out and surrender. The gallantry, tenacity of purpose, and utter disregard for personal safety displayed by Cpl. Kelly were an incentive to his comrades and worthy of emulation by all.

KELLY, THOMAS J.

Rank and organization: Corporal, U.S. Army, Medical Detachment, 48th Armored Infantry Battalion, 7th Armored Division. *Place and date:* Alemert, Germany, 5 April 1945. *Entered service at:* Brooklyn, N.Y. *Birth:* Brooklyn, N.Y. *G.O. No.:* 97, 1 November 1945. *Citation:* He was an aid man with the 1st Platoon of Company C during an attack on the town of Alemert, Germany. The platoon, committed in a flanking maneuver, had advanced down a small, open valley overlooked by wooded slopes hiding enemy machineguns and tanks, when the attack was stopped by murderous fire that inflicted heavy casualties in the American ranks. Ordered to withdraw, Cpl. Kelly reached safety with uninjured remnants of the unit, but, on realizing the extent of casualties suffered by the platoon, voluntarily retraced his steps and began evacuating his comrades under direct machinegun fire. He was forced to crawl, dragging the injured behind him for most of the 300 yards separating the exposed area from a place of comparative safety. Two other volunteers who attempted to negotiate the hazardous route with him were mortally wounded, but he kept on with his herculean task after dressing their wounds and carrying them to friendly hands. In all, he made 10 separate trips through the brutal fire, each time bringing out a man from the death trap. Seven more casualties who were able to crawl by themselves he guided and encouraged in escaping from the hail of fire. After he had completed his heroic, self-imposed task and was near collapse from fatigue, he refused to leave his platoon until the attack had been resumed and the objective taken. Cpl. Kelly's gallantry and intrepidity in the face of seemingly certain death saved the lives of many of his fellow soldiers and was an example of bravery under fire.

*KEPPLER, REINHARDT JOHN

Rank and organization: Boatswain's Mate First Class, U.S. Navy. *Born:* 22 January 1918, Ralston, Wash. *Accredited to:* Washington. *Other Navy award:* Navy Cross. *Citation:* For extraordinary heroism and distinguished courage above and beyond the call of duty while serving aboard the U.S.S. *San Francisco* during action against enemy Japanese forces in the Solomon Islands, 12–13 November 1942. When a hostile torpedo plane, during a daylight air raid, crashed on the after machinegun platform, Keppler promptly assisted in removal of the dead and, by his capable supervision of the wounded, undoubtedly helped save the lives of several shipmates who otherwise might have perished.

That night, when the ship's hangar was set afire during the great battle off Savo Island, he bravely led a hose into the starboard side of the stricken area and there, without assistance and despite frequent hits from terrific enemy bombardment, eventually brought the fire under control. Later, although mortally wounded, he labored valiantly in the midst of bursting shells, persistently directing firefighting operations and administering to wounded personnel until he finally collapsed from loss of blood. His great personal valor, maintained with utter disregard of personal safety, was in keeping with the highest traditions of the U.S. Naval Service. He gallantly gave his life for his country.

KERSTETTER, DEXTER J.

Rank and organization: Private First Class, U.S. Army, Company C, 130th Infantry, 33d Infantry Division. *Place and date:* Near Galiano, Luzon, Philippine Islands, 13 April 1945. *Entered service at:* Centralia, Wash. *Birth:* Centralia, Wash. *G.O. No.:* 97, 1 November 1945. *Citation:* He was with his unit in a dawn attack against hill positions approachable only along a narrow ridge paralleled on each side by steep cliffs which were heavily defended by enemy mortars, machineguns, and rifles in well-camouflaged spider holes and tunnels leading to caves. When the leading element was halted by intense fire that inflicted 5 casualties, Pfc. Kerstetter passed through the American line with his squad. Placing himself well in advance of his men, he grimly worked his way up the narrow steep hogback, meeting the brunt of enemy action. With well-aimed shots and rifle-grenade fire, he forced the Japs to take cover. He left the trail and moving down a cliff that offered only precarious footholds, dropped among 4 Japs at the entrance to a cave, fired his rifle from his hip and killed them all. Climbing back to the trail, he advanced against heavy enemy machinegun, rifle, and mortar fire to silence a heavy machinegun by killing its crew of 4 with rifle fire and grenades. He expended his remaining ammunition and grenades on a group of approximately 20 Japs, scattering them, and returned to his squad for more ammunition and first aid for his left hand, which had been blistered by the heat from his rifle. Resupplied, he guided a fresh platoon into a position from which a concerted attack could be launched, killing 3 hostile soldiers on the way. In all, he dispatched 16 Japs that day. The hill was taken and held against the enemy's counterattacks, which continued for 3 days. Pfc. Kerstetter's dauntless and gallant heroism was largely responsible for the capture of this key enemy position, and his fearless attack in the face of great odds was an inspiration to his comrades in their dangerous task.

*KESSLER, PATRICK L.

Rank and organization: Private First Class, U.S. Army, Company K, 30th Infantry, 3d Infantry Division. *Place and date:* Near Ponte Rotto, Italy, 23 May 1944. *Entered service at:* Middletown, Ohio. *Birth:* Middletown, Ohio. *G.O. No.:* 1, 4 January 1945. *Citation:* For conspicuous gallantry and intrepidity at risk of life above and beyond the call of duty. Pfc. Kessler, acting without orders, raced 50 yards through a hail of machinegun fire, which had killed 5 of his comrades and halted the advance of his company, in order to form an assault group to destroy the machinegun. Ordering 3 men to act as a base of fire, he left the cover of a ditch and snaked his way to a point within 50 yards of the enemy machinegun before he was discovered, whereupon he plunged headlong into the furious chain of automatic fire. Reaching a spot within 6 feet of the emplacement he stood over it and killed both the gunner and his assistant, jumped into the gun position, overpowered and captured a third German after a short struggle. The remaining member of the crew escaped, but Pfc. Kessler wounded him as he ran. While taking his prisoner to the rear, this soldier saw 2 of his comrades killed as they assaulted an enemy strongpoint, fire from which had already killed 10 men in the company. Turning his prisoner over to another man, Pfc. Kessler crawled 35 yards to the side of 1 of the casualties, relieved him of his BAR and ammunition and continued on toward the strongpoint, 125 yards distant. Although 2 machineguns concentrated their fire directly on him and shells exploded within 10 yards, bowling him over, Pfc. Kessler crawled 75 yards, passing through an antipersonnel minefield to a point within 50 yards of the enemy and engaged the machineguns in a duel. When an artillery shell burst within a few feet of him, he left the cover of a ditch and advanced upon the position in a slow walk, firing his BAR from the hip. Although the enemy poured heavy machine-gun and small-arms fire at him, Pfc. Kessler succeeded in reaching the edge of their position, killed the gunners, and captured 13 Germans. Then, despite continuous shelling, he started to the rear. After going 25 yards, Pfc. Kessler was fired upon by 2 snipers only 100 yards away. Several of his prisoners took advantage of this opportunity and attempted to escape; however, Pfc. Kessler hit the ground, fired on either flank of his prisoners, forcing them to cover, and then engaged the 2 snipers in a fire fight, and captured them. With this last threat removed, Company K continued its advance, capturing its objective without further opposition. Pfc. Kessler was killed in a subsequent action.

*KIDD, ISAAC CAMPBELL

Rank and organization: Rear Admiral, U.S. Navy. *Born:* 26 March 1884, Cleveland, Ohio. *Appointed from:* Ohio. *Citation:* For conspicuous devotion to duty, extraordinary courage and complete disregard of his own life, during the attack on the Fleet in Pearl Harbor, by Japanese forces on 7 December 1941. Rear Adm. Kidd immediately went to the bridge and, as Commander Battleship Division One, courageously discharged his duties as Senior Officer Present Afloat until the U.S.S *Arizona,* his Flagship, blew up from magazine explosions and a direct bomb hit on the bridge which resulted in the loss of his life.

*KIMBRO, TRUMAN

Rank and organization: Technician Fourth Grade, U.S. Army, Company C, 2d Engineer Combat Battalion, 2d Infantry Division. *Place and date:* Near Rocherath, Belgium, 19 December 1944. *Entered service at:* Houston, Tex. *Birth:* Madisonville, Tex. *G.O. No.:* 42, 24 May 1945. *Citation:* On 19 December 1944, as scout, he led a squad assigned to the mission of mining a vital crossroads near Rocherath, Belgium. At the first attempt to reach the objective, he discovered it was occupied by an enemy tank and at least 20 infantrymen. Driven back by withering fire, Technician 4th Grade Kimbro made 2 more attempts to lead his squad to the crossroads but all approaches were covered by intense enemy fire. Although warned by our own infantrymen of the great danger involved, he left his squad in a protected place and, laden with mines, crawled alone toward the crossroads. When nearing his objective he was severely wounded, but he continued to drag himself forward and laid his mines across the road. As he tried to crawl from the objective his body was riddled with rifle and machinegun fire. The mines laid by his act of indomitable courage delayed the advance of enemy armor and prevented the rear of our withdrawing columns from being attacked by the enemy.

*KINER, HAROLD G.

Rank and organization: Private, U.S. Army, Company F, 117th Infantry, 30th Infantry Division. *Place and date:* Near Palenberg, Germany, 2 October 1944. *Entered service at:* Enid, Okla. *Birth:* Aline, Okla. *G.O. No.:* 48, 23 June 1945. With 4 other men, he was leading in a frontal assault 2 October 1944, on a Siegfried Line pillbox near Palenberg, Germany. Machinegun fire from the strongly defended enemy position 25 yards away pinned down the attackers. The Germans threw handgrenades, 1 of which dropped between Pvt. Kiner and 2 other men. With no hesitation, Private Kiner hurled himself upon the grenade, smothering the explosion. By his gallant action and voluntary sacrifice of his own life, he saved his 2 comrades from serious injury or death.

*KINGSLEY, DAVID R. (Air Mission)

Rank and organization: Second Lieutenant, U.S. Army Air Corps, 97th Bombardment Group, 15th Air Force. *Place and date:* Ploesti Raid, Rumania, 23 June 1944. *Entered service at:* Portland, Oreg. *Birth:* Oregon. *G.O. No.:* 26, 9 April 1945. *Citation:* For conspicuous gallantry and intrepidity in action at the risk of life above and beyond the call of duty, 23 June 1944 near Ploesti, Rumania, while flying as bombardier of a B–17 type aircraft. On the bomb run 2d Lt. Kingsley's aircraft was severely damaged by intense flak and forced to drop out of formation but the pilot proceeded over the target and 2d Lt. Kingsley successfully dropped his bombs, causing severe damage to vital installations. The damaged aircraft, forced to lose altitude and to lag behind the formation, was aggressively attacked by 3 ME–109 aircraft, causing more damage to the aircraft and severely wounding the tail gunner in the upper arm. The radio operator and engineer notified 2d Lt. Kingsley that the tail gunner had been wounded and that assistance was needed to check the bleeding. 2d Lt. Kingsley made his way back to the radio room, skillfully applied first aid to the wound, and succeeded in checking the bleeding. The tail gunner's parachute harness and heavy clothes were removed and he was covered with blankets, making him as comfortable as possible. Eight ME–109 aircraft again aggressively attacked 2d Lt. Kingsley's aircraft and the ball turret gunner was wounded by 20-mm. shell fragments. He went forward to the radio room to have 2d Lt. Kingsley administer first aid. A few minutes later when the pilot gave the order to prepare to bail out, 2d Lt. Kingsley immediately began to assist the wounded gunners in putting on their parachute harness. In the confusion the tail gunner's harness, believed to have been damaged, could not be located in the bundle of blankets and flying clothes which had been removed from the wounded men. With utter disregard for his own means of escape, 2d Lt. Kingsley unhesitatingly removed his parachute harness and adjusted it to the wounded tail gunner. Due to the extensive damage caused by the accurate and concentrated 20-mm. fire by the enemy aircraft the pilot gave the order to bail out, as it appeared that the aircraft would disintegrate at any moment. 2d Lt. Kingsley aided the wounded men in bailing out and when last seen by the crewmembers he was standing on the bomb bay catwalk. The aircraft continued to fly on automatic pilot for a short distance, then crashed and burned. His body was later found in the wreckage. 2d Lt. Kingsley by his gallant heroic action was directly responsible for saving the life of the wounded gunner.

*KINSER, ELBERT LUTHER

Rank and organization: Sergeant, U.S. Marine Corps Reserve. *Born:* 21 October 1922, Greeneville, Tenn. *Accredited to:* Tennessee. *Citation:* For conspicuous gallantry and intrepidity at the risk of his life above and beyond the call of duty while acting as leader of a Rifle Platoon, serving with Company I, 3d Battalion, 1st Marines, 1st Marine Division, in action against Japanese forces on Okinawa Shima in the Ryukyu Chain, 4 May 1945. Taken under sudden, close attack by hostile troops entrenched on the reverse slope while moving up a strategic ridge along which his platoon was holding newly won positions, Sgt. Kinser engaged the enemy in a fierce handgrenade battle. Quick to act when a Japanese grenade landed in the immediate vicinity, Sgt. Kinser unhesitatingly threw himself on the deadly missile, absorbing the full charge of the shattering explosion in his own body and thereby protecting his men from serious injury and possible death. Stouthearted and indomitable, he had yielded his own chance of survival that his comrades might live to carry on the relentless battle against a fanatic enemy. His courage, cool decision and valiant spirit of self-sacrifice in the face of certain death sustained and enhanced the highest traditions of the U.S. Naval Service. He gallantly gave his life for his country.

KISTERS, GERRY H.

Rank and organization: Second Lieutenant (then Sergeant), U.S. Army, 2d Armored Division. *Place and date:* Near Gagliano, Sicily, 31 July 1943. *Entered service at:* Bloomington, Ind. *Birth:* Salt Lake City, Utah. *G.O. No.:* 13, 18 February 1944. *Citation:* On 31 July 1943, near Gagliano, Sicily, a detachment of 1 officer and 9 enlisted men, including Sgt. Kisters, advancing ahead of the leading elements of U.S. troops to fill a large crater in the only available vehicle route through Gagliano, was taken under fire by 2 enemy machineguns. Sgt. Kisters and the officer, unaided and in the face of intense small-arms fire, advanced on the nearest machinegun emplacement and succeeded in capturing the gun and its crew of 4. Although the greater part of the remaining small-arms fire was now directed on the captured machinegun position, Sgt. Kisters voluntarily advanced alone toward the second gun emplacement. While creeping forward, he was struck 5 times by enemy bullets, receiving wounds in both legs and his right arm. Despite the wounds, he continued to advance on the enemy, and captured the second machinegun after killing 3 of its crew and forcing the fourth member to flee. The courage of this soldier and his unhesitating willingness to sacrifice his life, if necessary, served as an inspiration to the command.

KNAPPENBERGER, ALTON W.

Rank and organization: Private First Class, U.S. Army, 3d Infantry Division. *Place and date:* Near Cisterna di Littoria, Italy, 1 February 1944. *Entered service at:* Spring Mount, Pa. *Birth:* Cooperstown, Pa. *G.O. No.:* 41, 26 May 1944. *Citation:* For conspicuous gallantry and intrepidity at the risk of his life above and beyond the call of duty in action involving actual conflict with the enemy, on 1 February 1944 near Cisterna di Littoria, Italy. When a heavy German counterattack was launched against his battalion, Pfc. Knappenberger crawled to an exposed knoll and went into position with his automatic rifle. An enemy machinegun 85 yards away opened fire, and bullets struck within 6 inches of him. Rising to a kneeling position, Pfc. Knappenberger opened fire on the hostile crew, knocked out the gun, killed 2 members of the crew, and wounded the third. While he fired at this hostile position, 2 Germans crawled to a point within 20 yards of the knoll and threw potato-masher grenades at him, but Pfc. Knappenberger killed them both with 1 burst from his automatic rifle. Later, a second machinegun opened fire upon his exposed position from a distance of 100 yards, and this weapon also was silenced by his well-aimed shots. Shortly thereafter, an enemy 20-mm. antiaircraft gun directed fire at him, and again Pfc. Knappenberger returned fire to wound 1 member of the hostile crew. Under tank and artillery shellfire, with shells bursting within 15 yards of him, he held his precarious position and fired at all enemy infantrymen armed with machine pistols and machineguns which he could locate. When his ammunition supply became exhausted, he crawled 15 yards forward through steady machinegun fire, removed rifle clips from the belt of a casualty, returned to his position and resumed firing to repel an assaulting German platoon armed with automatic weapons. Finally, his ammunition supply being completely exhausted, he rejoined his company. Pfc. Knappenberger's intrepid action disrupted the enemy attack for over 2 hours.

*KNIGHT, JACK L.

Rank and organization: First Lieutenant, U.S. Army, 124th Cavalry Regiment, Mars Task Force. *Place and date:* Near Loi-Kang, Burma, 2 February 1945. *Entered service at:* Weatherford, Tex. *Birth:* Garner, Tex. *G.O. No.:* 44, 6 June 1945. *Citation:* He led his cavalry troop against heavy concentrations of enemy mortar, artillery, and small-arms fire. After taking the troop's objective and while making preparations for a defense, he discovered a nest of Japanese pillboxes and foxholes to the right front. Preceding his men by a least 10 feet, he immediately led an attack. Singlehandedly he knocked out 2 enemy pillboxes and killed the occupants of several foxholes. While attempting to knock out a third pillbox, he was struck and blinded by an enemy grenade. Although unable to see, he rallied his platoon and continued forward in the assault on the remaining pillboxes. Before the task was completed he fell mortally wounded. 1st Lt. Knight's gallantry and intrepidity were responsible for the successful elimination of most of the Jap positions and served as an inspiration to officers and men of his troop.

*KNIGHT, RAYMOND L. (Air Mission)

Rank and organization: First Lieutenant, U.S. Army Air Corps. *Place and date:* In Northern Po Valley, Italy, 24–25 April 1945. *Entered service at:* Houston, Tex. *Birth:* Texas. *G.O. No.:* 81, 24 September 1945. *Citation:* He piloted a fighter-bomber aircraft in a series of low-level strafing missions, destroying 14 grounded enemy aircraft and leading attacks which wrecked 10 others during a critical period of the Allied drive in northern

Italy. On the morning of 24 April, he volunteered to lead 2 other aircraft against the strongly defended enemy airdrome at Ghedi. Ordering his fellow-pilots to remain aloft, he skimmed the ground through a deadly curtain of antiaircraft fire to reconnoiter the field, locating 8 German aircraft hidden beneath heavy camouflage. He rejoined his flight, briefed them by radio, and then led them with consummate skill through the hail of enemy fire in a low-level attack, destroying 5 aircraft, while his flight accounted for 2 others. Returning to his base, he volunteered to lead 3 other aircraft in reconnaissance of Bergamo airfield, an enemy base near Ghedi and one known to be equally well defended. Again ordering his flight to remain out of range of antiaircraft fire, 1st Lt. Knight flew through an exceptionally intense barrage, which heavily damaged his Thunderbolt, to observe the field at minimum altitude. He discovered a squadron of enemy aircraft under heavy camouflage and led his flight to the assault. Returning alone after this strafing, he made 10 deliberate passes against the field despite being hit by antiaircraft fire twice more, destroying 6 fully loaded enemy twin-engine aircraft and 2 fighters. His skillfully led attack enabled his flight to destroy 4 other twin-engine aircraft and a fighter plane. He then returned to his base in his seriously damaged plane. Early the next morning, when he again attacked Bergamo, he sighted an enemy plane on the runway. Again he led 3 other American pilots in a blistering low-level sweep through vicious antiaircraft fire that damaged his plane so severely that it was virtually nonflyable. Three of the few remaining enemy twin-engine aircraft at that base were destroyed. Realizing the critical need for aircraft in his unit, he declined to parachute to safety over friendly territory and unhesitatingly attempted to return his shattered plane to his home field. With great skill and strength, he flew homeward until caught by treacherous air conditions in the Appennines Mountains, where he crashed and was killed. The gallant action of 1st Lt. Knight eliminated the German aircraft which were poised to wreak havoc on Allied forces pressing to establish the first firm bridgehead across the Po River; his fearless daring and voluntary self-sacrifice averted possible heavy casualties among ground forces and the resultant slowing on the German drive culminated in the collapse of enemy resistance in Italy.

*KRAUS, RICHARD EDWARD

Rank and organization: Private First Class, U.S. Marine Corps Reserve. *Born:* 24 November 1925, Chicago, Ill. *Accredited to:* Minnesota. *Citation:* For conspicuous gallantry and intrepidity at the risk of his life above and beyond the call of duty while serving with the 8th Amphibious Tractor Battalion, Fleet Marine Force, in action against enemy Japanese forces on Peleliu, Palau Islands, on 5 October 1944. Unhesitatingly volunteering for the extremely hazardous mission of evacuating a wounded comrade from the front lines, Pfc. Kraus and 3 companions courageously made their way forward and successfully penetrated the lines for some distance before the enemy opened with an intense, devastating barrage of handgrenades which forced the stretcher party to take cover and subsequently abandon the mission. While returning to the rear, they observed 2 men approaching who appeared to be marines and immediately demanded the password. When, instead of answering, 1 of the 2 Japanese threw a handgrenade into the midst of the group, Pfc. Kraus heroically flung himself upon the grenade and, covering it with his body, absorbed the full impact of the explosion and was instantly killed. By his prompt action and great personal valor in the face of almost certain death, he saved the lives of his 3 companions, and his loyal spirit of self-sacrifice reflects the highest credit upon himself and the U.S. Naval Service. He gallantly gave his life for his comrades.

*KROTIAK, ANTHONY L.

Rank and organization: Private First Class, U.S. Army, Company I, 148th Infantry, 37th Infantry Division. *Place and date:* Balete Pass, Luzon, Philippine Islands, 8 May 1945. *Entered service at:* Chicago, Ill. *Born:* 15 August 1915, Chicago, Ill. *G.O. No.:* 18, 13 February 1946. *Citation:* He was an acting squad leader, directing his men in consolidating a newly won position on Hill B when the enemy concentrated small-arms fire and grenades upon him and 4 others, driving them to cover in an abandoned Japanese trench. A grenade thrown from above landed in the center of the group. Instantly pushing his comrades aside and jamming the grenade into the earth with his rifle butt, he threw himself over it, making a shield of his body to protect the other men. The grenade exploded under him, and he died a few minutes later. By his extraordinary heroism in deliberately giving his life to save those of his comrades, Pfc. Krotiak set an inspiring example of utter devotion and self-sacrifice which reflects the highest traditions of the military service.

*LA BELLE, JAMES DENNIS

Rank and organization: Private First Class, U.S. Marine Corps Reserve. *Born:* 22 November 1925, Columbia Heights, Minn. *Accredited to:* Minnesota. *Citation:* For conspicuous gallantry and intrepidity at the risk of his life above and beyond the call of duty while attached to the 27th Marines, 5th Marine Division, in action against enemy Japanese forces during the seizure of Iwo Jima in the Volcano Islands, 8 March 1945. Filling a gap in the front lines during a critical phase of the battle, Pfc. LaBelle had dug into a foxhole with 2 other marines and, grimly aware of the enemy's persistent attempts to blast a way through our lines with handgrenades, applied himself with steady concentration to maintaining a sharply vigilant watch during the hazardous night hours. Suddenly a hostile grenade landed beyond reach in his foxhole. Quickly estimating the situation, he determined to save the others if possible, shouted a warning, and instantly dived on the deadly missile, absorbing the exploding charge in his own body and thereby protecting his comrades from serious injury. Stouthearted and indomitable, he had unhesitatingly relinquished his own chance of survival that his fellow marines might carry on the relentless fight against a fanatic enemy. His dauntless courage, cool decision and valiant spirit of self-sacrifice in the face of certain death reflect the highest credit upon Pfc. LaBelle and upon the U.S. Naval Service. He gallantly gave his life in the service of his country.

LAWLEY, WILLIAM R., JR. (Air Mission)

Rank and organization: First Lieutenant, U.S. Army Air Corps, 364th Bomber Squadron, 305th Bomber Group. *Place and date:* Over Europe, 20 February 1944. *Entered service at:* Birmingham, Ala. *Born:* 23 August 1920, Leeds, Ala. *G.O. No.:* 64, 8 August 1944. *Citation:* For conspicuous gallantry and intrepidity in action above and beyond the call of duty, 20 February 1944, while serving as pilot of a B–17 aircraft on a heavy bombardment mission over enemy-occupied continental Europe. Coming off the target he was attacked by approximately 20 enemy fighters, shot out of formation, and his plane severely crippled. Eight crewmembers were wounded, the copilot was killed by a 20-mm. shell. One engine was on fire, the controls shot away, and 1st Lt. Lawley seriously and painfully wounded about the face. Forcing the copilot's body off the controls, he brought the plane out of a steep dive, flying with his left hand only. Blood covered the instruments and windshield and visibility was impossible. With a full bomb load the plane was difficult to maneuver and bombs could not be released because the racks were frozen. After the order to bail out had been given, 1 of the waist gunners informed the pilot that 2 crewmembers were so severely wounded that it would be impossible for them to bail out. With the fire in the engine spreading, the danger of an explosion was imminent. Because of the helpless condition of his wounded crewmembers 1st Lt. Lawley elected to remain with the ship and bring them to safety if it was humanly possible, giving the other crewmembers the option of bailing out. Enemy fighters again attacked but by using masterful evasive action he managed to lose them. One engine again caught on fire and was extinguished by skillful flying. 1st Lt. Lawley remained at his post, refusing first aid until he collapsed from sheer exhaustion caused by loss of blood, shock, and the energy he had expended in keeping control of his plane. He was revived by the bombardier and again took over the controls. Coming over the English coast 1 engine ran out of gasoline and had to be feathered. Another engine started to burn and continued to do so until a successful crash landing was made on a small fighter base. Through his heroism and exceptional flying skill 1st

Lt. Lawley rendered outstanding, distinguished and valorous service to our Nation.

LAWS, ROBERT E.

Rank and organization: Staff Sergeant, U.S. Army, Company G, 169th Infantry, 43d Infantry Division. *Place and date:* Pangasinan Province, Luzon, Philippine Islands, 12 January 1945. *Entered service at:* Altoona, Pa. *Birth:* Altoona, Pa. *G.O. No.:* 77, 10 September 1945. *Citation:* He led the assault squad when Company G attacked enemy hill positions. The enemy force, estimated to be a reinforced infantry company, was well supplied with machineguns, ammunition, grenades, and blocks of TNT and could be attacked only across a narrow ridge 70 yards long. At the end of this ridge an enemy pillbox and rifle positions were set in rising ground. Covered by his squad, S/Sgt. Laws traversed the hogback through vicious enemy fire until close to the pillbox, where he hurled grenades at the fortification. Enemy grenades wounded him, but he persisted in his assault until 1 of his missiles found its mark and knocked out the pillbox. With more grenades, passed to him by members of his squad who had joined him, he led the attack on the entrenched riflemen. In the advance up the hill, he suffered additional wounds in both arms and legs, about the body and in the head, as grenades and TNT charges exploded near him. Three Japs rushed him with fixed bayonets, and he emptied the magazine of his machine pistol at them, killing 2. He closed in hand-to-hand combat with the third, seizing the Jap's rifle as he met the onslaught. The 2 fell to the ground and rolled some 50 or 60 feet down a bank. When the dust cleared the Jap lay dead and the valiant American was climbing up the hill with a large gash across the head. He was given first aid and evacuated from the area while his squad completed the destruction of the enemy position. S/Sgt. Laws' heroic actions provided great inspiration to his comrades, and his courageous determination, in the face of formidable odds and while suffering from multiple wounds, enabled them to secure an important objective with minimum casualties.

LEE, DANIEL W.

Rank and organization: First Lieutenant, U.S. Army, Troop A, 117th Cavalry Reconnaissance Squadron. *Place and date:* Montreval, France, 2 September 1944. *Entered service at:* Alma, Ga. *Born:* 23 June 1919, Alma, Ga. *G.O. No.:* 14, 4 February 1946. *Citation:* 1st Lt. (then 2d Lt.) Daniel W. Lee was leader of Headquarters Platoon, Troop A, 117th Cavalry Reconnaissance Squadron, Mechanized, at Montreval, France, on 2 September 1944, when the Germans mounted a strong counterattack, isolating the town and engaging its outnumbered defenders in a pitched battle. After the fight had raged for hours and our forces had withstood heavy shelling and armor-supported infantry attacks, 2d Lt. Lee organized a patrol to knock out mortars which were inflicting heavy casualties on the beleaguered reconnaissance troops. He led the small group to the edge of the town, sweeping enemy riflemen out of position on a ridge from which he observed 7 Germans manning 2 large mortars near an armored halftrack about 100 yards down the reverse slope. Armed with a rifle and grenades, he left his men on the high ground and crawled to within 30 yards of the mortars, where the enemy discovered him and unleashed machine-pistol fire which shattered his right thigh. Scorning retreat, bleeding and suffering intense pain, he dragged himself relentlessly forward. He killed 5 of the enemy with rifle fire, and the others fled before he reached their position. Fired on by an armored car, he took cover behind the German halftrack and there found a panzerfaust with which to neutralize this threat. Despite his wounds, he inched his way toward the car through withering machinegun fire, maneuvered into range, and blasted the vehicle with a round from the rocket launcher, forcing it to withdraw. Having cleared the slope of hostile troops, he struggled back to his men, where he collapsed from pain and loss of blood. 2d Lt. Lee's outstanding gallantry, willing risk of life, and extreme tenacity of purpose in coming to grips with the enemy, although suffering from grievous wounds, set an example of bravery and devotion to duty in keeping with the highest traditions of the military service.

LEIMS, JOHN HAROLD

Rank and organization: Second Lieutenant, U.S. Marine Corps Reserve, Company B, 1st Battalion, 9th Marines, 3d Marine Division. *Place and date:* Iwo Jima, Volcano Islands, 7 March 1945. *Entered service at:* Chicago, Ill. *Born:* 8 June 1921, Chicago, Ill. *Citation:* For conspicuous gallantry and intrepidity at the risk of his life above and beyond the call of duty as commanding officer of Company B, 1st Battalion, 9th Marines, 3d Marine Division, in action against enemy Japanese forces on Iwo Jima in the Volcano Islands, 7 March 1945. Launching a surprise attack against the rock-imbedded fortifications of a dominating Japanese hill position, 2d Lt. Leims spurred his company forward with indomitable determination and, skillfully directing his assault platoons against the cave-emplaced enemy troops and heavily fortified pillboxes, succeeded in capturing the objective in the late afternoon. When it became apparent that his assault platoons were cut off in this newly won position, approximately 400 yards forward of adjacent units and lacked all communication with the command post, he personally advanced and laid telephone lines across the isolating expanse of open, fire-swept terrain. Ordered to withdraw his command after he had joined his forward platoons he immediately complied, adroitly effecting the withdrawal of his troops without incident. Upon arriving at the rear, he was informed that several casualties had been left at the abandoned ridge position beyond the front lines. Although suffering acutely from the strain and exhaustion of battle, he instantly went forward despite darkness and the slashing fury of hostile machine-gun fire, located and carried to safety 1 seriously wounded marine and then, running the gauntlet of enemy fire for the third time that night, again made his tortuous way into the bullet-riddled deathtrap and rescued another of his wounded men. A dauntless leader, concerned at all times for the welfare of his men, 2d Lt. Leims soundly maintained the coordinated strength of his battle-wearied company under extremely difficult conditions and, by his bold tactics, sustained aggressiveness, and heroic disregard of all personal danger, contributed essentially to the success of his division's operations against this vital Japanese base. His valiant conduct in the face of fanatic opposition sustains and enhances the highest traditions of the U.S. Naval Service.

*LEONARD, TURNEY W.

Rank and organization: First Lieutenant, U.S. Army, Company C, 893d Tank Destroyer Battalion. *Place and date:* Kommerscheidt, Germany, 4–6 November 1944. *Entered service at:* Dallas, Tex. *Birth:* Dallas, Tex. *G.O. No.:* 74, 1 September 1945. *Citation:* He displayed extraordinary heroism while commanding a platoon of mobile weapons at Kommerscheidt, Germany, on 4, 5, and 6 November 1944. During the fierce 3-day engagement, he repeatedly braved overwhelming enemy fire in advance of his platoon to direct the fire of his tank destroyer from exposed, dismounted positions. He went on lone reconnaissance missions to discover what opposition his men faced, and on 1 occasion, when fired upon by a hostile machinegun, advanced alone and eliminated the enemy emplacement with a handgrenade. When a strong German attack threatened to overrun friendly positions, he moved through withering artillery, mortar, and small-arms fire, reorganized confused infantry units whose leaders had become casualties, and exhorted them to hold firm. Although wounded early in battle, he continued to direct fire from his advanced position until he was disabled by a high-explosive shell which shattered his arm, forcing him to withdraw. He was last seen at a medical aid station which was subsequently captured by the enemy. By his superb courage, inspiring leadership, and indomitable fighting spirit, 1st Lt. Leonard enabled our forces to hold off the enemy attack and was personally responsible for the direction of fire which destroyed 6 German tanks.

*LESTER, FRED FAULKNER

Rank and organization: Hospital Apprentice First Class, U.S. Navy. *Born:* 29 April 1926, Downers Grove, Ill. *Accredited to:* Illinois. *Citation:* For conspicuous gallantry and intrepidity at the risk of his life above and beyond the call of duty while serving as a Medical Corpsman with an Assault Rifle Platoon, attached to the 1st Battalion, 22d Marines, 6th Marine Division, during action against enemy Japanese forces on Okinawa Shima in the Ryukyu Chain, 8 June 1945. Quick to spot a wounded marine lying in an open field beyond the front lines following the relentless assault against a strategic Japanese hill position, Lester unhesitatingly crawled toward the casualty under a concentrated barrage from hostile machineguns, rifles, and grenades. Torn by enemy rifle bullets as he inched forward, he stoically disregarded the mounting fury of Japanese fire and his own pain to pull the wounded man toward a covered position. Struck by enemy fire a second time before he reached cover, he exerted tremendous effort and succeeded in pulling his comrade to safety where, too seriously wounded himself to administer aid, he instructed 2 of his squad in proper medical treatment of the rescued marine. Realizing that his own wounds were fatal, he staunchly refused medical attention for himself and, gathering his fast-waning strength with calm determination, coolly and expertly directed his men in the treatment of 2 other wounded marines, succumbing shortly thereafter. Completely selfless in his concern for the welfare of his fighting comrades, Lester, by his indomitable spirit, outstanding valor, and competent direction of others, had saved the life of 1 who otherwise must have perished and had contributed to the safety of countless others. Lester's fortitude in the face of certain death sustains and enhances the highest traditions of the U.S. Naval Service. He gallantly gave his life for his country.

*LINDSEY, DARRELL R. (Air Mission)

Rank and organization: Captain, U.S. Army Air Corps. *Place and date:* L'Isle Adam railroad bridge over the Seine in occupied France, 9 August 1944. *Entered service at:* Storm Lake, Iowa. *Birth:* Jefferson, Iowa. *G.O. No.:* 43, 30 May 1945. *Citation:* On 9 August 1944, Capt. Lindsey led a formation of 30 B–26 medium bombers in a hazardous mission to destroy the strategic enemy held L'Isle Adam railroad bridge over the Seine in occupied France. With most of the bridges over the Seine destroyed, the heavily fortified L'Isle Adam bridge was of inestimable value to the enemy in moving troops, supplies, and equipment to Paris. Capt. Lindsey was fully aware of the fierce resistance that would be encountered. Shortly after reaching enemy territory the formation was buffeted with heavy and accurate antiaircraft fire. By skillful evasive action, Capt. Lindsey was able to elude much of the enemy flak, but just before entering the bombing run his B–26 was peppered with holes. During the bombing run the enemy fire was even more intense, and Capt. Lindsey's right engine received a direct hit and burst into flames. Despite the fact that his ship was hurled out of formation by the violence of the concussion, Capt. Lindsey brilliantly maneuvered back into the lead position without disrupting the flight. Fully aware that the gasoline tanks might explode at any moment, Capt. Lindsey gallantly elected to continue the perilous bombing run. With fire streaming from his right engine and his right wing half enveloped in flames, he led his formation over the target upon which the bombs were dropped with telling effect. Immediately after the objective was attacked, Capt. Lindsey gave the order for the crew to parachute from the doomed aircraft. With magnificent coolness and superb pilotage, and without regard for his own life, he held the swiftly descending airplane in a steady glide until the members of the crew could jump to safety. With the right wing completely enveloped in flames and an explosion of the gasoline tank imminent, Capt. Lindsey still remained unperturbed. The last man to leave the stricken plane was the bombardier, who offered to lower the wheels so that Capt. Lindsey might escape from the nose. Realizing that this might throw the aircraft into an uncontrollable spin and jeopardize the bombardier's chances to escape, Capt. Lindsey refused the offer. Immediately after the bombardier had bailed out, and before Capt. Lindsey was able to follow, the right gasoline tank exploded. The aircraft sheathed in fire, went into a steep dive and was seen to explode as it crashed. All who are living today from this plane owe their lives to the fact that Capt. Lindsey remained cool and showed supreme courage in this emergency.

LINDSEY, JAKE W.

Rank and organization: Technical Sergeant, U.S. Army, 16th Infantry, 1st Infantry Division. *Place and date:* Near Hamich, Germany, 16 November 1944. *Entered service at:* Lucedale, Miss. *Birth:* Isney, Ala. *G.O. No.:* 43, 30 May 1945. *Citation:* For conspicuous gallantry and intrepidity in action at the risk of his life above and beyond the call of duty: Technical Sergeant Jake W. Lindsey, Company C, 16th Infantry, led a platoon reduced to six of its original strength of forty, in the attack on an enemy position near Hamich, Germany, 16 November 1944. His men had captured their objective and were digging in when counterattacked by a German infantry company and five tanks. Armed with a rifle and grenades, Sergeant Lindsey took position on the left and in advance of the remnant of his platoon, and though exposed to heavy rifle, machine-gun and tank fire, beat off repeated enemy attacks. Tanks moved to within 50 yards of him but were forced to withdraw because of his accurate rifle/grenade fire. After driving off the tanks, he knocked out two machine guns to his front. Though painfully wounded, Sergeant Lindsey continued firing and throwing grenades until his ammunition was expended. An enemy squad attempted to set up a machinegun fifty yards from him. Unmindful of his wounds and enemy fire, he rushed these eight German soldiers, singlehandedly closed with them, killed three with his bayonet and captured three, the two others escaped. In his fearlessness, inspiring courage, and superb leadership, Sergeant Lindsey carried on a brilliant defense of his platoon's hard-won ground, securing the position and inflicting heavy casualties on the numerically superior enemy.

LINDSTROM, FLOYD K.

Rank and organization: Private First Class, U.S. Army, 3d Infantry Division. *Place and date:* Near Mignano, Italy, 11 November 1943. *Entered service at:* Colorado Springs, Colo. *Birth:* Holdredge, Nebr. *G.O. No.:* 32, 20 April 1944. *Citation:* For conspicuous gallantry and intrepidity at risk of life above and beyond the call of duty. On 11 November 1943, this soldier's platoon was furnishing machinegun support for a rifle company attacking a hill near Mignano, Italy, when the enemy counterattacked, forcing the riflemen and half the machinegun platoon to retire to a defensive position. Pfc. Lindstrom saw that his small section was alone and outnumbered 5 to 1, yet he immediately deployed the few remaining men into position and opened fire with his single gun. The enemy centered fire on him with machinegun, machine pistols, and grenades. Unable to knock out the enemy nest from his original position, Pfc. Lindstrom picked up his own heavy machinegun and staggered 15 yards up the barren, rocky hillside to a new position, completely ignoring enemy small-arms fire which was striking all around him. From this new site, only 10 yards from the enemy machinegun, he engaged it in an intense duel. Realizing that he could not hit the hostile gunners because they were behind a large rock, he charged uphill under a steady stream of fire, killed both gunners with his pistol and dragged their gun down to his own men, directing them to employ it against the enemy. Disregarding heavy rifle fire, he returned to the enemy machinegun nest for 2 boxes of ammunition, came back and resumed withering fire from his own gun. His spectacular performance completely broke up the German counterattack. Pfc. Lindstrom demonstrated aggressive spirit and complete fearlessness in the face of almost certain death.

*LLOYD, EDGAR H.

Rank and organization: First Lieutenant, U.S. Army, Company E, 319th Infantry, 80th Infantry Division. *Place and date:* Near Pompey, France, 14 September 1944. *Entered service at:* Blytheville, Ark. *Birth:* Blytheville, Ark. *G.O. No.:* 25, 7 April 1945. *Citation:* For conspicuous gallantry and intrepidity at the risk of his life above and beyond the call of duty. On 14 September 1944, Company E, 319th Infantry, with which 1st Lt. Lloyd was serving as a rifle platoon leader, was assigned the mission of expelling an estimated enemy force of 200 men from a heavily fortified position near Pompey, France. As the attack progressed, 1st Lt. Lloyd's platoon advanced to within 50 yards of the enemy position where they were caught in a withering machinegun and rifle crossfire which inflicted heavy casualties and momentarily disorganized the platoon. With complete disregard for his own safety, 1st Lt. Lloyd leaped to his feet and led his men on a run into the raking fire, shouting encouragement to them. He jumped into the first enemy machine-gun position, knocked out the gunner with his fist, dropped a grenade, and jumped out before it exploded. Still shouting encouragement he went from 1 machine-gun nest to another, pinning the enemy down with submachinegun fire until he was within throwing distance, and then destroyed them with handgrenades. He personally destroyed 5 machineguns and many of the enemy, and by his daring leadership and conspicuous bravery inspired his men to overrun the enemy positions and accomplish the objective in the face of seemingly insurmountable odds. His audacious determination and courageous devotion to duty exemplify the highest traditions of the military forces of the United States.

*LOBAUGH, DONALD R.

Rank and organization: Private, U.S. Army, 127th Infantry, 32d Infantry Division. *Place and date:* Near Afua, New Guinea, 22 July 1944. *Entered service at:* Freeport, Pa. *Birth:* Freeport, Pa. *G.O. No.:* 31, 17 April 1945. *Citation:* For conspicuous gallantry and intrepidity at the risk of his life above and beyond the call of duty near Afua, New Guinea, on 22 July 1944. While Pvt. Lobaugh's company was withdrawing from its position on 21 July, the enemy attacked and cut off approximately 1 platoon of our troops. The platoon immediately occupied, organized, and defended a position, which it held throughout the night. Early on 22 July, an attempt was made to effect its withdrawal, but during the preparation therefor, the enemy emplaced a machinegun, protected by the fire of rifles and automatic weapons, which blocked the only route over which the platoon could move. Knowing that it was the key to the enemy position, Pfc. Lobaugh volunteered to attempt to destroy this weapon, even though in order to reach it he would be forced to work his way about 30 yards over ground devoid of cover. When part way across this open space he threw a handgrenade, but exposed himself in the act and was wounded.

Heedless of his wound, he boldly rushed the emplacement, firing as he advanced. The enemy concentrated their fire on him, and he was struck repeatedly, but he continued his attack and killed 2 more before he was himself slain. Pfc. Lobaugh's heroic actions inspired his comrades to press the attack, and to drive the enemy from the position with heavy losses. His fighting determination and intrepidity in battle exemplify the highest traditions of the U.S. Armed Forces.

LOGAN, JAMES M.

Rank and organization: Sergeant, U.S. Army, 36th Infantry Division. *Place and date:* Near Salerno, Italy, 9 September 1943. *Entered service at:* Luling, Tex. *Birth:* McNeil, Tex. *G.O. No.:* 54, 5 July 1944. *Citation:* For conspicuous gallantry and intrepidity at risk of life above and beyond the call of duty in action involving actual conflict on 9 September 1943 in the vicinity of Salerno, Italy. As a rifleman of an infantry company, Sgt. Logan landed with the first wave of the assault echelon on the beaches of the Gulf of Salerno, and after his company had advanced 800 yards inland and taken positions along the forward bank of an irrigation canal, the enemy began a serious counterattack from positions along a rock wall which ran parallel with the canal about 200 yards further inland. Voluntarily exposing himself to the fire of a machinegun located along the rock wall, which sprayed the ground so close to him that he was splattered with dirt and rock splinters from the impact of the bullets, Sgt. Logan killed the first 3 Germans as they came through a gap in the wall. He then attacked the machinegun. As he dashed across the 200 yards of exposed terrain a withering stream of fire followed his advance. Reaching the wall, he crawled along the base, within easy reach of the enemy crouched along the opposite side, until he reached the gun. Jumping up, he shot the 2 gunners down, hurdled the wall, and seized the gun. Swinging it around, he immediately opened fire on the enemy with the remaining ammunition, raking their flight and inflicting further casualties on them as they fled. After smashing the machinegun over the rocks, Sgt. Logan captured an enemy officer and private who were attempting to sneak away. Later in the morning, Sgt. Logan went after a sniper hidden in a house about 150 yards from the company. Again the intrepid Sgt. ran a gauntlet of fire to reach his objective. Shooting the lock off the door, Sgt. Logan kicked it in and shot the sniper who had just reached the bottom of the stairs. The conspicuous gallantry and intrepidity which characterized Sgt. Logan's exploits proved a constant inspiration to all the men of his company, and aided materially in insuring the success of the beachhead at Salerno.

LOPEZ, JOSE M.

Rank and organization: Sergeant, U.S. Army, 23d Infantry, 2d Infantry Division. *Place and date:* Near Krinkelt, Belgium, 17 December 1944. *Entered service at:* Brownsville, Tex. *Birth:* Mission, Tex. *G.O. No.:* 47, 18 June 1945. *Citation:* On his own initiative, he carried his heavy machinegun from Company K's right flank to its left, in order to protect that flank which was in danger of being overrun by advancing enemy infantry supported by tanks. Occupying a shallow hole offering no protection above his waist, he cut down a group of 10 Germans. Ignoring enemy fire from an advancing tank, he held his position and cut down 25 more enemy infantry attempting to turn his flank. Glancing to his right, he saw a large number of infantry swarming in from the front. Although dazed and shaken from enemy artillery fire which had crashed into the ground only a few yards away, he realized that his position soon would be outflanked. Again, alone, he carried his machinegun to a position to the right rear of the sector; enemy tanks and infantry were forcing a withdrawal. Blown over backward by the concussion of enemy fire, he immediately reset his gun and continued his fire. Singlehanded he held off the German horde until he was satisfied his company had effected its retirement. Again he loaded his gun on his back and in a hail of small-arms fire he ran to a point where a few of his comrades were attempting to set up another defense against the onrushing enemy. He fired from this position until his ammunition was exhausted. Still carrying his gun, he fell back with his small group to Krinkelt. Sgt. Lopez's gallantry and intrepidity, on seemingly suicidal missions in which he killed at least 100 of the enemy, were almost solely responsible for allowing Company K to avoid being enveloped, to withdraw successfully and to give other forces coming up in support time to build a line which repelled the enemy drive.

LUCAS, JACKLYN HAROLD

Rank and organization: Private First Class, U.S. Marine Corps Reserve, 1st Battalion, 26th Marines, 5th Marine Division. *Place and date:* Iwo Jima, Volcano Islands, 20 February 1945. *Entered service at:* Norfolk, Va. *Born:* 14 February 1928, Plymouth, N.C. *Citation:* For conspicuous gallantry and intrepidity at the risk of his life above and beyond the call of duty while serving with the 1st Battalion, 26th Marines, 5th Marine Division, during action against enemy Japanese forces on Iwo Jima, Volcano Islands, 20 February 1945. While creeping through a treacherous, twisting ravine which ran in close proximity to a fluid and uncertain frontline on D-plus-1 day, Pfc. Lucas and 3 other men were suddenly ambushed by a hostile patrol which savagely attacked with rifle fire and grenades. Quick to act when the lives of the small group were endangered by 2 grenades which landed directly in front of them, Pfc. Lucas unhesitatingly hurled himself over his comrades upon 1 grenade and pulled the other under him, absorbing the whole blasting forces of the explosions in his own body in order to shield his companions from the concussion and murderous flying fragments. By his inspiring action and valiant spirit of self-sacrifice, he not only protected his comrades from certain injury or possible death but also enabled them to rout the Japanese patrol and continue the advance. His exceptionally courageous initiative and loyalty reflect the highest credit upon Pfc. Lucas and the U.S. Naval Service.

*LUMMUS, JACK

Rank and organization: First Lieutenant, U.S. Marine Corps Reserve. *Born:* 22 October 1915, Ennie, Tex. *Appointed from:* Texas. *Citation:* For conspicuous gallantry and intrepidity at the risk of his life above and beyond the call of duty as leader of a Rifle Platoon attached to the 2d Battalion, 27th Marines, 5th Marine Division, in action against enemy Japanese forces on Iwo Jima in the Volcano Islands, 8 March 1945. Resuming his assault tactics with bold decision after fighting without respite for 2 days and nights, 1st Lt. Lummus slowly advanced his platoon against an enemy deeply entrenched in a network of mutually supporting positions. Suddenly halted by a terrific concentration of hostile fire, he unhesitatingly moved forward of his front lines in an effort to neutralize the Japanese position. Although knocked to the ground when an enemy grenade exploded close by, he immediately recovered himself and, again moving forward despite the intensified barrage, quickly located, attacked, and destroyed the occupied emplacement. Instantly taken under fire by the garrison of a supporting pillbox and further assailed by the slashing fury of hostile rifle fire, he fell under the impact of a second enemy grenade but, courageously disregarding painful shoulder wounds, staunchly continued his heroic 1-man assault and charged the second pillbox, annihilating all the occupants. Subsequently returning to his platoon position, he fearlessly traversed his lines under fire, encouraging his men to advance and directing the fire of supporting tanks against other stubbornly holding Japanese emplacements. Held up again by a devastating barrage, he again moved into the open, rushed a third heavily fortified installation and killed the defending troops. Determined to crush all resistance, he led his men indomitably, personally attacking foxholes and spider traps with his carbine and systematically reducing the fanatic opposition, until, stepping on a land mine, he sustained fatal wounds. By his outstanding valor, skilled tactics, and tenacious perseverance in the face of overwhelming odds, 1st Lt. Lummus had inspired his stouthearted marines to continue the relentless drive northward, thereby contributing materially to the success of his regimental mission. His dauntless leadership and unwavering devotion to duty throughout sustain and enhance the highest traditions of the U.S. Naval Service. He gallantly gave his life in the service of his country.